The Art of
Staying Together

A NEW
CONSCIOUSNESS
READER

This *New Consciousness Reader* is part of a new series of original and classic writing by renowned experts on leading-edge concepts in personal development, psychology, spiritual growth, and healing. Other books in this series include:

The Art of
Staying Together

*Embracing Love, Intimacy,
and Spirit in Relationships*

EDITED BY

Mark Robert Waldman

Jeremy P. Tarcher/Putnam
a member of
Penguin Putnam Inc.
New York

Most Tarcher/Putnam books are available at special quantity
discounts for bulk purchases for sales promotions, premiums,
fund-raising, and educational needs. Special books or book excerpts
also can be created to fit specific needs.
For details, write Putnam
Special Markets, 375 Hudson Street
New York, NY 10014

Permissions appear on page 225.

Jeremy P. Tarcher/Putnam
a member of
Penguin Putnam Inc.
375 Hudson Street
New York, NY 10014
www.penguinputnam.com

Library of Congress Cataloging-in-Publication Data

The art of staying together : embracing love, intimacy, and spirit in relationships/
    edited by Mark R. Waldman.
        p.   cm.—(A new consciousness reader)
    Includes bibliographical references.
    ISBN 0-87477-914-6 (alk. paper)
    1. Love.   2. Intimacy (Psychology).   3. Man-woman relationships.
    I. Waldman, Mark R.   II. Series.
    BF575.L8A8 1998
    158.2'4—dc21   97-41472 CIP

Book design by Lee Fukui
Cover design by Shelly Meadows

Printed in the United States of America
10   9   8   7   6   5

This book is printed on acid-free paper. ∞

To Adam

I will teach my son to write one day.
I will teach him about the absence of words
and the spaces between them,
where the whiteness of the page
reminds us of a greater silence,
a truth to be held and savored until
the next few letters intrude.

Contents

PART III

What Can We Do When It Isn't Working?

PART IV

Sacred Bodies, Sacred Selves

Introduction

Mark Robert Waldman

MY FIRST SERIOUS relationship began at the age of six, when the girls next door invited me over to play house. It was here, in my neighbors' back yard, that I discovered the possibilities of an ideal marital love. It was wonderful! I came home to the playhouse from work and greeted my two wives, ages three and five respectively. I told them what I wanted to eat and they prepared a sumptuous feast: mud, if I recall. Afterward, they made a bed and tucked me in, and climbed under the sheets, giggling. It was a perfect marriage: two minutes of work, dinner, and a hug. I thought I had it made.

But the fantasy didn't last for long. In a few hours I would go home to a real house and real dinner and experience my parents' marriage in progress, where a busy wife prepared a hurried meal for a very tired man. We ate, I did my homework, watched TV, and tucked myself in bed, feeling lonely and ignored. Confused about the notions of marriage and love, I slipped quietly into sleep, dreaming about the fantasy next door. And there I stayed, emotionally, for the next six years of life.

When puberty came, I was too afraid to try playing house again, and so I turned to literature to enrich my education—science fiction, short stories, and an occasional *Playboy* or two. But it was a book by Henry Miller that awakened me to the forbidden fruits of love. I burned that book, primarily out of guilt (remember *Portnoy's Complaint?*), but the words remained alive. Miller only opened the door; others—in person and print—pushed me ever more deeply into the passions of life. And so, over the years, I moved back and forth between fantasy and fact, searching for the ideal way to love—sometimes through the eyes of a six-year-old, or with the yearnings of an adolescent heart, and occasionally with the wisdom of a maturing young man.

We all have a six-year-old inside, an adolescent boy or girl in search of the perfect love. Our stories may be different, but we bring them nonetheless into all the realms of adult relationship, influencing our styles of communication, our notions of intimacy, our degree of sexual openness, our values, our hopes and our dreams. And because our stories are different, we eventually collide, facing the inevitable conflicts of love. Unless we become deeply aware of these internal processes, and are willing to fully explore them with our partners—with understanding, patience, and compassion—we may lose a valued intimacy or turn away too soon.

Without intimacy, life withers away. As the great poet Rilke once said, we need each other, profoundly, to survive. In love, we find ourselves in the eyes of another and hold each other through the stormy ports of life. In love, we can unfold. We embrace, we discover each other, we grow, but still the mystery remains.

I never found the perfect love I dreamed of as a child, but instead I found myself. And the voices that I've encountered along the way—the books I've read, the people I've met and the stories I've shared with others—these are the seeds from which this book has grown.

The Art of Staying Together

To love and be loved, to be seen and understood, these are the treasures we seek.

We live in a society that is flooded by images and words of love. It permeates our senses, our reason, the very core of our being. Without definition, we immediately grasp the meaning of love, seeking its essence throughout our lives.

Our culture places extraordinary emphasis on the value of love, building it into the fabric of our psychology, our work, and our spiritual beliefs. We are expected to love. We marry for love. We divorce for lack of love. Without it, we somehow feel incomplete.

But we are also a society that is starved for love. The problem lies not in our capacity to love but in our need *to be loved,* a need that is born out of the dependency of childhood, fueled by the ambiguities of adolescence, and frustrated by the ever-increasing demands of life. Few people are given the quality of love that they need.

"People think that to *love* is simple," Erich Fromm once wrote, that it is only a matter of acting lovable and falling in love with the "right" person.[1] For Fromm, love was not a natural act; it was an *art,* a process of learning that demanded practice, patience, discipline, and dedication. Yet, despite all evidence to the contrary, people continue to treat love casually. We keep our views on love primarily to ourselves, sharing a sentence or two, with a flower or a hug, never really knowing what our partners need.

What is the nature of this beast called love? Is it real, or a fantasy? Is it a feeling or a thought, an ethic or a moral, a sacred ideal? What must we do to really love another person, to communicate our need to be loved and resolve the inevitable conflicts that arise? These questions, pondered by the Platos and Freuds of their times, seem underexplored today. Let us take a moment to look at what love has meant in the past, what it has become today, and where it may lead to in the next few years ahead.

A Brief History of Love[2]

In the past, love denoted a simpler form of experience, one that was rarely attached to the contract of marriage. Throughout most of history, it was looked upon as an emotion, a feeling, an un-thought-through expression of devotion, admiration, infatuation, or lust. Often, love was seen as an epiphany of beauty and sensuality, a feminine ideal that can be traced back three thousand years to the hieroglyphic poetry of Egypt. The Greek and Roman philosophers elevated it to the higher realms of the soul—

agape, eros, philos, charity, esteem—but it was a love outside of marriage, separate from the physical and sexual embrace. The early Christians took this notion to its extreme and thrust a profound asceticism upon the Western world. For nearly a thousand years, sensual and marital love remained taboo:

> The Christian code was based, quite simply, on the conviction that the sexual act was to be avoided like the plague, except for the bare minimum necessary to keep the race in existence. Even when performed for this purpose it remained a regrettable necessity. Those who could were exhorted to avoid it entirely, even if married. For those incapable of such heroic self-denial there was a great spider's web of regulations whose overriding purpose was to make the sexual act as joyless as possible. . . . Not only the pleasure of the sexual act was held sinful, but also the sensation of desire for a person of the opposite sex, even when unconsummated.[3]

The underlying premise was that no man should ever love his wife, for it would detract him from his love of God. Furthermore, the integration of love and sex was considered a sin, an act that was treated with more severity than adultery. But ultimately, it was the woman who was held to blame.

Over time, the powers of the church began to wane, allowing for a certain freedom of desire. In the twelfth century, hints of a transformation began to appear, most notably in the poems and songs of troubadours who spoke of a "courtly love." More literary than real, this code held great significance for the emerging consciousness of the times, reaffirming the ideals and tragedies once portrayed in Greek and Roman myth. From these tales of chivalry and adventure, the romantic era was born.

Still, no integration of love and sex emerged until the influence of the Renaissance took hold. It was a time of great social and political upheaval that eventually gave birth to our modern notions of intimacy. For the first time in history, people married for love, and although they were still influenced by family preferences and cultural mores, individuals were relatively free to marry the partner of their choice. Sex and sensuality were no longer sins, and all that was once considered perverse became the unalienable rights of lovers. In such an environment, women's standards improved, equalizing to some degree the balance of marital power.

From the sixteenth century on, the seeds of contemporary love took root. Passion was no longer the secret affair but a voice that cried out to all. Throughout Europe, the yearnings of the heart were heard: on stage, in music, in paintings and sculptures and poems. "Romeo! humours! madman! passion! lover!" Mercutio laments of his friend's desire: "The ape is dead and I must conjure him." In these brief lines from *Romeo and Juliet*[4] we grasp the essence of the lover's soul, of the suffering and joy and the darker corners of the self. In Shakespeare's plays we see the erotic metaphors of ancient Greece being offered as templates for a liberating romance, to be taken as a model for royalty and common folk alike. In many ways, the sensuality and boldness of those times have yet to be transcended or matched. Witness the seduction of Adonis by Venus, unfettered and autonomous in her strength:

> *"A thousand honey secrets shalt thou know:*
> *Here come and sit, where never serpent hisses,*
> *And being set, I'll smother thee with kisses . . ."*
>
> *With this she seizeth on his sweating palm,*
> *The precedent of pith and livelihood,*
> *And, trembling in her passion, calls it balm,*
> *Earth's sovereign salve to do a goddess good:*
> *Being so enraged, desire doth lend her force*
> *Courageously to pluck him from his horse. . . .*
>
> *He burns with bashful shame; she with her tears*
> *Doth quench the maiden burning of his cheeks;*
> *Then with her windy sighs and golden hairs*

To fan and blow them dry again she seeks:
He saith she is immodest, blames her miss;
What follows more she murders with a kiss.[5]

And so, with the aid of a popular press, the *language* of romance was born: a rich vocabulary of intimacy and love, exchanged with neighboring towns, crossing social and ethnic lines to be embraced throughout the Western world.

The culmination of the romantic ideal took place, not in Europe, but on American soil, where its unique vision of love became a constitutional right, where each individual was guaranteed the privilege to love separate from the edicts of church or state. "It is difficult for Americans today to appreciate fully the revolutionary significance of this concept," Nathaniel Branden writes:

> We who live in twentieth-century America enjoy unprecedented freedom in the conduct of our private lives, and in particular of our sexual lives. We are learning to see sex not as "the darker side" of our nature but as a normal expression of our total personality. We are less inclined to glamorize tragedy in the style of so many nineteenth-century Romanticists. As the influence of religion continues to decline, we feel less need to rebel and "prove" our "enlightenment" by means of debauchery. As a consequence, the "naturalness" of romantic love is far more accepted today than ever before.[6]

While the rest of the world regarded such standards with suspicion, Americans continued to expand their relational and marital ideals. In the first few decades of this century, love was viewed by the behaviorists as a purely physical event, a motivation that was built into our biological selves. It simply existed, without question or embellishment, in every human being. Others disagreed, believing that love was a supreme development of a rational mind. Still others took issue and argued that it was an impulse emerging out of the unconscious depths of an irrational soul.

And with the diversity of religious thought, a thousand moral issues clamored for support.

As the years progressed, new concepts emerged. In the 1920s, the notion of sexual *satisfaction* became a major criterion for a meaningful marital union. In the 1930s, the emphasis shifted to cooperation, teamwork, and tolerance—values that paralleled the ethics of the working class society. In the 1940s, the postwar "American Dream" encouraged ambition, aggressiveness, and independence for the husband, and emotional and domestic support from the wife.

Perhaps the most radical change came in the 1950s, when therapists became the experts on love and the language of psychology became the norm. In the past, love and intimacy were seen primarily as external experiences—a relationship that took place *between* two people. Now they were seen as *internal* processes that took shape in the hidden processes of the mind. Styles of intimacy could be traced to childhood events and parental introjects, carried out within a matrix of unconscious acts. We were not in charge of our lives. Instead, we were governed by unknown forces within, dark and potent energies that could turn a relationship into chaos or pain. But, said the psychologists, if we could become aware of these unseen dimensions of the soul, we could redirect them toward more satisfactory goals.

And so we began to question everything down to its core, redefining the meaning of love in psychological terms. Consciousness became the new ideal. In an article published in 1950, a Jungian analyst named Helen Henley eloquently captured these themes:

> A conscious relationship must always presuppose two individuals able to make a commitment to a meaningful life together. Each has his own contribution to make that life. But growing relationship does not follow a smooth and even course; because a man or woman, who is sincerely self-acceptant, must often express the dark aspect of his nature without which he can never become himself. For nobody is whole without negative qualities and one begins to

grow free only through the assimilation of the shadow. In that process of assimilation other persons in one's environment are the immediate "beneficiaries"! And the husband or the wife is the first in line. Conscious relationship is always dearly won. Its achievement is both an art and a discipline, seldom consummated in the early years of married life. First—so goes the rule—bride and groom find themselves in an enchanted garden of young love. But between blossom time and harvest lies summer with its blistering heat and its wind and storm, the trial season which must be weathered if the harvest is to bring forth ripened fruit. In the marriage also there must be a testing time when crucial matters arise to challenge the very fundamentals of relationship. When such hazards can be overcome with mature consciousness, then the adult relationship ripens.[7]

In the 1960s, another subtle shift took place, where individuals began to value internal ideals to the same degree that the previous generation valued material worth. We began to seek higher standards of happiness and pleasure. We strived to become more authentic, more real, seeking the limits of human potential. We were becoming a society in search of the perfect self.

But something seemed missing and ill at ease, and so we developed a culture of movements—civil rights movements, feminist movements, countercultural movements—designed to transform the inequities of the past. We broke the rules, challenged traditional values, deconstructed the meaning of love, and gained a sense of freedom that was never dreamed of before. But with this transformation came an unexpected burden: the loss of a sense of self. Bruno Bettelheim explains:

While a traditionally ordered society tightly shackled both females and males to narrowly defined social and sexual roles, society thus provided people with certainty regarding their identities. . . . They more or less accepted and settled into the roles which society decreed. Where there is not doubt there is also little insecurity . . . [but]

there was also little need for developing a strong personal identity. . . . With the breaking down of ancient customs and traditional sex-related traits, and the new freedom to be oneself in whatever way one wishes, comes the difficult task of achieving personal identity, and the related task of gaining autonomy. . . . But the internal difficulties of achieving a secure personal and sexual identity have, if anything, become even more of a problem. Persons who have not achieved a secure identity for themselves cannot provide each other with those complementary experiences that make for a happy marital relationship. Although in many more cases both partners in a marriage now have an independent life in society, this has not necessarily made it easier for them to be happier with each other.[8]

Love, marriage, and intimacy—all had been revisioned to embrace consciousness, freedom, and autonomy, but at the cost of disrupting our sense of personal and relational identity. In the 1970s and 1980s we became a generation of seekers, testing and promoting a multitude of lifestyles from which to choose. Today, our definitions of intimacy have become so complexly interwoven that it is almost impossible to grasp, leading us into a confusing world of subjective realities where seemingly opposite viewpoints appear equally valid. One hypothesis even suggests that the importance of identity no longer matters, that we do not need an individualized sense of self. In terms of relationships, love is nothing more than a convenient mental construction. This postmodern perspective suggests that individual, social, and cultural identities are dissolving into an informational global community where familiar boundaries between people and cultures disappear. Kenneth Gergen, a leading proponent of this "constructivist" view, describes the psychological environment we now embrace:

Emerging technologies saturate us with the voices of humankind—both harmonious and alien. As we absorb their varied rhymes and reasons, they become part of us and we of them. Social saturation furnishes us with a multiplicity of incoherent and unrelated languages of the self. For everything that we "know to be true" about ourselves, other voices within respond with doubt and even derision. This fragmentation of self-conceptions corresponds to a multiplicity of incoherent and disconnected relationships. These relationships pull us in myriad directions, inviting us to play such a variety of roles that the very concept of an "authentic self" with knowable characteristics recedes from view.[9]

This startling shift in consciousness may actually be beneficial, for current research suggests that people's attitudes are becoming more open and tolerant of the differences in others. There is no melancholy Generation X. Instead, we find a generation of young adults who are less shy, more emotionally expressive and responsive, more positive in their attitudes toward others and less distressed about their personal and collective futures. This new breed may be able to explore relationships more openly than previous generations, comfortably experimenting with a multiplicity of love: platonic, romantic, traditional, pragmatic, long distance, genderless, futuristic, etc. For this generation, an intriguing redefinition of intimacy has begun.

Constructing a Recipe for Love

Turning away from these more speculative scenarios, let us examine the major themes that have emerged in the past and have shaped our concepts today. What do we mean when we speak of love and intimacy? What do we desire in our partners and what do we seek as a standard for living together? In the past, we settled for simple definitions, relying on tradition to set the tone and pace, less conscious of our inner and outer needs. But now, we seem to want it all.

Throughout history we have sought a partner who was attractive, financially and emotionally stable, capable of having children, and who was willing to commit to the responsibilities of family life. These are universal values, upheld by nearly every culture worldwide, from ancient times to the present. They are survival skills, guaranteed to keep us alive in the best way possible, ensuring us an adequate mate and providing us with the needed security to carry out the tasks of life. In the behavioral and sexual strategies we use to select a partner, many subtle evaluations are made in order to support our fundamental desires. Is the potential mate in good health? Is the woman beautiful and young, of reputable character and kind? Is the man ambitious and generous, intelligent and of high social status—all criteria to ensure safety and support. Although we are unaware of it, these ancient strategies continue to govern our selection process for a mate. Indeed, throughout most of the world, this is the extent to which relationships aspire.[10]

But Americans have radically expanded upon these basic needs. We seek not just sexual union but sexual satisfaction in so many subtle ways: we want love, romance, passion, eros, ecstasy, a gentle embrace, the little death. We seek transcendence in the moment and more, believing that these ideal states are the everyday norms of life. In such a state of love, we run the risk of seeking wholeness exclusively in the other, struggling between the extremes of overdependence and isolation. In no other country has the romantic vision played such a fundamental role. Here we are free to dissolve the traditional rules of the game. We see the emergence of a new woman, liberated from the gender stereotypes of the past, engaged in political action, assertive, creative, and independent. A new man, too, has arisen, no longer tied to the false masculinity society used to expect: silent, defended by pride, ambitiously married to his work yet distant from child and wife. In writing in favor of the sensitive man, Anaïs Nin captured these changing roles and the unexpected challenge it brought:

> The empathy these new men show women is born of their acceptance of their own emotional, intuitive, sensory, and humanistic approach to relationships. They allow themselves to weep (men never wept), to show vulnerability, to expose their fantasies, share their inmost selves. . . . The new type of young man I have met is exceptionally fitted for the new woman, but she is not yet totally appreciative of his tenderness, his growing proximity to woman, his attitude of

twinship rather than differentiation. People who once lived under a dictatorship often are at a loss to govern themselves. This loss is a transitional one: It may mean the beginning of a totally new life and freedom. The man is there. He is an equal. He treats you like an equal. In moments of uncertainty you can still discuss problems with him you could not have talked about twenty years ago.[11]

Nin wrote these words over twenty years ago yet we are still struggling to define ourselves and our relationships with each other. Today, we have to *consciously* build a life together, reconstructing meaning at every step and turn. This is the legacy of contemporary American love.

The Art of Communication

Because we do not have a template to go by, we must forge between us a new cooperative alliance, one that attempts to embrace the unique desires of the other. In other parts of the world, cooperation is primarily governed by rules of conduct traditionally determined by culture and family. But in our society, we develop cooperation through dialogue and negotiation. In other words, to make our relationships work, we have to focus upon the art of communication. It is the key to successful relating: for discovering who the other person is, for identifying what his or her values are, for developing trust and emotional support, for resolving conflicts, and for recognizing the inherent differences that naturally exist between two people.

Here I make a distinction between everyday conversation and intimate dialogue. In our day-to-day communications, our feelings are often concealed, a useful strategy when dealing with the business aspects of our lives. At work or in school, or with casual acquaintances, we are expected to conform in behavior *and* speech, muting the nuances of our personality. We learn to talk by the rules. To an observant eye, one may be able to detect an underlying emotion or stress, but for the most part we remain hidden. At home or with friends, we may disclose a little more about our internal state of affairs. We might voice an opinion, crack a joke, or hint at an underlying disturbance. But because we have learned to be cautious about sharing our feelings, we continue to express ourselves through a protective veil. "What a lousy day at work," the husband says, avoiding a discussion of his internal feelings of inadequacy. "Let's go out to dinner," replies his wife, insinuating a need for affection. In a way, indirect communication is safe, a roundabout approach to test the waters of intimacy or gauge the degree of closeness our partners will allow. But because the messages are disguised, our intentions may be misconstrued.[12]

In contrast, intimate communication is direct and personal. It takes courage and trust to expose our more vulnerable feelings, to show our weaknesses and fears and deeper desires. Can we depend upon our partners to support us, to try to understand and not to judge? And when our lovers open their hearts to us, can we tolerate what they have to say? In intimate dialogue, we need to listen carefully, reflecting as much upon ourselves as upon the other, finding ways to let our partners know that they have been correctly understood. To respond to someone else's intimacy *in the way he or she needs to be responded to* takes practice, dialogue, and patience.

We often forego a deeper inquiry in the early stages of romance for fear that our questions may appear intrusive. Yet it is essential that we explore compatibility beyond the emotional bond. Do our social, religious, and political values mesh? Are our styles of dealing with money akin? Do we share similar parenting values? Do our personalities complement each other? A young woman caught in the throes of passion may presume that her lover shares complementary values and beliefs, while a young man's infatuation may blind him to his sexual insensitivity. Romance, it seems, obscures the logic that communication demands.

If we are willing to risk opening the doors of communication, we may begin to discover the deeper qualities of our partners and the hidden sides of our personality—our shadow, as the Jungians say. When we begin to share our fantasies and histories, we can discover who we once were, who we currently are, and what we may potentially become, together, with each other. We learn to talk not only *to* the other person but also *from* our selves, sharing what we are internally thinking and feeling. But to speak deeply from one's self involves great emotional risk. It feels vulnerable, for we are open to criticism, misunderstanding, and rejection at nearly every turn.

At this stage of communication, we often pierce the romantic veil that initially brought us together. Now disillusionment sets in and reality intrudes. We see behind the curtain: the differences, the subtle incompatibilities, the sexual inequalities. We notice how often we disagree about issues formerly taken for granted. But if we continue to share our intimate concerns, we may form a deeper bond and establish the framework for a genuine working relationship. Now we can creatively address the imbalances between autonomy and overdependence. We can negotiate the financial and family concerns that so often drive a couple to divorce. And we can embrace the challenges that a relational life provides, through marriage and midlife to the last few moments we share. When older couples tell us what made their marriages work, they invariably say that it was the kindness, the flexibility, the shared values, and the respectful companionship that each provided the other.[13] But for our generation, it will be the ability to communicate that will bring us the satisfaction we seek.

Communication provides the basic structure for contemporary relationships, but emotional support sustains its growth. It comes in many forms—acknowledgment, appreciation, recognition, compassion, understanding, respect—and, like communication, is often understated. We forget, or do not realize, that our partners have special vulnerabilities and needs, which change as we grow older and enter different stages of life. But the conveyance of emotional support is elusive. Words do not seem to capture it, and actions often fail. Like love, support means so many different things to others, and we can never take for granted that the person we are talking with feels understood and cared for. We have to ask, and ask again, never presuming that our partners feel embraced. Relationships are fragile, needing constant feedback and repair.

When we feel cared for, when we feel seen and heard and loved, then we can begin to establish the trust that is necessary for a meaningful and satisfying relationship.[14] One of the more serious mistakes that lovers make is presuming trust without substantiation. We enter a relationship with implied goodwill, but we need to seek verification through action, knowing that words, once again, are not enough. Trust involves integrity, honesty, and dependability, to be demonstrated in every aspect of life, in work and love, with family and social concerns. And any inconsistency in communication, support, or trust may be a trigger for conflict and discord. It may be caused by a simple empathic failure, a psychological problem, or an underlying weakness in personality.

In spite of all these difficulties, a rich and satisfying relationship can still be forged. And with a little knowledge and care we can transform the occasional nightmare that reality metes out.

Sometimes I wish that love was simple, but when I look inside, I have to admit that I really want it all. The wish itself is nothing new, spoken by Rilke a hundred years ago:

> *You see, I want a lot.*
> *Perhaps I want everything:*
> *the darkness that comes with every infinite fall*
> *and the shivering blaze of every step up. . . .*
> *You love most of all those who need you*
> *as they need a crowbar or a hoe.*[15]

What follows is a summary of relationship values that contemporary research has identified: the biological and evolutionary goals of love, the qualities of relationship that are highly valued throughout the world, those additional qualities that are desired by Americans, and the developmental tasks that have been recognized as essential for maintaining a meaningful and satisfactory relationship.[16] By no means is this list complete, nor is it intended to capture all the nuances and preferences that an individual may desire. Ultimately, each relationship is a unique constellation of complex attributes and compromises that remain in a state of flux through each developmental stage of life.

Making Relationships Work: A Summary of Contemporary World Research on Relationships

FOUR BIOLOGICAL GOALS OF LOVE:

- sexual attractiveness and intimacy
- the ability to provide for physical, economic, emotional, and family security
- sharing of resources
- commitment, marriage, and fidelity

These goals ultimately contribute to an increase in reproductive success, the basic survival goal for any living species. Evolutionary psychologists argue that these are the fundamental criteria that unconsciously govern our selection process for a mate.[17]

EIGHT QUALITIES THAT ARE HIGHLY VALUED IN RELATIONSHIPS WORLDWIDE:

- love
- dependable character
- good health
- emotional stability and maturity
- compatibility (necessary for sustaining a cooperative alliance and minimizing conflicts)
- ambition and industriousness (for men)
- physical beauty and youth (for women)
- education and intelligence

High social status and similarities in personality, race, and ethnicity also are highly valued throughout the world.[18] However, these characteristics are given much less import in the United States.

SIX ADDITIONAL QUALITIES SEEN AS ESSENTIAL BY AMERICAN COUPLES TODAY:

- communication
- sexual satisfaction (fantasy, romance, pleasure, passion, etc.)
- emotional support (understanding, compassion, appreciation, respect, empathy, etc.)
- trust (integrity, honesty, dependability)
- shared values (social, financial, spiritual, child, and family, etc.)
- friendship and companionship

A seventh attribute, psychological awareness—of self, other, and family dynamics—is also becoming highly valued, particularly in view of the tasks that are now required to develop and maintain relational stability.

EIGHT DEVELOPMENTAL TASKS NEEDED TO MAINTAIN A MEANINGFUL RELATIONSHIP:

- developing communication and listening skills
- exercising creative and flexible attitudes throughout all stages of relational development
- confronting challenges at each stage of life (dating, marriage, children, midlife, old age)
- establishing a balanced interdependence (autonomy versus overdependence)
- recognizing how personal history, family dynamics, and values influence relationships
- co-developing realistic and satisfactory financial and parenting plans
- maintaining an optimal balance between romantic idealization and disillusionment
- resolving conflicts in a safe and supportive environment

The Spirit of Love

Today, many American couples are beginning to seek an integration of spirituality and love. This pursuit is fueled, in part, by contemporary research which validates the importance that spirituality can play in maintaining physical and emotional health and providing meaning to relationship, work, and love.

Historically, many religious traditions attempted to separate love from the physical, reserving it solely for the higher realms of the soul. Islamic, Christian, and orthodox religions have been notorious for suppressing the carnal desire, but other religions have been more tolerant. Many forms of Judaism, for example, openly encourage a sensual and sexual involvement in life. And in the tantric arts of Asia, one may learn to savor the divine within the sexual embrace.

In India, where the Hindu temples are engraved with erotic delights, we find a culture and a religion that is based on the love affairs of the gods. In the Sahaja tradition of the eleventh and twelfth centuries, each man was Krishna and each woman Radha, and if they desired to reach ultimate consciousness, they must make their love as passionate as the gods:

> Clasped to my breasts you are far from me.
> Stay as my veil close to my face,
> How I fear when you turn your eyes away!
> We spend the night: one body,
> Sinking in the fathomless ocean of joy.
> As the dawn comes our anxious hearts watch
> Life deserting us.[19]

These stories, still sung today as part of the Bengali folk tradition, are filled with amorosity, desire, and jealousy, of the adulterous heart and the suicidal remorse. "A woman of one husband knows nothing of love," Radha implies to her virtuous friend, encouraging her to have an affair. But the equally unfaithful Krishna responds: "Have you no heart, no faith? Die then, sinful woman, die. I shall not live either for this sadness."[20] It is a familiar story, echoed in Shakespeare's plays and in the tragedies from ancient Greece, but it is also a religious theme that portrays the human side of love.

The eros of the Sahaja poets found its way across the borders where it eventually influenced the Sufi mystics. The affair with the Beloved continued: Rumi drank with his god, and Hafiz wedded her: "If love leads me to a musky, thick wine, it must be what I need. . . . The beautiful bride of the world approaches . . . and if we kissed, could I endure the love?"[21] Similar godly trysts can be found in the sixteenth-century memoirs of Saint Teresa and Saint John of the Cross.

These examples of mystical union may not have been fully embraced in the flesh, but they seem to have inspired, today, a generation of seekers who wish to invest their passion with a metaphysical tinge. Stripped of the religious conservatism that permeated the first half of this century, many young people turned to nontraditional and non-Western sources in search of inspiration and a newer definition of self. They discovered a different spirituality, a wholeness that could embrace love and sensitivity and the sensual pleasures of this earth. Today, we can see the emergence of a new set of spiritual preferences, borrowed from Asian and tribal philosophies and integrated with contemporary psychodynamics. From Jung to Frankl and Fromm, to the prevailing theories of object-relations and mind-body medicine, our society and our sciences have come to appreciate these subtle dimensions of the soul.

By integrating self-love and the love for another with spirituality, we can incorporate values that are equally recognized by psychology and religion, qualities that have been respected throughout culture and time. Beginning with Aristotle's cardinal virtues—strength, tranquility, wisdom, and justice—we might add any number of attributes that merit consideration, such as compassion, honesty, kindness, commitment, or forgiveness. For each person, the list will be different, yet these values are essential to the stability of any intimate relationship, whether we are conscious of them or not.

On the spiritual roads we travel, we sense the transformational powers of love, to the love within and between, and to the lover beyond. And we may even discover the spirituality of everyday life, where the sacred is found in the trees and the rocks and the ripple of a stream. With patience, these values can be integrated into every stage of human relationship: in conversations, in a heated debate, or in the midst of a passionate embrace. This is what Thomas Moore means when he invites us to care for the soul: to appreciate the mysteries of love, to embrace the sacredness of life, and to discover ourselves in the caring eyes of another.

In my own relationships, I have come to appreciate a certain truth the mystics talk about in their poems: that love is a tenuous and fluid path—impermanent as the Buddhists like to say. Life is impermanent. The flowers and trees are impermanent. They grow and dissolve with the seasons and eventually return anew. When we enter a relationship with such awareness, with an appreciation of its delicacy and vulnerability, we can approach our partners with grace.

All this, and more, we may find as we walk the path of love.

PART I

The Nature of
the Beast

All relationships are
laboratories in which we can
solve problems, engage in bold
and courageous acts of change,
and work toward defining
ourselves. Even small steps in
this direction will allow us to
know ourselves and our
partners better, a worthwhile
venture whether we stay
together over the long haul
or move on.

HARRIET LERNER

Relationship is complex and
difficult, and few can come
out of it unscathed. Though
we would like it to be static,
enduring, continuous,
relationship is a movement, a
process which must be deeply
and fully understood and
not made to conform to an
inner or outer pattern.

KRISHNAMURTI

Wild Nights

Wild nights! Wild nights!
Were I with thee,
Wild nights should be
Our luxury!

Futile the winds
To a heart in port—
Done with the compass,
Done with the chart.

Rowing in Eden!
Ah! The sea!
Might I but moor
Tonight in thee!

EMILY DICKINSON

Abiquiu

We were fighting, you know, as we drove through the deserts of New Mexico, and it was the sands of Abiquiu to which you made love. It was the colors and tones within those barren mountains that you courted, the reflection of daylight between the shadows, the dried parched mud of the land embracing you from every side.

I was jealous, I wanted to fight, resist. Slowly, painfully, I let the colors in. Mile after highway mile, hill after hill, I was inched down-ward into the clay, moistened now by my tears of shame for having never seen. You took me down into the clay, through your own uncovered soul, and I saw you for the very first time in the hills of Abiquiu.

M. R. WALDMAN

I n 1972, an anthropologist named Colin Turnbull came to a startling conclusion about human behavior and survival: that an emphasis upon individuality could eventually destroy all human goodness and condemn society to a cruel and meaningless existence.[1] For the most part, his ominous words fell on deaf ears, for we lived in a society that fully embraced the ideals of individualism and autonomy. Feelings of neediness and attachment were seen as faults, and couples were encouraged to develop separate lives and interests. We did not see the damage we were doing to ourselves and others.

Today, these views are changing as recent developments in science and medicine support a new relational paradigm: that closeness and interdependence are fundamental to survival and health. In psychology, we now give fuller attention to the complex interaction between internal and external forces, focusing upon the *interrelatedness* of people and the ways in which we influence one another. From this new perspective, our goal is to come closer to each other, to strengthen and deepen our bonds.

The opening chapter by Ruthellen Josselson captures this new vision of relationship. "People create their lives within a web of connection to others," she writes, noting that "the nuances of interconnection provide the richness, the intricacy, the abrasion, and much of the interest in living." In her groundbreaking research, she looks at relationships through the metaphor of space and how we navigate ourselves through this unseen realm of intimacy. Her theme provides, essentially, a new way to understand many of the problems that couples struggle with—love addictions, affairs, communication breakdowns, sexual insensitivities— issues that are the topic of many other chapters in this book.

The theme of connectedness continues in Nathaniel Branden's essay, "A New Vision of Romance," as he examines many of our psychological needs of companionship and the role that romance can play in developing a healthy and lasting intimacy. He defines romantic love as "a passionate spiritual-emotional-sexual *attachment* between two people that reflects a high regard for the value of each other's person."

These new dimensions of relationship do not preclude the lessons we've learned from the past. In Judith Viorst's essay, she reminds us how much Freud's insights remain relevant today: that in every aspect of our lives we are partially motivated by unconscious processes shaped by our childhood memories and encounters. Unless we become cognizant of these influences, we are bound to repeat our past, bringing undeserved suffering to ourselves and to those for whom we care.

On the biological side of relationships, modern neuroscience provides a wealth of information showing that many experiences of love—desire, romance, infatuation, attachment, disappointment, even the urge to divorce—are shaped as much by the body's chemistry as they are by conscious and unconscious decisions. Diane Ackerman's discussion of these "cuddle chemicals" challenges us to rethink many of the notions we hold about feelings and choice when it comes to matters of the heart.

Deepak Chopra expands upon the physiological models of love by exploring how a state of loving can positively affect the immune system. Indeed, there are hundreds of studies that confirm the connections between intimacy and health, for when we are in a good relationship, we get ill less often, recover from surgery faster, have less depression and anxiety, and even live longer after an encounter with a terminal disease. Without adequate social support—friends, family, even pets—our lives just fade away. Overall, we are happier in relationship than when we are alone. Thus, as Chopra suggests, the more we consciously love, the healthier we become in body, mind, and soul.

Cultural historian Riane Eisler provides yet another link between biology and love, using evolutionary studies to show how sex, language, and consciousness have emerged within the human species to promote an interconnectedness with others. But she argues that the history of Western religion, with its insistence upon a separation between physical and spiritual love, has interfered with our natural development, contributing to many of the relational problems of today. She sees the current interest in altered states of consciousness providing a doorway to a more natural and integrative spirituality, one that facilitates greater intimacy between people and cultures throughout the world: "Since this will be a spirituality that derives from a sense of connection rather than detachment, it will also be a spirituality in which love is not otherworldly but very much of this world."

In a world where the components of relationship seem to grow more complicated every day, one might suspect that intimacy would become more difficult to achieve or maintain. But Mihaly Csikszentmihalyi's research on the psychology of optimal experience suggests the opposite: that the increasing complexity of any experience—be it work, relationship, or spirituality—creates an opportunity to grow, thereby improving the flow of intimacy and love. Csikszentmihalyi demonstrates that in any activity, like a game or sport, the more challenging it is, the more pleasure we receive. The same is true in relationships, sex, and family life. When we immerse ourselves more deeply in challenging aspects of love, we experience a state of consciousness called *flow* and our relationships become more meaningful and satisfying. When we "play" with intimacy in this way, we become more psychologically integrated and able to enjoy life more fully. "Flow helps to integrate the self because in that state of deep concentration consciousness is unusually well ordered," writes Csikszentmihalyi. "It makes the present instant more enjoyable, and . . . it builds the self-confidence that allows us to develop skills and make significant contributions to humankind."

I.

The Space Between Us

RUTHELLEN JOSSELSON

In the past, independence was considered a psychological treasure, but now it is seen as a potential threat to intimacy. Today, our views have changed to embrace the notions of interdependency, where love is seen as an intricate web of personal and interpersonal dynamics. In the following essay, Ruthellen Josselson, a professor at Towson State University, makes an important contribution to our understanding of the psycho-physical dimensions of intimacy and love, describing eight dimensions of relatedness as seen through the metaphor of space.

AT BIRTH, the cord that tied us prenatally to our mother is cut, and we are alone. We are thrust into separateness, physically bound within the confines of our body. If we are women, we can contain another, in pregnancy, within our physical body space. But we can never again be physically joined to another. Relationship becomes the only means of overcoming the space between us.

Psychologically, we are also doomed to separateness. No one else can ever think exactly my thoughts as I think them or know precisely how I feel. We cannot even know, for example, that what I see and call blue is not what you see when you say red. But we reach out and try to overcome that separateness. With speech, we try to describe our inner experiences to one another. Or we share our lives and needs in various ways. Or we get as close as we can physically. When we do these things, we feel as if there is something "between" us. And we speak in those terms: "Is there something between you and him?" Interpersonal life, then, is an effort to connect and, in connecting, to overcome this psychological and physical space. Different ways of interrelating are different methods of transcending the chasm that parts us. The "between"—the way the space is filled or reverberates—becomes all-important.

There are many ways in which we reach through the space that separates us to make connections—ways that vary throughout life—and many motives that impel us to do so. Relatedness involves other people as objects of desire (as when we need someone to satisfy a particular need), but relatedness also serves as a context for the experience of the self. Theorists who have taken on the task of explicating relational experience have tended to do so emphasizing a particular aspect of connection. D. W. Winnicott, for example, taught us much about holding, and John Bowlby called our attention to attachment. Sigmund Freud, of course, viewed all relational connection as an aspect of sexual (libidinal) drive. More recent writers, such as Jean Baker Miller and her colleagues at the Stone Center, have highlighted the importance of responsiveness and mutuality, and Carol Gilligan has gotten us thinking about the dilemmas of care and connection, fundamental to selfhood, that are organizers of identity as well as moral thinking. Each theorist, however, ends up with a unidimensional model. By putting these models together, we can construct a figure with many sides.

The psychological and the physical are always metaphorically (and often linguistically) linked. Thus, when we feel deeply the experience of another, we say that we feel "touched."

Conversely, we might hold the hand of another to feel emotionally close to him or her. We can have sex with a stranger and feel psychologically "untouched," and we can have profound intimate contact by looking in someone else's eyes. . . .

There are eight primary ways in which we overcome the space between us. They involve, actually or metaphorically, a way of transcending space, of reaching through space (or being reached) and being in contact with each other. As each dimension emerges in the developmental history of the individual, each is concrete and basic. As development proceeds, each way of connecting becomes more symbolic, less physical and spatial, but no less crucial. Each dimension of relatedness has its own channel, its own origin and course. Understanding each dimension uniquely allows us to understand the confluence of the streams that create the character of relatedness in adult life.

Holding is the first interpersonal experience and represents security and a basic trust that what is essential will be provided. In holding, we experience ourselves as contained by another; powerful arms keep us from falling. Throughout life, we need to feel held in developmentally more mature idioms, but we continue to need to be contained, bounded, and grounded in order to grow.

A bit later in earliest development, babies learn to discriminate their mothers from the other people around, making possible *attachment* to this one very particular other person. The innate propensity to attach to others structures some of the most fundamental processes throughout life, including the painful vulnerability to loss that is part of our human core. When we are attached, it is as though we were clinging to someone, holding on with our limbs, keeping close. Throughout life, we continue to form attachments (if we are fortunate), and these are often at the center of our existence.

From the beginning of life, basic biological drives seek gratification. In infancy, the need to suck—the earliest form of libidinal life—forms a third configuration of interpersonal experience. Here, in the realm of *passionate experience,* others are objects of drive gratification. This pleasure-seeking orientation will organize experience in different ways and at different levels of intensity throughout the life course. Contacting others through our drives is the mode of passionate relating: overcoming separateness through sexual union or its symbolic expression. The pleasures of touch and the possibilities of uniting in boundaryless bliss are powerful means of transcending space.

In eye-to-eye relating, we overcome space through the communication of eye contact, finding ourselves in the other's eyes, having a place in the other. In *eye-to-eye validation,* we connect by existing in and for someone else. As early in development as we become able to know an other as an Other, we begin to use the other as a mirror to learn about ourselves. What the infant first sees in the mother's eyes forms a core of the infant's sense of self—the beginning of a process that continues in more refined and complex ways throughout life.

After existing for a time in this world of Others, we begin to notice that some are bigger, stronger, and more able to do things than we are ourselves. When we idealize and identify with others, we reach up for them, try to climb through the distance that separates us; we try to be where they are as a way of expanding ourselves. *Idealization and identification* are ways of linking to powerful others and striving to become like them (or to control them).

As the person grows through childhood and the self matures and becomes more aware of others, the child eventually discovers the possibilities of engaging the self with others and becomes able to experience companionship, which is a form of *mutuality.* In mutuality, we stand side by side with someone, moving in harmony, creating a bond that is the product of both people—an emergent *we* in the space between.

When we are embedded with others, we "fit in" like a piece of a jigsaw puzzle; we are comfortable in our role, our "place." It is not usually until adolescence that the concern with having a place in society becomes paramount. Yet younger children also make important their sense of belonging to one group rather than another, differentiating themselves and at the same time experiencing communality. The experience is one of being part of, belonging—the dimension of *embeddedness* with others.

Finally, but all along, the developing person has been learning about taking care of others, offering the self to others' needs, bridging the space through *tending and care.* In tending, we hold others, cradling them (actually or symbolically) in our arms.

All of these modalities, then, are forms of reaching through the space that separates us, both physically and psychologically. Any given relationship may involve more than one of these dimensions, simultaneously or sequentially. The metaphor of spatial orientation is useful in cutting through confusing verbalizations to clarify how people are oriented toward each other and what they need to feel connected.

These dimensions of relatedness unfold simultaneously and often independently, although they may interpenetrate and incorporate each other. They are not, however, reducible one to another. Because human life is of a piece, the dimensions shade into one another; they do not stay separate and distinct (as well they should not). But each has its own coherent center, its own fundamental phenomenology; each has its own metaphor and form of expression. Thinking in these terms allows us to move beyond thinking of all human connection as rooted in and metaphorically experienced as "good feeding."

How and toward whom love is expressed varies by culture. Yet there are certain fundamental human propensities for connection that find expression in some form universally. Social mores and traditions regulate the rituals and forms through which people are held or recognized or idealized, but the processes of these eight dimensions remain identifiable.

No doubt there are other ways to describe a multidimensional relational space; perhaps there are even more than eight dimensions. The dimensions chosen here are drawn from the modalities that theorists have already brought into focus, juxtaposed with one another so that relatedness emerges as a multifaceted process.

The first four dimensions are primary: holding, attachment, passionate experience, and eye-to-eye validation. They are present either from the beginning of life (the need to be held and the need for drive gratification) or shortly thereafter (as in attachment and awareness of eye-to-eye response). The second four dimensions require cognitive maturation and may not develop until late childhood. Idealization and embeddedness require a concept and experience of the self, as well as the capacity to think about how one is positioned in regard to others. Mutuality and tending, also very much concerned with responsiveness to others, require development out of egocentrism and into a world of others. . . .

In this fundamental existential sense, we can love and can be loved on any of the dimensions, exclusively or in combination. We love the one who holds us, because without that person we could not exist; and we love those we hold, because we mean so much to them. We love those to whom we are attached, because they are our emotional "home," where we will be taken in no matter what, and they are the people with whom our lives are intertwined. And we love those who mirror and recognize us, because without them we could not be. All these people we love with gratitude, for they give us ourselves. We also love those who are the objects of our passions, because they arouse and excite us and seem to embody all that would complete us. This person we wish to possess, exclusively and eternally. And we love those who embody our ideals, who stimulate us to reach beyond ourselves, who represent our becoming. We love those with whom we share ourselves, in play and in knowledge of one another. These are the people who walk with us through life, and they are irreplaceable. And we love those whom we tend and nurture, because they contain a part of us and testify to our value as human beings. We love, too, those with whom we are embedded; these people we love less personally but, especially in times of group distress, no less profoundly.

It may be that there are higher and lower forms of love, each building on the other. People who grew up deprived of adequate attachment experiences, for example, seek, above all, enduring attachment in later life. Such people—for example, child survivors of the Holocaust whose parents were taken from them and murdered—speak little as adults about a quest for passion or mutuality. For them, feeling bonded to special others in new attachments overshadows all other forms of relatedness.

Maslow was working with the idea of higher and lower forms of love in his notions of deficiency and being needs. While healthy development requires some relational connection on all of the dimensions, the higher orders of mutuality, passion, and tenderness, for example, are probably available only to those who have had adequate experiences of attachment, holding, and (later) embeddedness. (Perhaps there are also forms of self-actualization that we have not yet conceptualized in loyal bonding or in serving group goals.)

The labyrinths of our relationships with each other are created by our unique recipes for love. The arguments between spouses, between brothers and sisters, and between friends all begin with built-in—perhaps even unconscious—expectations of how one would treat and be treated if love bound the relationship. Thus "If you loved me, you would . . ." is a fundamental phrase of human misunderstanding.

Love and Culture

We have to be wary of love ideology that is based on cultural assumptions. Only recently, with the triumph of "therapeutic" ideals, has "authentic feeling" become the ideological basis of love relationships. In contrast to previous eras, in which kinship or class or duty served to lead people to each other, our age anchors relationship in feeling. The ideal is the heterosexual pair who are "in love," experiencing passion, tenderness, and attachment. Real relatedness among people—relatedness that sustains life, powers development, and shapes identity—is, however, far more complex.

Expectations about love are, to a large extent, dictated by culture. That is dangerous only when people are confused as to what is a cultural ideal and what they can expect in reality. People are alarmed when they find themselves loving differently from others, for example. They are also confused by the idealization of love in a materialistic environment. When love is promoted as a commodity, it is hard to know when we have gotten our share. How much exactly are we entitled to? How do we know whether to stay with a relationship and try to improve it or simply move on? Beneath the symptoms of psychopathology is always relational pain—wounds inflicted through commission or omission by another. But our actions with others exist in a context of interpretation. Between our experience with another and our integration of that experience are multiple steps of meaning-making. Consider the following stories of Sandra and Janet:

Sandra is married to Jack, a businessman who is preoccupied with his work and spends most of his time at his office. He makes a large income and gives Sandra complete freedom in spending it. He has been generous about financial assistance to Sandra's brother, who is always on the brink of bankruptcy, and he is forbearing about taking in other members of Sandra's family in their recurring crises and disasters. He is devoted to Sandra and tries to comply with anything she asks of him. But what Sandra wants most from Jack is emotional investment in her. She wants him to talk to her about his feelings, to initiate sex, to try to get to know her more deeply, to plan activities for them. Sandra works part-time as a nurse, takes college courses, and has many friends. But she feels depressed and unfulfilled, in conflict over whether she should leave Jack and find a partner with whom she can have a more emotionally intense and mutual relationship.

Janet was thrilled when Marty, the high school football hero, finally asked her to marry him. Their friends viewed them as the ideal couple, and Janet thought she had everything she would ever want. Two years after their marriage, they had a much-wanted son, but Marty began spending more and more time at work and playing golf. Now Janet is feeling increasingly isolated. With great simplicity and great pain, she speaks of the collapse of her dream: "I thought we would be together and build a family together. Now I hardly ever see him."

If they were members of another society or subculture, Sandra and Janet would not expect anything else from their husbands. (Men are similarly culture-bound in their expectations of women and in their interpretation of opposite-sex behavior. We might remember that Freud could not figure out what women want.) If they were Victorian women, for example, they would expect to be living their emotional lives apart from their husbands in distinct, sex-segregated worlds. They would expect to satisfy their interpersonal needs through kinship, friendship, and community. The relational networks of our highly mobile, loosely organized society force people into increasingly smaller units of relational connection and at the same time idealize these units beyond their capacity to deliver. The current emphasis on marital "togetherness" often burdens the relationship beyond its endurance and so gives rise to an industry of self-help books and marriage counselors to try to keep it intact.

Similarly, the nuclear family is now asked to perform functions formerly carried out by a whole community, and when it fails in its task, it is usually the mother who is "blamed." As the extended family was fading out of existence in urban America in the 1950s, in response to rapidly increasing geographical mobility and the turn to the suburbs, the extremely popular television program "Father Knows Best" was romanticizing the nuclear family. No other television program has appeared so frequently in my patients' associations—associations related to their intense disappointment in their own families for not being like the TV family. They yearned for the calm understanding and compassion of that all-wise, ideal father, whom they were afraid all others had and they alone lacked.

We all secretly suspect that the reason that we do not get more from others is that we are undeserving, unacceptable. ("If only I could lose ten pounds, I would be loved as much as I want.") We compare our own experience of what others offer us with media images and come up short. We are ashamed to compare our experiences with others, because we may be exposed in our inadequacy. Thus many people live with the painful sense of having less loyal and interested friends than others do, less passionate spouses, less reliable attachment figures. To comfort and distract themselves, they seize on the current cultural and therapeutic message that what we really ought to do in life is learn to do it all ourselves. Love ourselves, take care of ourselves, draw wider boundaries. Be our own best friend! (I wonder how anything so absurd could have captured so many people.) Let's just not need each other, our culture urges.

Conflict and the Irrationalities of Love

The dimensional model of relatedness emphasizes the yearning for connection, but power, competition, and conflict are also present throughout. Within each of the dimensions of connection lurks the threat (and experience) of the opposite. We are most aware of being held when we begin to fall or feel smothered, for example. Nothing sharpens our sense of ourselves and our meaning for others as much as a heated argument or contest. Sometimes we most heighten our experience of a dimension of love when we veer into its absence or excess.

Conflict is itself a form of connection, existing on each of the dimensions. Anger, envy, and contempt color all relationships. To speak of relational connection is not to imply seamless harmony or warm fuzziness or anything static and unchanging. Above all, relationships *move*. We discover the self through our connections with others, and our heightening of self-knowledge makes possible more complex and deeper ways of reaching others. As we grow, we refine and modify our connections. We never fully bridge the space between us, but we experience within our lives many ways of reaching across. I agree with Bowlby that we are not inherently aggressive. Rather, our fears of aloneness and loss make us rageful, and we learn to use our anger to try to compel others to meet our needs.

To be unloved is unbearable because it means that we have no real meaning or importance to anyone. As humans, we are stuck with our inescapable need for the emotional responsiveness of another—a need kindled by the sparkle in our mother's eye, a need that serves no biological purpose and often causes us tremendous pain. But unless we know that we are somewhere part of the affective life of another, we cannot feel our own existence. This is why people who fear that they are unloved often work to be hated (hate being just another face of love in its intensity and its selectivity).

Conflict between us and those whom we take into our relational networks, conflict among the dimensions of our relational needs—these conflicts generally must be lived with rather than "resolved." We can try to achieve a higher order of understanding and integration, or we can tear ourselves apart trying to insist on relational illusions or relational consistency.

People live with both their fantasies of love and their experiences of love. Inner representations of loving relationships may have little to do with how they appear to observers (or even to the other person in the relationship). What we learn about love, then, depends a great deal on what we ask people. Studies of the mythology of love tell us little about people's actual experience. We sigh cathartically over *Antigone* or *Casablanca* but carry on with the less romantic folks at home.

Marge, a thirty-five-year-old research subject, told of her own dreams of love. For years, while she was in her twenties, she was involved with a married man whom she idealized. He was in her profession, and she was always very stimulated talking to him about ideas. There was much mutuality between them, and wonderful sex. Yet she knew that his attachment to his wife was so strong that he would never leave her. What Marge was focused on was wanting just once to hear him tell her that he loved her. She felt that these would be the magic words that would let her know that she was a person of value. (He often told her that he loved being with her or loved making love to her, but he never said that he loved *her*.) Finally, after a five-year relationship, he said the magic words. And Marge said that she felt nothing. The declaration meant nothing. As in the wonderful "Do You Love Me?" song from *Fiddler on the Roof,* it did not change a thing. And she left him.

Consider also the insightful scene in the movie *Tootsie* where the Jessica Lange character confides to the female Dustin Hoffman character that her deepest fantasy is that someday a man will come up to her and say, with no ritual or small talk, "The simple truth is—I find you really interesting—and I'd really like to make love to you." Some days later, the Dustin Hoffman character, back as a man, obligingly does just that. And she throws her drink in his face.

Relatedness and love may be to psychology what chaos is to physics—a new but necessary frontier where the phenomena will not hold still for analysis. (In physics, if they do hold still, they change.) To understand relatedness, we must be able to encompass paradox and contradiction. Inner and outer, self and other, love and hate, fantasy and reality, rational and irrational, conscious and unconscious—all coexist within the relational frame.

Always there is the fear that love, in its many manifestations and dimensions, is not very scientific. And so we try to make love problems appear to be something else. People go to psychiatrists because they are lonely and feel unloved, and they are given medication: the "scientific" response.

A patient consults me for intractable stomach pain that physicians have been unable to treat medically. I am her fifth therapist. Others have told her that her problem is her oral dependency, her inhibited sexuality, possible sexual abuse (which she does not remember), repressed rage. She is talented, attractive, and sensitive but has no friends. What does she feel she needs? I ask her. "I need to have someone in my corner," she says. And that, I think, is the essence of it. So do we all.

2.

A New Vision of Romance

NATHANIEL BRANDEN

For centuries, philosophers and psychologists have warned us about the dangers of romantic love, but current research has found that it is an essential component in relationships. Nathaniel Branden, well-known author and psychotherapist, outlines nine psychological needs that romantic love satisfies. He reminds us, though, that the journey into romantic love takes courage and mutual responsibility .

THERE ARE ... different kinds of love that can unite one human being with another. There is love between parents and children. There is love between siblings. There is love between friends. There is a love made of caring and affection but devoid of sexual feeling. And there is the kind of love we call "romantic."

Romantic love is *a passionate spiritual-emotional-sexual attachment between two people that reflects a high regard for the value of each other's person.* When I write of romantic love, this is the meaning I intend.

I do not describe a relationship as romantic if the couple does not experience their attachment as passionate or intense, at least to some significant extent (allowing, of course, for the normal ebb and flow of feeling that is intrinsic to life). I do not describe a relationship as romantic love if there is not some experience of spiritual affinity, by which I mean some deep mutuality of values and outlook, some sense of being soul mates; if there is not a deep emotional involvement; if there is not a strong sexual attraction (allowing, once more, for normal fluctuations of feeling). And if there is not mutual admiration—if, for example, there is mutual contempt instead (which can certainly coexist with sexual attraction)—again I do not describe the relationship as romantic love. . . .

What is unique about romantic love is that it incorporates or draws on more aspects of the self than any other kind of love—our sense of life, our sexuality, our body, our deepest fantasies or longings regarding man or woman, our self-concept, the cardinal values that energize our existence. Our spiritual-emotional-sexual response to our partner is a consequence of seeing him or her as the embodiment of our highest values and as being crucially important to our personal happiness. "Highest," in this context, does not necessarily mean noblest or most exalted; it means most important, in terms of our personal needs and desires and in terms of what we wish to find and experience in life. As an integral part of that response—and this differentiates romantic love from the love for a friend, a parent, or a child—we see the loved object as being crucially important to our *sexual* happiness. The needs of our spirit and body melt into each other; we experience a unique sense of wholeness. . . .

What are the psychological needs that romantic love satisfies? There are, I believe, a network of complementary needs involved.

1. There is our need for *human companionship:* for someone with whom to share values, feelings, interests, and goals; for someone with whom to share the joys and burdens of existence.

2. There is our need *to love:* to exercise our emotional capacity in the unique way that love makes possible. We need to find persons to admire, to feel stimulated and excited by, persons toward whom we can direct our energies.

3. There is our need *to be loved:* to be valued, cared for, and nurtured by another human being.

4. There is our need to experience *psychological visibility:* to see ourselves in and through the responses of another person, one with whom we have important affinities. This is, in effect, our need for a psychological mirror. (The concept of psychological visibility,

developed in considerable detail in *The Psychology of Romantic Love,* is basic to my understanding of man/woman relationships.)

5. There is the need for *sexual fulfillment:* for a counterpart as a source of sexual satisfaction.

6. There is our need for *an emotional support system:* for at least one person who is genuinely devoted to our well-being, an emotional ally who, in the face of life's challenges, is reliably there.

7. There is our need for *self-awareness and self-discovery:* for expanded contact with the self, which happens continually and more or less naturally through the process of intimacy and confrontation with another human being. Self-awareness and self-discovery attend the joys and conflicts, harmonies and dissonances of a relationship.

8. There is our need *to experience ourselves fully as a man or woman:* to explore the potentials of our maleness or femaleness in ways that only romantic love optimally makes possible. Just as we need a sense of identity as human beings, so we need a sense of identity related to gender—of a kind most successfully realized through interaction with the opposite sex.

9. There is our need *to share our excitement in being alive and to enjoy and be nourished by the excitement of another.*

I call these needs, not because we die without them, but because we live with ourselves and in the world so much better with them. They have survival value.

This list does not seem to me to be the slightest bit speculative. I believe common experience, observation, and reason support it. But if I were to be speculative, I might posit a tenth need—the need *to encounter, unite with, and live out vicariously our opposite-gender possibilities:* the need, in males, to find an embodiment in the world of the internal feminine; the need, in females, to find an embodiment in the world of the internal masculine. . . .

If romantic love is to succeed, it asks far more of us in terms of our personal evolution and maturity than is ordinarily understood.

The first thing it asks is a reasonably good level of self-esteem. If we enjoy healthy self-esteem—if we feel competent, lovable, deserving of happiness—we are very likely to choose a mate who will reflect and support our self-concept. If we feel inadequate, unlovable, undeserving of happiness, again we are likely to become involved with a person who will confirm our deepest vision of ourselves.

If we enjoy good self-esteem, we are likely to treat our partner well and to expect that he or she will treat us well, which tends to become a self-fulfilling prophecy. We will not see ourselves as a martyr or a victim. We will not feel that suffering is our natural destiny, and we will not put up with it in passive resignation—let alone go looking for it. If we lack good self-esteem, we are unlikely to treat our partner well, despite our good intentions, because of our fears and excessive dependency. And if our partner treats us badly, some part of us will feel, "But of course." And if and when our relationship ends and we go looking for a new partner, despair can make us not more thoughtful but more blind—so our self-esteem goes on deteriorating and so does our love life.

If we are to choose a mate wisely, we need to feel that we are deserving of love, admiration, and respect—and that only someone we can truly love, admire, and respect is appropriate for us. If we are to treat our relationship with the care and nurturing it deserves, we need to feel that we are deserving of happiness—that happiness is not a miracle or a mirage but our natural and appropriate birthright.

Our sense of self, the way we perceive and assess ourselves, crucially affects virtually *every* aspect of our existence. That has been the central theme of all my work. As regards love, the first love affair we must consummate successfully is with ourselves. Only then are we ready for other relationships. And how well can we practice "mutual self-disclosure" if we are strangers to ourselves, alienated from our inner life, cut off from feelings and emotions and longings? Self-alienation is the enemy of intimacy and therefore of romantic love (or any other kind of love). Or if we are estranged from our sexuality, or in an adversary relationship to our body, we lack the mind-body integration that romantic love celebrates. If we have not attained a reasonably mature level of individuation and autonomy, chances are we will overburden our relationship with demands that can't be met—such as to create (rather than express) our self-esteem and our happiness or to support the illusion that we are not ultimately responsible for our own existence.

Romantic love requires courage—the courage to stay vulnerable, to stay open to our feelings for our partner, even when we are temporarily in conflict, even when we are frustrated, hurt, angry—the courage to remain connected with our love, rather than shut down emotionally, even when it is terribly difficult to do so. When a couple lacks this courage and seeks "safety" from pain in the refuge of withdrawal, as so commonly happens, it is not romantic love that has failed them but they who have failed romantic love.

3.

Lessons in Love

JUDITH VIORST

The ways in which we experience love as a child will often shape our other relationships throughout life. In this essay, Judith Viorst, recipient of many awards for her writings on poetry, journalism, and psychoanalysis, reminds us how often the past can influence and interfere with our ability to love and be loved, and how important it is for us to develop our self-reflective skills.

WE DISCOVER from early experiences of passionate intensity, the pleasures love can offer, and the pain. We repeat and repeat our lessons all our life. And maybe . . . we may even be able to say, "Hey, there I go again."

But sometimes the repetitions are outside of our awareness.

And sometimes the lessons we learn are not too terrific.

I play with a little girl who has traumatically lost her mother and her father. In the midst of our fun she stops, stands up, says "Bye." Her style seems to be: "I'm leaving you first, before you go off and leave me." And I wonder if she will grow up compelled to always leave what she loves before it can hurt her, a practitioner of relationship interruptus.

I know a little boy whose mother pushes him away. "I'm busy," she tells him. "Not now. You're bothering me." Watching him pester and whine and plead and ragingly kick at her always locked bedroom door, I wonder what he will be doing with women twenty years from now and what he will want, need, women to do to him.

There is in human nature a compulsion to repeat. Indeed it is called the repetition compulsion. It impels us to do again and again what we have done before, to attempt to restore an earlier state of being. It impels us to transfer the past—our ancient longings, our defenses against those longings—onto the present.

Thus whom we love and how we love are revivals—unconscious revivals—of early experience, even when revival brings us pain. And although we may play Iago instead of Othello, Desdemona instead of Iago, we will act out the same old tragedies unless awareness and insight intervene.

That little boy, for instance, may play out his helplessness as a passive, submissive husband. He may play out his murderous rage as a wife-beating husband. He may choose his mother's role and become a cold you-have-to-beg-me-for-it husband. Or he may, like his absent father, simply abandon his wife and his own son to their fate.

That little boy may marry the psychological spitting image of his mother. He may work his wife over until she becomes that mother. He may ask his wife the impossible and then, when she refuses him, he may rail, "You always refuse me—just like my mother."

In repeating the past that boy might repeat his fury or humiliation or grief. Or he might repeat the tactics by which he beat back fury, humiliation, grief. In repeating the past he will update the script to include the shadings of subsequent experience. But whom he loves and how he loves will reflect that whining, pleading, raging boy.

For many men the denial of dependency on their mother is repeated in their subsequent relationships, sometimes by an absence of any sexual interest in women, sometimes by a pattern of loving and leaving them. For other men and women, however, dependency is the point of love relationships; and whomever they take to bed will always be (at least in their head) the ever-yearned-for, gratifying mother.

A lesbian relationship—like the one Karen Snow describes in her novel *Willo*—may also repeat love patterns of early childhood:

> Out of boredom, Pete takes a job welding in an aircraft plant. But the
> long hours of manual labor do not change her into the man. She is

still the self-sacrificing one who will continue to cook and wash and iron and scrub floors. She will spend large chunks of her wages on Willo. . . .

The masculine-feminine bond is frail compared with this mother-daughter bond. Each girl is merely moving in grooves that were carved deep into her early in childhood. Willo has always been the aloof princess served and scolded by a coarse, martyred woman; in fact, by two martyred women: her mother and her sister. Pete has always been subservient to a glamorous mother, who was usually away from home, achieving. She has been housekeeper and cook, too, for a busy, burly father who had wanted a son.

In describing his taste in women, baby doctor/political activist Benjamin Spock also reveals a repetition compulsion, for, as he points out, "I have always been fascinated by rather severe women, women I then could charm despite their severity." The model for these women—as Dr. Spock is well aware—was his own demanding and highly critical mother. And if, in his early eighties, he is indeed a most exceptionally charming man, the wish to win over his mother may help explain why.

"I have always been amazed," he says, "at men who were able to love somewhat soft women." Such conquests, he suggests, are too easy to matter. "I always needed someone who thought I was special but who also offered a challenge." He says that both his first wife, Jane, and his second wife, Mary Morgan, are versions—although in quite different ways—of this type.

(Because Dr. Spock volunteered "to give permission for you and Mary to talk about me behind my back," let me note here that Mary Morgan disagrees. She maintains that she isn't this critical type of woman that Spock is describing. But, she adds, "He keeps trying to make me into that person"—which is also, of course, a compulsion to repeat.)

We repeat the past by reproducing earlier conditions, challenging as that can sometimes be, like the woman described by Freud who managed to find not one, not two, but three different husbands, all of whom fell fatally ill soon after they were married and subsequently had to be nursed by her on their deathbed.

We also repeat the past by superimposing parental images onto the present, myopic as that frequently can be, failing to recognize that being gentle doesn't have to mean being weak (daddy, alas, was gentle but he was weak), that silence may be companionable not punishing (mother's silences were always punishing) and that gentle, quiet people may be offering something new—if we could but see it.

We even repeat the past when we quite consciously are trying not to repeat it, hopeless as that may turn out to be, like the woman who disdained her parents' conventional and patriarchal marriage and decided that hers would have an entirely new format. Was her mother completely ruled by her bossy husband? Well, then, this lady's mate would be the ruled-over type. And furthermore she would be so unconventional, modern and free that she would openly bring her lovers into their house. But she then allowed her lovers to abuse her and humiliate her—I suppose her notion of modern was anything goes—and so, in her freewheeling life as an autonomous woman and wife she arranged to repeat her mother's despised submissiveness.

The repetition compulsion, writes Freud, explains why this one is always betrayed by his friends and why that one is always abandoned by his protégés and why each of a lover's love affairs may pass through similar stages and end the same way. For although there are people, writes Freud, who seem to be "pursued by a malignant fate, or possessed by some 'daemonic' power . . . their fate is for the most part arranged by themselves and determined by early infantile influences."

It seems reasonable to us to wish to transfer the pleasing past onto the present, to seek to repeat the delights of earlier days, to fall in love with those who resemble the first beloved objects of our affection, to do it again because we loved it the first time. If mom was truly wonderful, why shouldn't her son want to marry a girl like the girl who married dear old dad? Surely all normal love—it needn't be kinky, it needn't be blatantly incestuous—is bound to partake in part of transference love.

Repeating the good makes sense but we have trouble understanding the compulsion to repeat what causes pain. And while Freud has tried to explain this compulsion as part of a dubious concept called the death instinct, it can also be understood as our hopeless effort to undo—rewrite—the past. In other words, we do it and do it and do it and do it again in the hope that this time the ending will be different. We keep repeating the past—when we were helpless and acted upon—trying to master and change what has already happened.

In repeating painful experience we are refusing to lay to rest our childhood ghosts. We continue to clamor for something that cannot be. No matter how hard they clap for us now, she will never clap for us *then.* We have to relinquish that hope. We have to let go.

For we cannot climb into a time machine, become that long-gone child and get what we want when we oh so desperately wanted it. The days for that getting are over, finished, done. We have needs we can meet in different ways, in better ways, in ways that create new experience. But until we can mourn that past, until we can mourn and let go of that past, we are doomed to repeat it.

Weaving the past with the present, we can experience many kinds and stages of love. We can love, one way or another, throughout our life. "Only connect!" a character in E. M. Forster's *Howards End* exhorts us. And needy, tender, romantic, ecstatic, fearful, heedless, hopeful—how we do try!

We try through sexual love—the physical thrum and orgastic release; through eros—the urge for union and creation; through motherly love and brotherly love and neighborly love and friendship; through *caritas*—an altruistic loving. We try through human relationships that draw on one, or all, of the above. Shaped in whole or in part and for good or for ill by the instructors of our childhood, we try to love.

We try and we keep on trying because an unconnected life is not worth living. A life of solitude cannot be borne. In an eloquent passage, Erich Fromm writes:

Man is gifted with reason; he is *life being aware of itself*. . . . This aware-ness of himself as a separate entity, the awareness of his own short life span, of the fact that without his will he is born and against his will he dies, that he will die before those whom he loves, or they be-fore him, the awareness of his aloneness and separateness, of his helplessness before the forces of nature and of society, all this makes his separate, disunited existence an unbearable prison. He would be-come insane could he not liberate himself from this prison and reach out, unite. . . .

And so our noble achievement—the winning of separateness, of self—will also always be our grievous loss. That loss is necessary—there can be no human love without that loss. But through our love that loss may be transcended.

4.

The Cuddle Chemical

DIANE ACKERMAN

When it comes to matters of the heart, we like to believe that we are in control. But recent findings in neuroscience suggest that we are more influenced by our own body chemicals and hormones than we ever realized before. Historian and poet Diane Ackerman explores how our desires to fall in love, to bond, or even divorce, are governed by these tiny creatures within.

OXYTOCIN, a hormone that encourages labor and the contractions during childbirth, seems to play an important role in mother love. The sound of a crying baby makes its mother's body secrete more oxytocin, which in turn erects her nipples and helps the milk to flow. As the baby nurses, even more oxytocin is released, making the mother want to nuzzle and hug it. It's been called the "cuddle chemical" by zoologists who have artificially raised the oxytocin level in goats and other animals and produced similar behavior. Oxytocin has many functions, some of them beneficial for the mother. The baby feels warm and safe as it nurses, and its digestive and respiratory systems run smoothly. The baby's nursing, which also coaxes the oxytocin level to rise in the mother, results, too, in contractions of the uterus that stop bleeding and detach the placenta. So mother and baby find themselves swept away in a chemical dance of love, interdependency, and survival.

Later in life, oxytocin seems to play an equally important role in romantic love, as a hormone that encourages cuddling between lovers and increases pleasure during lovemaking. The hormone stimulates the smooth muscles and sensitizes the nerves, and snowballs during sexual arousal—the more intense the arousal, the more oxytocin is produced. As arousal builds, oxytocin is thought to cause the nerves in the genitals to fire spontaneously, bringing on orgasm. Unlike other hormones, oxytocin arousal can be generated both by physical and emotional cues—a certain look, voice, or gesture is enough—and can become conditioned to one's personal love history. The lover's smell or touch may trigger the production of oxytocin. So might a richly woven and redolent sexual fantasy. Women are more responsive to oxytocin's emotional effects, probably because of the important role it plays in mothering. Indeed, women who have gone through natural childbirth sometimes report that they felt an orgasmic sense of pleasure during delivery. Some nonorgasmic women have found it easier to achieve orgasm after they've been through childbirth; the secretion of oxytocin during delivery and nursing melts their sexual blockade. This hormonal outpouring may help explain why women more than men prefer to continue embracing after sex. A woman may yearn to feel close and connected, tightly coiled around the mainspring of the man's heart. In evolutionary terms, she hopes the man will be staying around for a while, long enough to protect her and the child he just fathered.

Men's oxytocin levels quintuple during orgasm. But a Stanford University study showed that women have even higher levels of oxytocin than men do during sex, and that it takes more oxytocin for a woman to achieve orgasm. Drenched in this spa of the chemical, women are able to have more multiple orgasms than men, as well as full body orgasms. Mothers have told me that during their baby's first year or so they were surprised to find themselves "in love" with it, "turned on" by it, involved with it in "the best romance ever." Because the same hormone controls a woman's pleasure during orgasm, childbirth, cuddling, and nursing her baby, it makes perfect sense that she should feel this way. The brain may have an excess of gray matter, but in some things it's economical. It likes to reuse convenient pathways and chemicals for many purposes. Why plow fresh paths through the snow of existence when old paths already lead part of the way there? New fathers feel gratified by their babies, too, and their oxytocin levels rise, but not as high.

How about cuddling among other animals? At the National Institute of Mental Health, neuroscientists Thomas R. Insel and Lawrence E. Shapiro have been studying the romantic lives of mountain voles, promiscuous wild rodents that live alone in remote burrows until it's time to mate, which they do often and indiscriminately. Mother voles leave their pups soon after birth; father voles don't see their pups at all; and when a researcher removes a pup from its nest it doesn't cry for its mother or seem particularly stressed. They have nothing like what we might call a sense of family. What the researchers have found is that mountain voles have fewer brain receptors for oxytocin than their more affectionate and family-oriented relatives, the prairie voles. Despite this, but just as one might predict, the oxytocin levels of the mountain voles do climb steeply in mothers right after birth, while they're nursing their pups. Such a study makes one wonder about the complex role that oxytocin plays in human relationships. Are oxytocin levels lower in people characterized as "loners," in abusing parents, in children suffering from the solitary nightmare of autism?

The Infatuation Chemical

First, a small correction of something we take for granted. The mind is not located in the brain alone. The mind travels the body on an endless caravan of hormones and enzymes. An army of neuropeptides carries messages between the brain and the immune system. When things happen to the body—like pain, trauma, or illness—they affect the brain, which is a part of the body. When things happen in the brain—like shock, thought, or feeling—they affect the heart, the digestive system, and all the rest of the body. Thought and feeling are not separate. Mental health and physical health are not separate. We are one organism. Sometimes hunger pangs override morality. Sometimes our senses wantonly crave novelty, for no other reason than that it feels good. Sometimes a man does indeed *think with his dick*. Because we prize reason and are confused about our biology, we refer to our body's cravings and demands as our "baser" motives, instincts, or drives. So it is craven to yearn for sex, but noble to yearn for music, for example. Depraved to devote hours to finding sex, but admirable to devote hours to searching out beautiful music. Perverted to spend an afternoon fantasizing and masturbating repeatedly, but wholesome to spend the same afternoon enraptured by music. When love becomes obsession, the whole body hears the trumpet blast, the call to arms.

"The meeting of two personalities is like the contact of two chemical substances," Carl Jung wrote, "if there is any reaction, both are transformed." When two people find each other attractive, their bodies quiver with a gush of PEA (phenylethylamine), a molecule that speeds up the flow of information between nerve cells. An amphetaminelike chemical, PEA whips the brain into a frenzy of excitement, which is why lovers feel euphoric, rejuvenated, optimistic, and energized, happy to sit up talking all night or making love for hours on end. Because "speed" is addictive, even the body's naturally made speed, some people become what Michael Liebowitz and Donald Klein of the New York State Psychiatric Institute refer to as "attraction junkies," needing a romantic relationship to feel excited by life. The craving catapults them from high to low in an exhilarating, exhausting cycle of thrill and depression. Driven by a chemical hunger, they choose unsuitable partners, or quickly misconstrue a potential partner's feelings. Sliding down the slippery chute of their longing, they fall head over heels into a sea of all-consuming, passionate love. Soon the relationship crumbles, or they find themselves rejected. In either case, tortured by lovesick despair, they plummet into a savage depression, which they try to cure by falling in love again. Liebowitz and Klein think that this roller coaster is fueled by a chemical imbalance in the brain, a craving for PEA. When they gave some attraction junkies MAO inhibitors—antidepressants that work by disabling certain enzymes that can subdue PEA and other neurotransmitters—they were amazed to find how quickly the therapy worked. No longer craving PEA, the patients were able to choose partners more calmly and realistically. Other studies with humans seem to confirm these findings. Researchers have also found that injecting mice, rhesus monkeys, and other animals with

PEA produces noises of pleasure, courting behavior, and addiction (they keep pressing a lever to get more PEA). All this strongly suggests that when we fall in love the brain drenches itself in PEA, a chemical that makes us feel pleasure, rampant excitement, and well-being. A sweet fix, love.

The body uses PEA for more than infatuation. The same chemical soars in thrill-seeking of any kind, because it keeps one alert, confident, and ready to try something new. That may help explain a fascinating phenomenon: people are more likely to fall in love when they're in danger. Wartime romances are legendary. I am part of a "baby boom" produced by such an event. Love thrives especially well in exotic locales. When the senses are heightened because of stress, novelty, or fear, it's much easier to become a mystic or feel ecstasy or fall in love. Danger makes one receptive to romance. Danger is an aphrodisiac. To test this, researchers asked single men to cross a suspension bridge. The bridge was safe, but frightening. Some men met women on the bridge. Other men encountered the same women—but not on the bridge—in a safer setting such as a campus or an office.

The men who met the women on the trembling bridge were much more likely to ask them out on dates.

The Attachment Chemical

While the chemical sleigh ride of infatuation carries one at a fast clip over uneven terrain, lives become blended, people mate and genes mix, and babies are born. Then the infatuation subsides and a new group of chemicals takes over, the morphinelike opiates of the mind, which calm and reassure. The sweet blistering rage of infatuation gives way to a narcotic peacefulness, a sense of security and belonging. Being in love is a state of chaotic equilibrium. Its rewards of intimacy, warmth, empathy, dependability, and shared experiences trigger the production of that mental comfort food, the endorphins. The feeling is less steep than falling in love, but it's steadier and more addictive. The longer two people have been married, the more likely it is they'll stay married. And couples who have three or more children tend to be lifelong spouses. Stability, friendship, familiarity, and affection are rewards the body clings to. As much as we love being happily unsettled, not to mention dizzied by infatuation, such a state is stressful. On the other hand, it also feels magnificent to rest, to be free of anxiety or fretting, and to enjoy one's life with a devoted companion who is as comfortable as a childhood playmate, as predictable if at times irksome as a sibling, as attentive as a parent, and also affectionate and loving: a longtime spouse. This is a tonic that is hard to give up, even if the relationship isn't perfect, and one is tempted by rejuvenating affairs. Shared events, including shared stresses and crises, are rivets that draw couples closer together. Soon they are fastened by so many it becomes difficult to pull free. It takes a vast amount of courage to leap off a slowly moving ship and grab a lifebuoy drifting past, not knowing exactly where it's headed or if it will keep one afloat. As the "other women" embroiled with long-married men discover, the men are unlikely to divorce, no matter how mundane their marriages, what they may promise, or how passionately in love they genuinely feel.

The Chemistry of Divorce

"Philandering," we call it, "fooling around," "hanky-panky," "skirt chasing," "man chasing," or something equally picturesque. Monogamy and adultery are both hallmarks of being human. Anthropologist Helen Fisher proposes a chemical basis for adultery, what she calls "The Four-Year Itch." Studying the United Nations survey of marriage and divorce around the world, she noticed that divorce usually occurs early in a marriage, during the couple's first reproductive and parenting years. Also, that this peak time for divorce coincides with the period in which infatuation normally ends, and a couple has to decide if they're going to call it quits or stay together as companions. Some couples do stay together and have other children, but even more don't. "The human animal," she concludes, "seems built to court, to fall in love, and to marry one person at a time; then, at the height of our reproductive years, often with a single child, we divorce; then, a few years later, we remarry once again."

Our chemistry makes it easy to follow that plan, and painful to avoid it. After the seductive fireworks of first attraction, which may last a few weeks or a few years, the body gets bored with easy ecstasy. The nerves no longer quiver with excitement. Nothing new has been happening for ages, why bother to rouse oneself? Love is exhausting. Too much of anything feels overwhelming, even too much thrill. Then the attachment chemicals roll in their thick cozy carpets of marital serenity. Might as well relax and enjoy the calm and security, some feel. Separated even for a short while, the partners crave the cradle of the other's embrace. Is it a chemical craving? Possibly so, a hunger for the soothing endorphins that flow when they're together. It is a deep, sweet river, just right for dangling one's feet in while the world waits.

Other people grow restless and search for novelty. They can't stand the tedium of constancy. Eventually the ghost of old age stalks them. They are becoming their parents. Elsewhere, life is storied with new horizons, and new flanks. Everyone else seems to be enjoying a feast of sensual delicacies, and they want to smother themselves in a sauce of sensations. So they begin illicit affairs or divorce proceedings, or both.

One way or another the genes survive, the species prevails. Couples who stay together raise more kids to adulthood. When couples part, they almost always marry again and raise at least one child. Even when the chemical cycle falters and breaks, it picks itself up and starts again. Both systems work, so both reward the players. As Oscar Wilde once said, "The chains of marriage are heavy and it takes two to carry them—sometimes three."

5.

Timeless Love: A Cure for the Common Cold?

DEEPAK CHOPRA

In this essay, Deepak Chopra explores how love positively affects our immune systems and our health. It is, if you will forgive my pun, nothing to sneeze at. Chopra, well known for his books on spirituality and love, has served on the panel for alternative medicine with the National Institutes of Health.

IN A SERIES of revealing experiments, Harvard psychologist David C. McClelland probed the physiology of love. He had a group of subjects view a short film of Mother Teresa in her daily work of caring for sick and abandoned children in Calcutta. The film displayed a profound outpouring of love. As the audience watched the film, McClelland discovered that a marker in their immune systems increased—this was SIgA, or salivary immunoglobulin antigen. High levels of SIgA, as measured in people's saliva, indicates a high immune response; as it happens, an elevated immune response is also characteristic of people who have recently fallen in love. (The popular saying "If you don't want to catch a cold, fall in love" recognizes this connection between emotions and physiology.)

Curiously, when the film was over and the audience was asked their opinion of Mother Teresa, not everyone found her work laudable. Some had objections of one kind or another, centering on differences in religious belief, while others reported feeling disturbed by the sight of children who were starving or suffering from leprosy. Yet all the audience members experienced an increase in SIgA levels; their physical response to love appeared to be more powerful than their rational attitudes. This led McClelland to question one of the most popular definitions of love in modern psychology, which holds that love is a reflexive response that arises when two people meet to fill each other's needs. According to that definition, love would depend on a person's conscious evaluation of the benefits he or she was getting in a relationship. But here were people whose bodies were responding at a much deeper level, deeper even than pleasure.

McClelland also found that the positive effect on the viewers' immune response declined and disappeared an hour or two after they had viewed the film. It remained highest among those subjects who reported a strong sense of being loved in their own lives and having strong ties to family and friends. This implied that some people are already in a state conducive to love. Instead of experiencing it as a passing state, they had incorporated it as a trait. In other words, the statement of the enlightened sage, "I am love," was present in these people, if to a smaller degree.

What is love as a trait rather than as a passing phase? Even the most passionate experience of being in love eventually cools off, leaving people dismayed to find that little real love, in a lasting sense, remains. Pondering this problem, McClelland wondered what had become of the experiences described in the poetry of love. These experiences did not refer to the selfish advantages of being in love but to altruistic, undying devotion. Was Shakespeare simply wrong when he declared, "Love is not love which alters when it alteration finds, or bends with the remover to remove. Oh no! It is an ever-fixed mark that looks on tempest and is never shaken." McClelland also knew of instances cited in the psychological literature where people were in loving relationships that made no sense in terms of gaining any objective benefits. Such people felt deep love and devotion despite the fact that they had no rational reason for feeling that way.

What all this implied to McClelland was that love is a state that transcends reason and whose purpose is simply to allow the experience of a larger shared reality. One critical matter in this regard was a person's reaction to the death of a loved one. If two people were in love just for what they could get, their interdependence would form the basis for loving and being loved. Thus, the death of the loved one would cause great pain as the bond was ripped apart. Certainly this could be observed in real-life relationships, but McClelland felt from personal experience that something very different was possible:

> The death of a loved partner should cause intense suffering and grief, according to this theory. Yet when my wife died of cancer a few years ago, I did not react in this way. We had been very much in love, happily married for 42 years, had raised five children to well-adjusted maturity . . . yet when she died I did not feel the amount of pain that the theory would require that I should feel. . . . What the experience felt like was much closer to the poet's view of love. We had felt that we were part of something that was much bigger than ourselves—which had nurtured and supported us throughout our long life together and which continued to support me after her death.

This describes a step into the realm of timeless love. When two people use their love for each other as a doorway into this realm, the death of the loved one does not close the door or deprive the other of the flow of love. Ultimately, all love comes from within. We are deluding ourselves when we believe that another person is who we love; the other person is a pretext by which we give ourselves permission to feel love. Only you can open and close your heart. The power of love to nurture and sustain us depends on our commitment to it "in here."

6.

Language, Consciousness, and the Yearning for Connection

RIANE EISLER

Cultural historian Riane Eisler looks at love within the context of evolution. She sees a complex relationship among language, consciousness, and sexuality, all of which provide for the sense of intimacy and connectedness we feel for each other. Furthermore, she argues that many of our relationship problems occur when we try to separate physical and spiritual love, a situation that for centuries has been imposed on us by Western religious beliefs.

I THINK ONE OF the great tragedies of Western religion as most of us have known it has been its compartmentalized view of human experience, and particularly its elevation of disembodied or "spiritual" love over embodied or "carnal" love. As we have seen, this compartmentalized view of human experience is not unique to the West. And it is certainly not unique to religion. For instance, the common wisdom (part of our legacy from both ancient Greek philosophers and medieval Christian savants) is that sexual sensations are of a "lower order," that love resides in the heart, and that what we today call higher consciousness is connected only with mental rather than physical states.

In fact, contemporary scientific research indicates that the locus of the sex drive is not in our genitals but in our brains. Even experiments on rats show that electrical stimulation of certain regions of the brain directly results in erections and/or ejaculations, without any genital stimulation whatsoever. And it is not only scientific studies but our everyday experiences and observations that verify this. We know that sexual arousal can come from sexual pictures, or even sexual thoughts. Who a woman or man is sexually attracted to, in all its idiosyncratic variations, is largely a function of something that happens in our minds. And how we interpret states of both sexual and emotional arousal, and what actions we take or do not take as a consequence, are largely determined by what we have learned to think and feel rather than by any innate or mechanical physical drives or "instincts."

The emotion of love likewise involves our brains. In fact, all feelings and sensations—be they associated with sex, spirituality, or love—are in humans mediated by what psychologists call cognition or thought, which is processed in our brains. But since our brains are part of our bodies, it is in our bodies that we physically experience all feelings and sensations, regardless of whether they are conventionally labeled higher or lower.

Thus, it is actually what happens in our bodies that brings on spiritual or trancelike states. People experiencing "higher" states of consciousness, such as yoga masters, often engage in rigorous bodily exercises and are able to sit for hours in positions that most of us could sustain for only a few minutes. This physical dimension of spiritual states is now also being documented in a growing scientific literature on what researchers call altered states of consciousness (in scientific shorthand, ASCs). Experiments show that meditative or trancelike states involve measurable changes in the electrical activity of the brain (or brain waves) as measured by electroencephalographs.

Most interesting, and relevant to what we are exploring, is that sexual orgasm is also increasingly recognized as an altered state of consciousness—as indeed it is. As Julian Davidson writes in *The Psychobiology of Consciousness,* although there are immense individual differences (as there also are in the experiences of individuals in other ASCs), "all orgasms share some of the criteria found in full-blown ASCs." These include changes in "the senses of space, time, identity, as well as strong emotions and great changes in motor output." And as Davidson also notes, "orgasms have been used extensively to induce mystical states."

So it is not surprising that . . . mystics have often described their experiences in the language of sex. Or that the common, and central—word in the language of both sexual passion and spiritual illumination is love.

This common theme of love in the literature (and experience) of both sexuality and spirituality is not coincidental. It reflects an underlying link that prehistoric civilizations seem to have intuited and modern science is beginning to rediscover. For while we have been taught that human sexuality (which is a striving for connection or oneness), the emotion of love (which is again a striving for connection or oneness), and the spiritual striving for union or oneness with what we call the divine are completely different from one another, at opposite poles, in reality they all stem from the same deeply rooted human need: our powerful human yearning for connection.

Because this yearning is in our species so powerful and so persistent, I believe it is biologically based. This is not to say that only humans have a strong striving for connection. Actually this striving is a recurrent evolutionary theme. Its earliest roots go back billions of years, to the symbiotic union of single cells into the first multicelled organisms that the biologist Lynn Margulis aptly called the first partnership between life forms on our planet.[1] Among colonies of insects, swarms of birds, schools of fish, and herds of mammals, this need for connection is expressed in what we call the grouping or herding instinct, which enhances survival through the greater safety of being close together in large numbers. In life forms as diverse as ladybugs, kittens, monkeys, and humans, we see evidence of a need for physical connection through touch. This physical connection through touch is integral to the survival of species that reproduce by sexual mating. And particularly in mammals, touching is essential for the survival of offspring, who would die without adult protection and care.

But although the striving for connection is by no means unique to our species, it is most highly developed in humans. This is due to a number of peculiarly human traits. Notable among these are the much longer period of helpless dependency of human infants, the human female's capacity for nonseasonal sex and multiple orgasms, and humanity's much greater mental capacities, which play such an important part in the phenomenon we call consciousness.

Looked at from this larger perspective, it becomes apparent that, contrary to prevailing views, humanity's highly developed mental capacities are not of such a different evolutionary order from our highly developed capacities (and needs) for female-male and adult-infant connection. Rather, these are all related evolutionary developments: developments that came together in the emergence of our species. Specifically, they are the evolutionary developments that together give our species the potential for two uniquely human—and related—characteristics. One is the phenomenon we call higher consciousness. The second is the complex of feelings and behaviors that in the realm of both spirituality and sexuality we call love.

Obviously unloving, cruel, and violent sexual and nonsexual relations are also possibilities for our species. But the evolution in humans of our highly developed potential for the conscious and caring connectivity we call love offers us the basis for a more balanced and fulfilling way of relating to one another and our planet—a way that recognizes our essential interconnection with one another and the rest of nature.

The main evolutionary development emphasized in the emergence of our species is the human brain. And it is our brain (combined with our vocal cords) that directly accounts for the fact that ours is the only species that can communicate through the complex symbols we call words. But as the biologists Humberto Maturana and Francisco Varela note, it is our frontal and nonseasonal human sexuality (combined with the long period of physical dependency of the products of that sexuality) that seems to have provided a major impetus for what they call "a biology of cooperation and a linguistic coordination of action."[2]

Other scholars, for example Adrienne Zihlman and Nancy Tanner, also attribute both the first human social bonds and the origin of language to the need, in a species where there is such a long maturation period, for mothers and infants to communicate. They point out that those infants whose mothers could interact with them through language, instructing, cautioning, and supporting their development, would have a greater chance of survival. And they note that this in turn would have tended to further promote physiological changes (such as larger brain capacity, smaller mandibles, and a large space for a larynx) that also mark the shift to our human species, and with it, the development of language.[3]

Maturana and Varela, however, specifically relate the emergence of language as a human tool to facilitate sharing and cooperation to sex, arguing that the development of language as a means of communicating in intimate relations was facilitated by the human female's year-round sexuality. They note that this would have tended to promote more sustained and cooperative contacts between females and males, and thus more need and opportunity to communicate. And they stress that although many species of birds and fish as well as a number of mammals and primates also have strong male participation in the care of the young, the possibility in humans for year-round sexual bonding between females and males would encourage males to take a more active caretaking role—an important development for a species with an extremely long period of early helplessness.

So, in contrast to what we still find in much of the sociobiological literature, Maturana and Varela emphasize the differences between human and animal sexuality. They also recognize that we are fundamentally different from other animals in still another major respect: our highly developed capacity for awareness of self as distinct from (and at the same time interconnected with) others—in other words, for consciousness. And once again they believe that this too is a development inextricably connected with the emergence of human sexuality.

As they put it, it is "in the intimacy of recurrent individual interactions, which personalize the other individual with a linguistic distinction such as a name," that "the conditions may have been present for the appearance of a self as a distinction in a linguistic domain." And while a few other life forms, such as our primate cousins the gorillas and the chimpanzees, seem to have some capacity to reflect upon themselves, the capacity for conceptual thinking and imaging is clearly most highly developed in our species.

It should therefore also not surprise us that it is in humans that we see the highest development of consciousness. Nor should it surprise us—given our much more developed capacity for communication as well as our capacity for year-round sexual bonding and our need for intimate childhood connections—that we find in humans the highest development of what Maturana calls the "biology of love."

Maturana's use of the term love may seem to border on the poetic—after all, poetry is the characteristic literature of love. But although the phrase "biology of love" initially takes one aback, there is little question that the human need for love stems from a biological fact: that without love, without at least some measure of caring connections or bonds, we humans do not survive.

7.

The Flow of Relationship

MIHALY CSIKSZENTMIHALYI

Mihaly Csikszentmihalyi, professor and former chairman of the psychology department at the University of Chicago, has made a significant contribution to our understanding of optimal health and how we can learn to enjoy life fully. In this article, he applies his theory of "flow" to love, intimacy, and family life.

EVERY RELATIONSHIP requires a reorienting of attention, a repositioning of goals. When two people begin to go out together, they must accept certain constraints that each person alone did not have: schedules have to be coordinated, plans modified. Even something as simple as a dinner date imposes compromises as to time, place, type of food, and so on. To some degree the couple will have to respond with similar emotions to the stimuli they encounter—the relationship will probably not last long if the man loves a movie that the woman hates, and vice versa. When two people choose to focus their attention on each other, both will have to change their habits; as a result, the pattern of their consciousness will also have to change. Getting married requires a radical and permanent reorientation of attentional habits. When a child is added to the pair, both parents have to readapt again to accommodate the needs of the infant: their sleep cycle must change, they will go out less often, the wife may give up her job, they may have to start saving for the child's education.

All this can be very hard work, and it can also be very frustrating. If a person is unwilling to adjust personal goals when starting a relationship, then a lot of what subsequently happens in that relationship will produce disorder in the person's consciousness, because novel patterns of interaction will conflict with old patterns of expectation. A bachelor may have, on his list of priorities, to drive a sleek sports car and to spend a few weeks each winter in the Caribbean. Later he decides to marry and have a child. As he realizes these latter goals, however, he discovers that they are incompatible with the prior ones. He can't afford a Maserati any longer, and the Bahamas are out of reach. Unless he revises the old goals, he will be frustrated, producing that sense of inner conflict known as psychic entropy. And if he changes goals, his self will change as a consequence—the self being the sum and organization of goals. In this manner entering any relationship entails a transformation of the self.

Until a few decades ago, families tended to stay together because parents and children were forced to continue the relationship for extrinsic reasons. If divorces were rare in the past, it wasn't because husbands and wives loved each other more in the old times, but because husbands needed someone to cook and keep house, wives needed someone to bring home the bacon, and children needed both parents in order to eat, sleep, and get a start in the world. The "family values" that the elders spent so much effort inculcating in the young were a reflection of this simple necessity, even when it was cloaked in religious and moral considerations. Of course, once family values were taught as being important, people learned to take them seriously, and they helped keep families from disintegrating. All too often, however, the moral rules were seen as an outside imposition, an external constraint under which husbands, wives, and children chafed. In such cases the family may have remained intact physically, but it was internally riven with conflicts and hatred. The current "disintegration" of the family is the result of the slow disappearance of external reasons for staying married. The increase in the divorce rate is probably more affected by changes in the labor market that have increased women's employment opportunities, and by the diffusion of labor-saving home appliances, than it is by a lessening of love or of moral fiber.

But extrinsic reasons are not the only ones for staying married and for living together in families. There are great opportunities for joy and for growth that can only be experienced in family life, and these intrinsic rewards are no less present now than they were in the past; in fact, they are probably much more readily available today than they have been at any previous time. If the trend of traditional families keeping together mainly as a convenience is on the wane, the number of families that endure because their members enjoy each other may be increasing. Of course, because external forces are still much more powerful than internal ones, the net effect is likely to be a further fragmentation of family life for some time to come. But the families that do persevere will be in a better position to help their members develop a rich self than families held together against their will are able to do.

There have been endless discussions about whether humans are naturally promiscuous, polygamous, or monogamous; and whether in terms of cultural evolution monogamy is the highest form of family organization. It is important to realize that these questions deal only with the extrinsic conditions shaping marriage relationships. And on that count, the bottom line seems to be that marriages will take the form that most efficiently ensures survival. Even members of the same animal species will vary their patterns of relationship so as to adapt best in a given environment. For instance the male long-billed marsh wren (*Cistothorus palustris*) is polygamous in Washington, where swamps vary in quality and females are attracted to those few males who have rich territories, leaving the less lucky ones to a life of enforced bachelorhood. The same wrens are monogamous in Georgia, not so much because that state is part of the Bible Belt, but because the marshes all have roughly the same amount of food and cover, and so each male can attract a doting spouse to an equally comfortable nesting site.

The form the human family takes is a response to similar kinds of environmental pressures. In terms of extrinsic reasons, we are monogamous because in technological societies based on a money economy, time has proven this to be a more convenient arrangement. But the issue we have to confront as individuals is not whether humans are "naturally" monogamous or not, but whether we *want* to be monogamous or not. And in answering that question, we need to weigh all the consequences of our choice.

It is customary to think of marriage as the end of freedom, and some refer to their spouses as "old ball-and-chain." The notion of family life typically implies constraints, responsibilities that interfere with one's goals and freedom of action. While this is true, especially when the marriage is one of convenience, what we tend to forget is that these rules and obligations are no different, in principle, than those rules that constrain behavior in a game. Like all rules, they exclude a wide range of possibilities so that we might concentrate fully on a selected set of options.

Cicero once wrote that to be completely free one must become a slave to a set of laws. In other words, accepting limitations is liberating. For example, by making up one's mind to invest psychic energy exclusively in a monogamous marriage, regardless of any problems, obstacles, or more attractive options that may come along later, one is freed of the constant pressure of trying to maximize emotional returns. Having made the commitment that an old-fashioned marriage demands, and having made it willingly instead of being compelled by tradition, a person no longer needs to worry whether she has made the right choice, or whether the grass might be greener somewhere else. As a result a great deal of energy gets freed up for living, instead of being spent on wondering about how to live.

If one decides to accept the traditional form of the family, complete with a monogamous marriage, and with a close involvement with children, with relatives, and with the community, it is important to consider beforehand how family life can be turned into a flow activity. Because if it is not, boredom and frustration will inevitably set in, and then the relationship is likely to break up unless there are strong external factors keeping it together.

To provide flow, a family has to have a goal for its existence. Extrinsic reasons are not sufficient: it is not enough to feel that, well, "Everybody else is married," "It is natural to have children," or "Two can live as cheaply as one." These attitudes may encourage one to start a family, and may even be strong enough to keep it going, but they cannot make family life enjoyable. Positive goals are necessary to focus the psychic energies of parents and children on common tasks.

Some of these goals might be very general and long-term, such as planning a particular life-style—to build an ideal home, to provide the best possible education for the children, or to implement a religious way of living in a modern secularized society. For such goals to result in interactions that will help increase the complexity of its members, the family must be both *differentiated* and *integrated*. Differentiation means that each person is encouraged to develop his or her unique traits, maximize personal skills, set individual goals. Integration, in contrast, guarantees that what happens to one person will affect all others. If a child is proud of what she accomplished in school, the rest of the family will pay attention and will be proud of her, too. If the mother is tired and depressed, the family will try to help and cheer her up. In an integrated family, each person's goals matter to all others.

In addition to long-term goals, it is imperative to have a constant supply of short-term objectives. These may include simple tasks like buying a new sofa, going on a picnic, planning for a vacation, or playing a game of Scrabble together on Sunday afternoon. Unless there are goals that the whole family is willing to share, it is almost impossible for its members to be physically together, let alone involved in an enjoyable joint activity. Here again, differentiation and integration are important: the common goals should reflect the goals of individual members as much as possible. If Rick wants to go to a motocross race, and Erica would like to go to the aquarium, it should be possible for everyone to watch the race one weekend, and then visit the aquarium the next. The beauty of such an arrangement is that Erica is likely to enjoy some of the aspects of bike racing, and Rick might actually get to appreciate looking at fish, even though neither would have discovered as much if left to his or her own prejudices.

As with any other flow activity, family activities should also provide clear feedback. In this case, it is simply a matter of keeping open channels of communication. If a husband does not know what bothers his wife, and vice versa, neither has the opportunity to reduce the inevitable tensions that will arise. In this context it is worth stressing that entropy is the basic condition of group life, just as it is of personal experience. Unless the partners invest psychic energy in the relationship, conflicts are inevitable, simply because each individual has goals that are to a certain extent divergent from those of all other members of the family. Without good lines of communication the distortions will become amplified, until the relationship falls apart.

Feedback is also crucial to determine whether family goals are being achieved. My wife and I used to think that taking our children to the zoo on a Sunday every few months was a splendid educational activity, and one that we could all enjoy. But when our oldest child turned ten, we stopped going because he had become seriously distressed with the idea of animals being confined in restricted spaces. It is a fact of life that sooner or later all children will express the opinion that common family activities are "dumb." At this point, forcing them to do things together tends to be counterproductive. So most parents just give up, and abandon their teenagers to the peer culture. The more fruitful, if more difficult, strategy is to find a new set of activities that will continue to keep the family group involved.

The balancing of challenges and skills is another factor as necessary in enjoying social relationships in general, and family life in particular, as it is for any other flow activity. When a man and a woman are first attracted to each other, the opportunities for action are usually clear enough. Ever since the dawn of time, the most basic challenge for the swain has been "Can I make her?" and for the maid, "Can I catch him?" Usually, and depending on the partners' level of skill, a host of more complex challenges are also perceived: to find out what sort of a person the other really is, what movies she likes, what he thinks about South Africa, and whether the encounter is likely to develop into a "meaningful relationship." Then there are fun things to do together, places to visit, parties to go to and talk about afterward, and so on.

With time one gets to know the other person well, and the obvious challenges have been exhausted. All the usual gambits have been tried; the other person's reactions have become predictable. Sexual play has lost its first excitement. At this point, the relationship is in danger of becoming a boring routine that might be kept alive by mutual convenience, but is unlikely to provide further enjoyment, or spark a new growth in complexity. The only way to restore flow to the relationship is by finding new challenges in it.

These might involve steps as simple as varying the routines of eating, sleeping, or shopping. They might involve making an effort to talk together about new topics of conversation, visiting new places, making new friends. More than anything else they involve paying attention to the partner's own complexity, getting to know her at deeper levels than were necessary in the earlier days of the relationship, supporting him with sympathy and compassion during the inevitable changes that the years bring. A complex relationship sooner or later faces the big question: whether the two partners are ready to make a lifelong commitment. At that point, a whole new set of challenges presents itself: raising a family together, getting involved in broader community affairs when the children have grown up, working alongside one another. Of course, these things cannot happen without extensive inputs of energy and time; but the payoff in terms of the quality of experience is usually more than worth it.

PART II

Making Relationships Work

> Love . . . is a constant
> challenge; it is not a resting
> place, but a moving, growing,
> working together, even
> whether there is harmony
> or conflict.
> **ERICH FROMM**

> Love is the only way to grasp another human
> being in the innermost core of his personality.
> No one can become fully aware of the very
> essence of another human being unless he
> loves him. By the spiritual act of love he is en-
> abled to see the essential traits and features in
> the beloved person; and even more, he sees
> that which is potential in him; which is not
> yet actualized but yet ought to be actualized.
> Furthermore, by his love, the loving person
> enables the beloved person to actualize these
> potentialities. By making him aware of what
> he can be and what he should become, he
> makes these potentialities come true.
> **VIKTOR FRANKL**

How Do I Love Thee?

How do I love thee? Let me count the ways.
I love thee to the depth and breadth and height
My soul can reach, when feeling out of sight
For the ends of Being and ideal Grace.
I love thee to the level of everyday's
Most quiet need, by sun and candle-light.
I love thee freely, as men strive for Right;
I love thee purely, as they turn from Praise.
I love thee with the passion put to use
In my old griefs, and with my childhood's faith.
I love thee with a love I seemed to lose
With my lost saints,——I love thee with the breath,
Smiles, tears, of all my life!——and, if God choose,
I shall but love thee better after death.

ELIZABETH BARRETT BROWNING

In Praise of Lovers Unfound

You ask me what I want and I say I want it all——the sun and the
trees and the faint spirit beneath your lips, the sigh of the wind and
your hand against my skin. The fires, the world, no less of God or the
fragrance of a memory turned wine. Baruch atoh adonai——blessed
art thou who flows with the night, in the ripple of wind and the skin
of the time. Blessed art thou unknown to me, of the hint of confusion,
the hour unseen.

M. R. WALDMAN

Consciousness and communication are two major themes reflected throughout this book. Without them, love remains unknown. Without intimate dialogue, we cannot know what our partners need, nor will we know if we are hurting each other through unconscious patterns of behavior.

The elements of a conscious relationship are clearly stated in Harville Hendrix's book *Getting the Love You Want.* Most relationships, he feels, are lived unconsciously, with little awareness or appreciation of our partners. Hendrix argues for the development of a conscious relationship, a sophisticated endeavor that incorporates the lessons of psychology with many of the philosophical teachings drawn from spiritual tradition:

> Marriage is not a static state between two unchanging people. Marriage is a psychological and spiritual journey that begins in the ecstasy of attraction, meanders through a rocky stretch of self-discovery, and culminates in the creation of an intimate, joyful, lifelong union. Whether or not you realize the full potential of this vision depends not on your ability to attract the perfect mate, but on your willingness to acquire knowledge about hidden parts of yourself.[1]

A central theme in Hendrix's model is that we can use relationships to heal the wounds of childhood. This is a radical notion, differing substantially from other relational theorists, for he asks us to take on the role that a therapist normally assumes. And yet, when we do so, an intimacy emerges that is profoundly meaningful and rich. In Hendrix's essay, he outlines ten essential qualities that need to be developed in a conscious relationship.

When we talk about ways to improve communication, we usually focus on the dialogue, on what we are *saying* to each other. But a complementary aspect is equally important, which involves the art of listening and paying attention. In M. Scott Peck's essay, he approaches listening by breaking it down into several types: casual listening, where we superficially pay attention to what the other is saying; selective listening, in which we filter out what we don't want to hear; and true listening, in which we give our fullest attention to every aspect of what the other person says. Peck believes that our difficulties in listening come from our parents' failure to pay full attention to us when we are young, and that "the need for one's parents to listen is never outgrown." Without deep listening, no true dialogue takes place. Once again we can see how childhood experiences can limit our adult relational skills.

The differences in communication styles between women and men have received tremendous publicity, popularized by authors like Deborah Tannen and John Gray. Tannen, a professor of linguistics, feels that it is essential to recognize such differences:

> Once people realize that their partners have different conversational styles, they are inclined to accept differences without blaming themselves, their partners, or their relationships.... Understanding the other's ways of talking is a giant leap across the communication gap between women and men, and a giant step toward opening lines of communication.[2]

Tannen's research has had a profound effect upon how we view communication between the sexes, but recent studies challenge some of her views, suggesting that the differences are not so much gender-biased but more related to social, ethnic, and childhood influences. Furthermore, many believe that such views promote stereotypes concerning men's and women's behavior, causing greater distance, frustration, and hostility between the sexes. In trying to unravel the cause for these potential gender wars, Elizabeth Aries reminds us that there are many ways to interpret the research and what we see, that no observation or fact is ultimately objective, and that there are many perspectives on the truth.[3] The two chapters by Tannen and Aries present both sides to this controversial issue.

Research into language and communication confirms that each person, regardless of sex, has a unique style of communication, and that we must listen carefully and communicate more deeply if we are to avoid the misinterpretations that occur when we do not question our assumptions. When we fail to do this, conflict is certain to emerge.

Even in the act of sex, communication plays an essential role. In Leonore Tiefer's provocative essay, she tears apart the belief that sex is a *natural* act, pointing out that we often fall into a painful trap when we believe that romantic and sexual experiences are automatic events. Sexual satisfaction is not a biological act; an orgasm is not intimacy. Tiefer points out that each aspect of sexuality is a unique experience between two individuals, to be talked about and shared. In this respect, sex is simply another form of communication through which we develop intimacy.

Friendship has reemerged as a valued quality in relationships, but the dynamics of friendship differ significantly from the dynamics of love. Historically, many philosophers believed that friendship between women and men was limited, a notion strongly put forth by Aristotle. A similar attitude is echoed in the movie *When Harry Met Sally,* which, in Gilbert Meilaender's article, is analyzed with self-reflective humor. In Bhikhu Parekh's chapter, he takes a deeper look at the subject by identifying six primary characteristics of friendship. Parekh also explores the unique dimensions of friendship that have emerged in Eastern cultures through their spiritual practice and texts.

Today, the element of trust has come to be recognized as one of the most essential ingredients to relational stability, for without it, there is simply no framework in which to talk openly and honestly. Without trust, we cannot develop intimacy, and in a marriage, when trust disappears, divorce will often follow. In her comprehensive analysis of the subject, Susan D. Boon describes four key issues that partners must address in order to develop a mature capacity to trust: dependability, responsiveness, a capacity to resolve conflict, and faith. Her essay, grounded in substantial research, makes one of the most important contributions to this book.

Throughout the world, the institution of marriage implies the deepest form of commitment between two people. Judith S. Wallerstein and Sandra Blakeslee, known for their authoritative work with divorce, have recently turned their attention to marriages. In their article, they identify a number of qualities that contribute to a satisfying marriage, which include comfort, respect, mutual care, support, commitment, and equality. Another characteristic cited was *integrity,* a complex moral ethic made up of "honesty, compassion, generosity of spirit, decency, loyalty to the family and fairness," principles that are deeply embedded in today's spiritual and transpersonal views. Wallerstein and Blakeslee conclude their study with a list of nine essential tasks that, if not addressed, may lead to a collapse and failure of the marriage.

8.

The Ten Characteristics of a Conscious Relationship

HARVILLE HENDRIX

Harville Hendrix was one of the first therapists to encourage the development of a conscious relationship for couples. It is a courageous but difficult path to take, as you will see from the following ten criteria, but the rewards can lead you into one of the most intimate relationships you have known. Share this article with your partner and a friend and see how they respond.

A CONSCIOUS MARRIAGE is a marriage that fosters maximum psychological and spiritual growth; it's a marriage created by becoming conscious and cooperating with the fundamental drives of the unconscious mind: to be safe, to be healed, and to be whole.

The idea of "becoming conscious" refers to processes common to psychology and the spiritual traditions. Long before Freud's development of his theory of the unconscious, which states that our lives are directed largely by forces not in our consciousness nor under its control, the ancient mystical traditions of the East and the West perceived our ordinary, everyday consciousness as an illusion, a state of "waking sleep." While there are important technical distinctions between the "unconscious" and "waking sleep," both views are in agreement in perceiving that things are not the way they appear and that a fundamental change in mental life is necessary if we are to know the "truth." These changes consist of "insight" and "awakening," respectively.

Insight brings unconscious contents into consciousness, and awakening gives us direct experience of "reality" that has been hidden behind our symbolic constructions. I use the phrase "becoming conscious" to combine these two processes as they apply to marriage.

What are some of the differences when you become conscious? The following list highlights some of the essential differences in attitude and behavior:

1. *You realize that your love relationship has a hidden purpose—the healing of childhood wounds.* Instead of focusing entirely on surface needs and desires, you learn to recognize the unresolved childhood issues that underlie them. When you look at marriage with this X-ray vision, your daily interactions take on more meaning. Puzzling aspects of your relationship begin to make sense to you, and you have a greater sense of control.

2. *You create a more accurate image of your partner.* At the very moment of attraction, you began fusing your lover with your primary caretakers. Later you projected your negative traits onto your partner, further obscuring your partner's essential reality. As you move toward a conscious marriage, you gradually let go of these illusions and begin to see more of your partner's truth. You see your partner not as your savior but as another wounded human being, struggling to be healed.

3. *You take responsibility for communicating your needs and desires to your partner.* In an unconscious marriage, you cling to the childhood belief that your partner automatically intuits your needs. In a conscious marriage, you accept the fact that, in order to understand each other, you have to develop clear channels of communication.

4. *You become more intentional in your interactions.* In an unconscious marriage, you tend to react without thinking. You allow the primitive response of your old brain to control your behavior. In a conscious marriage, you train yourself to behave in a more constructive manner.

5. *You learn to value your partner's needs and wishes as highly as you value your own.* In an unconscious marriage, you assume that your partner's role in life is to take care of your needs magically. In a conscious marriage, you let go of

this narcissistic view and divert more and more of your energy to meeting your partner's needs.

6. You embrace the dark side of your personality. In a conscious marriage, you openly acknowledge the fact that you, like everyone else, have negative traits. As you accept responsibility for this dark side of your nature, you lessen your tendency to project your negative traits onto your mate, which creates a less hostile environment.

7. You learn new techniques to satisfy your basic needs and desires. During the power struggle, you cajole, harangue, and blame in an attempt to coerce your partner to meet your needs. When you move beyond this stage, you realize that your partner *can indeed be a resource for you*—once you abandon your self-defeating tactics.

8. You search within yourself for the strengths and abilities you are lacking. One reason you were attracted to your partner is that your partner had strengths and abilities that you lacked. Therefore, being with your partner gave you an illusory sense of wholeness. In a conscious marriage, you learn that the only way you can truly recapture a sense of oneness is to develop the hidden traits within yourself.

9. You become more aware of your drive to be loving and whole and united with the universe. As a part of your God-given nature, you have the ability to love unconditionally and to experience unity with the world around you. Social conditioning and imperfect parenting made you lose touch with these qualities. In a conscious marriage, you begin to rediscover your original nature.

10. You accept the difficulty of creating a good marriage. In an unconscious marriage, you believe that the way to have a good marriage is to pick the right partner. In a conscious marriage you realize you have to be the right partner. As you gain a more realistic view of love relationships, you realize that a good marriage requires commitment, discipline, and the courage to grow and change; marriage is hard work.

9.

True Listening and the Work of Attention

M. Scott Peck

> "Most people never truly listen to each other," notes Dr. Peck in this rich and challenging essay. But, if we bring our attention to this most essential skill and learn to practice it daily, we can begin to open fully the doors to love, intimacy, and mutual respect. Without true listening, a conscious relationship will stall.

WHEN WE EXTEND OURSELVES, when we take an extra step or walk an extra mile, we do so in opposition to the inertia of laziness or the resistance of fear. Extension of ourselves or moving out against the inertia of laziness we call work. Moving out in the face of fear we call courage. Love, then, is a form of work or a form of courage. Specifically, it is work or courage directed toward the nurture of our own or another's spiritual growth. We may work or exert courage in directions other than toward spiritual growth, and for this reason all work and all courage is not love. But since it requires the extension of ourselves, love is always either work or courage. If an act is not one of work or courage, then it is not an act of love. There are no exceptions.

The principal form that the work of love takes is attention. When we love another we give him or her our attention; we attend to that person's growth. When we love ourselves we attend to our own growth. When we attend to someone we are caring for that person. The act of attending requires that we make the effort to set aside our existing preoccupations (as was described in regard to the discipline of bracketing) and actively shift our consciousness. Attention is an act of will, of work against the inertia of our own minds. As Rollo May says, "When we analyze will with all the tools modern psychoanalysis brings us, we shall find ourselves pushed back to the level of attention or intention as the seat of will. The effort which goes into the exercise of the will is really effort of attention; the strain in willing is the effort to keep the consciousness clear, i.e., the strain of keeping the attention focused."

By far the most common and important way in which we can exercise our attention is by listening. We spend an enormous amount of time listening, most of which we waste, because on the whole most of us listen very poorly. An industrial psychologist once pointed out to me that the amount of time we devote to teaching certain subjects to our children in school is inversely proportional to the frequency with which the children will make use of the subject when they grow up. Thus a business executive will spend roughly an hour of his day reading, two hours talking and eight hours listening. Yet in school we spend a large amount of time teaching children how to read, a very small amount of time teaching them how to speak, and usually no time at all teaching them how to listen. I do not believe it would be a good thing to make what we teach in school exactly proportional to what we do after school, but I do think we would be wise to give our children some instruction in the process of listening—not so that listening can be made easy but rather that they will understand how difficult it is to listen well. Listening well is an exercise of attention and by necessity hard work. It is because they do not realize this or because they are not willing to do the work that most people do not listen well.

Not very long ago I attended a lecture by a famous man on an aspect of the relationship between psychology and religion in which I have long been interested. Because of my interest I had a certain amount of expertise in the subject and immediately recognized the lecturer to be a great sage indeed. I also sensed love in the tremendous effort that he was exerting to communicate, with all manner of examples, highly abstract concepts that were difficult for us, his audience, to comprehend. I therefore listened to him with all the intentness of which I was capable. Throughout the hour and a half he talked sweat was literally dripping down my face in the air-conditioned auditorium. By the time he was finished I had a throbbing headache, the muscles in my neck were rigid from my effort at concentration, and I felt completely drained and exhausted. Although I estimated that I had understood no more than 50 percent of what this great man had said to us that afternoon, I was amazed by the large number of brilliant insights he had given me. Following the lecture, which was well attended by culture-seeking individuals, I wandered about through the audience during a coffee break listening to their comments. Generally they were disappointed. Knowing his reputation, they had expected more. They found him hard to follow and his talk confusing. He was not as competent a speaker as they had hoped to hear. One woman proclaimed to nods of agreement, "He really didn't tell us anything."

In contradistinction to the others, I was able to hear much of what this great man said, precisely because I was willing to do the work of listening to him. I was willing to do this work for two reasons: one, because I recognized his greatness and that what he had to say would likely be of great value; second, because of my interest in the field I deeply wanted to absorb what he had to say so as to enhance my own understanding and spiritual growth. My listening to him was an act of love. I loved him because I perceived him to be a person of great value worth attending to, and I loved myself because I was willing to work on behalf of my growth. Since he was the teacher and I the pupil, he the giver and I the receiver, my love was primarily self-directed, motivated by what I could get out of our relationship and not what I could give him. Nonetheless, it is entirely possible that he could sense within his audience the intensity of my concentration, my attention, my love, and he may have been thereby rewarded. Love, as we shall see again and again, is invariably a two-way street, a reciprocal phenomenon whereby the receiver also gives and the giver also receives. . . .

True listening, total concentration on the other, is always a manifestation of love. An essential part of true listening is the discipline of bracketing, the temporary giving up or setting aside of one's own prejudices, frames of reference and desires so as to experience as far as possible the speaker's world from the inside, stepping inside his or her shoes. This unification of speaker and listener is actually an extension and enlargement of ourself, and new knowledge is always gained from this. Moreover, since true listening involves bracketing, a setting aside of the self, it also temporarily involves a total acceptance of the other. Sensing this acceptance, the speaker will feel less and less vulnerable and more and more inclined to open up the inner recesses of his or her mind to the listener. As this happens, speaker and listener begin to appreciate each other more and more, and the duet dance of love is again begun. The energy required for the discipline of bracketing and the focusing of total attention is so great that it can be accomplished only by love, by the will to extend oneself for mutual growth. Most of the time we lack this energy. Even though we may feel in our business dealings or social relationships that we are listening very hard, what we are usually doing is listening selectively, with a preset agenda in mind, wondering as we listen how we can achieve certain desired results and get the conversation over with as quickly as possible or redirected in ways more satisfactory to us.

Since true listening is love in action, nowhere is it more appropriate than in marriage. Yet most couples never truly listen to each other. Consequently, when couples come to us for counseling or therapy, a major task we must accomplish if the process is to be successful is to teach them how to listen. Not infrequently we fail, the energy and discipline involved being more than they are willing to expend or submit themselves to. Couples are often surprised, even horrified, when we suggest to them that among the things they should do is talk to each other by appointment. It seems rigid and unromantic and unspontaneous to them. Yet true listening can occur only when time is set aside for it and conditions are supportive of it. It cannot occur when people are driving, or cooking or tired and anxious to sleep or easily interrupted or in a hurry. Romantic "love" is effortless, and couples are frequently reluctant to shoulder the effort and discipline of true love and listening. But when and if they finally do, the results are superbly gratifying. Again and again we have the experience of hearing one spouse say to another with real joy, once the process of true listening has been started, "We've been married twenty-nine years and I never knew that about you before." When this occurs we know that growth in the marriage has begun.

While it is true that one's capacity to truly listen may improve gradually with practice, it never becomes an effortless process. Perhaps the primary requisite for a good psychiatrist is a capacity to truly listen, yet half a dozen times during the average "fifty-minute hour" I will catch myself failing to truly listen to what my patient is saying. Sometimes I may lose the thread of my patient's associations entirely, and it is then necessary for me to say, "I'm sorry, but I allowed my mind to wander for a moment and I was not truly listening to you. Could you run over the past few sentences again?" Interestingly, patients are usually not resentful when this occurs. To the contrary, they seem to understand intuitively that a vital element of the capacity to truly listen is being on the alert for those lapses when one is not truly listening, and my acknowledgment that my attention has wandered actually reassures them that most of the time I am truly listening. This knowledge that one is being truly listened to is frequently in and of itself remarkably therapeutic. In approximately a quarter of our cases, whether patients are adults or children, considerable and even dramatic improvement is shown during the first few months of psychotherapy, before any of the roots of problems have been uncovered or significant interpretations have been made. There are several reasons for this phenomenon, but chief among them, I believe, is the patient's sense that he or she is being truly listened to, often for the first time in years, and perhaps for the first time ever.

10.

Conversational Styles

DEBORAH TANNEN

Deborah Tannen, professor of linguistics at Georgetown University, opened up a world of controversy and debate when she argued that men and women communicate differently. There is great truth and value in what she has to say, but such a view may also reinforce gender stereotypes and inadvertently increase hostility between women and men (a counter-argument that is presented in the next chapter by Elizabeth Aries, a specialist in gender studies).

ONE OF THE MOST common stereotypes of American men is the strong silent type. Jack Kroll, writing about Henry Fonda on the occasion of his death, used the phrases "quiet power," "abashed silences," "combustible catatonia," and "sense of power held in check." He explained that Fonda's goal was not to let anyone see "the wheels go around," not to let the "machinery" show. According to Kroll, the resulting silence was effective on stage but devastating to Fonda's family.

The image of a silent father is common and is often the model for the lover or husband. But what attracts us can become flypaper to which we are unhappily stuck. Many women find the strong silent type to be a lure as a lover but a lug as a husband. Nancy Schoenberger begins a poem with the lines "It was your silence that hooked me,/ so like my father's." Adrienne Rich refers in a poem to the "husband who is frustratingly mute." Despite the initial attraction of such quintessentially male silence, it may begin to feel, to a woman in a long-term relationship, like a brick wall against which she is banging her head.

In addition to these images of male and female behavior—both the result and the cause of them—are differences in how women and men view the role of talk in relationships as well as how talk accomplishes its purpose. These differences have their roots in the settings in which men and women learn to have conversations: among their peers, growing up.

Children whose parents have foreign accents don't speak with accents. They learn to talk like their peers. Little girls and little boys learn how to have conversations as they learn how to pronounce words: from their playmates. Between the ages of five and fifteen, when children are learning to have conversations, they play mostly with friends of their own sex. So it's not surprising that they learn different ways of having and using conversations.

Anthropologists Daniel Maltz and Ruth Borker point out that boys and girls socialize differently. Little girls tend to play in small groups or, even more common, in pairs. Their social life usually centers around a best friend, and friendships are made, maintained, and broken by talk—especially "secrets." If a little girl tells her friend's secret to another little girl, she may find herself with a new best friend. The secrets themselves may or may not be important, but the fact of telling them is all-important. It's hard for newcomers to get into these tight groups, but anyone who is admitted is treated as an equal. Girls like to play cooperatively; if they can't cooperate, the group breaks up.

Little boys tend to play in larger groups, often outdoors, and they spend more time doing things than talking. It's easy for boys to get into the group, but not everyone is accepted as an equal. Once in the group, boys must jockey for their status in it. One of the most important ways they do this is through talk: verbal display such as telling stories and jokes, challenging and sidetracking the verbal displays of other boys, and withstanding other boys' challenges in order to maintain their own story—and status. Their talk is often competitive talk about who is best at what. . . .

Adult men and women struggling to communicate often sound like children: "You said so!" "I did not!" The reason is that when they grow up, women and men keep the divergent attitudes and habits they learned as children—which they don't recognize as attitudes and habits but simply take for granted as ways of talking.

Women want their partners to be a new and improved version of a best friend. This gives them a soft spot for men who tell them secrets. As Jack Nicholson once advised a guy in a movie: "Tell her about your troubled childhood—that always gets 'em." Men expect to *do* things together and don't feel anything is missing if they don't have heart-to-heart talks all the time.

If they do have heart-to-heart talks, the meaning of those talks may be opposite for men and women. To many women, the relationship is working as long as they can talk things out. To many men, the relationship isn't working out if they have to keep working it over. If she keeps trying to get talks going to save the relationship, and he keeps trying to avoid them because he sees them as weakening it, then each one's efforts to preserve the relationship appear to the other as reckless endangerment. . . .

We expect partners to be both romantic interests and best friends. Though women and men may have fairly similar expectations for romantic interests, obscuring their differences when relationships begin, they have very different ideas about how to be friends, and these are the differences that mount over time.

In conversations between friends who are not lovers, small misunderstandings can be passed over or diffused by breaks in contact. But in the context of a primary relationship, differences can't be ignored, and the pressure cooker of continued contact keeps both people stewing in the juice of accumulated minor misunderstandings. And stylistic differences are sure to cause misunderstandings—not, ironically, in matters such as sharing values and interests or understanding each other's philosophies of life. These large and significant yet palpable issues can be talked about and agreed on. It is far harder to achieve congruence—and much more surprising and troubling that it is hard—in the simple day-to-day matters of the automatic rhythms and nuances of talk. Nothing in our backgrounds or in the media (the present-day counterpart to religion or grandparents' teachings) prepares us for this failure. If two people share so much in terms of point of view and basic values, how can they continually get into fights about insignificant matters?

If you find yourself in such a situation and you don't know about differences in conversational style, you assume something's wrong with your partner or you, or you for having chosen your partner. At best, if you are forward thinking and generous minded, you may absolve individuals and blame the relationship. But if you know about differences in conversational style, you can accept that there are differences in habits and assumptions about how to have conversation, show interest, be considerate, and so on. You may not always correctly interpret your partner's intentions, but you will know that if you get a negative impression, it may not be what was intended—and neither are your responses unfounded.

II

Are Men and Women Really Worlds Apart?

ELIZABETH ARIES

In her many essays and books, Professor Aries strongly criticizes the writings of Deborah Tannen (whose essay appears in the previous chapter) and John Gray for ignoring the substantial evidence that contradicts their views. In reality, men are not from Mars, nor women from Venus; rather, each of us has a unique style of relating, shaped in part by our cultural and family histories. If we truly desire intimacy, we must be very careful of simplistic generalizations which can generate stereotypical views and even greater distance between us.

ALTHOUGH WE ARE likely to perceive many differences between the behavior of men and women in our daily lives, gender may not account for the differences; they may result from differences in power and social roles held by men and women. Research shows that men and women act quite similarly when we place them in identical roles and give them equal access to power.

Do gender differences in conversational style emerge consistently regardless of context, or do they only appear in selected contexts? Gender is only one of many determinants of behavior in interaction. The characteristics of the participants (e.g., sex, age, race, class, ethnicity, sexual orientation) in an encounter, the setting of the interaction, the topic of conversation, and the sex composition of the group all influence the way people behave in an interaction and thereby influence the degree to which gender differences are manifested.

Our cultural stereotypes of men and women are based on White middle- to upper-middle-class samples. Caution must be exercised in extending this portrayal to "men" and "women" in general. We must be wary of talking about "men" differing from "women" when our findings pertain only to selective groups of men and women. . . .

Deborah Tannen argues that "women feel men don't communicate" and attributes the problem to conversational style. She cites the case of a woman, married for thirty-eight years, who claimed that her husband had gone quiet on her after ten years of marriage. Tannen takes this husband as typical of men's failure to talk to their wives, overlooking the fact that this man *did* talk to his wife for the first ten years of his marriage. The problem could not, then, have arisen from gender differences in style but must have resulted from other changes in the context of their marriage.

Men are capable of sharing intimately and can do so when the situation demands it. When Harry Reis and his colleagues asked men and women to come to the laboratory and to have an intimate conversation with their same-sex best friend—to discuss something important and to reveal thoughts, feelings, and emotions—they found no gender differences in self-disclosure.

In summary, these studies demonstrate that men and women do not show a single style of behavior; rather, they display different styles depending on the demands of the situation, the characteristics of their conversational partners, the length of their interaction, or the setting of the interaction. Men and women select a style depending on the context in which they find themselves. In some contexts the styles of men and women will be different; in others they will be similar. . . .

Gender stereotypes should concern us for several reasons. First, they may dictate what we notice and bias our perceptions in the direction of expectation. Deborah Tannen elucidates gender differences with the goal of helping women and men to understand and respond to one another better. In the process, however, her work encourages people to notice and attend to differences rather than to similarities, to perceive men and women in accordance with stereotypes that may not accurately depict their behavior or intentions.

A second cause for concern is that gender stereotypes shape behavior. They not only describe behavior but prescribe it, dictating how men and women "should" behave. People behave in ways that are not internalized but that are prescribed for them because those who deviate from traditional sex-role norms pay a price. Punishment for deviation helps to maintain gender distinctions. Women who violate feminine norms and talk in a masculine way or display masculine behavior in male roles are evaluated more negatively than men who display the same behaviors or speech.

Stereotypes also shape behavior by serving as self-fulfilling prophecies. People begin to act in ways that support other people's gender-role expectations about them. Finally, stereotypes have a critical effect on the evaluation of speakers. A bias favors male speakers on the dimension of instrumental competency; men are evaluated more positively than women on this dimension even when men and women display the same behavior. . . .

Knowledge of people's gender alone will not lead to an accurate prediction of how they will behave. Behavior depends on more than the internalization into personality of unique styles associated with masculinity and femininity. People's behavior can be accounted for by race, class, ethnicity, and sexual orientation; by how they are situated in the social hierarchy; by differences in social roles and the normative expectations of particular settings; by cultural norms about how men and women should behave toward each other; and by the consequences of deviating from expectations. When the norms, roles, and expectations change, so do men's and women's behavior. Gender is not the primary determinant of behavior. In many settings other explanatory variables, such as race, class, and social position, are much more powerful predictors of behavior than gender. Gender is sometimes central and definitive, sometimes marginal and contingent. The fostering of gender stereotypes by books such as Deborah Tannen's sustains current realities, justifies current social inequalities, and keeps those inequalities in place. We must think carefully about the difference we choose to make out of gender differences.

12

Sex Is Not a Natural Act

LEONORE TIEFER

There is no such thing as spontaneous sex. It is not the ultimate intimacy or communication, nor is it even a natural act! In this provocative and witty essay, our notions of sexual intimacy are challenged to their stereotypical cores by Dr. Tiefer, associate professor of urology and psychiatry at the Albert Einstein College of Medicine. Share this story with your lover as soon as you can!

The Myth of Spontaneity

Nowadays we are expected to be sexually spontaneous. Scheming and playing games are out. But good sex doesn't strike like lightning. Only in romantic novels do lovers swoon from a single glance or pant from a passing touch. Getting turned on in real life is more like warming up an engine than flicking on a light switch.

Such is the power of our ignorance on this subject that many people suspect organic or hormonal weakness if they are not aroused at a moment's notice. Even those informed about the importance of mental preparation may wrongly label themselves psychologically undersexed. Not to mention the names they hurl at their partners.

In fact, seasoned lovers often deliberately put themselves in the mood. Thinking about sex usually tops their list of preliminaries. Like John Travolta, leisurely and lovingly combing his hair before going out to disco in *Saturday Night Fever,* anyone can tune into sensual, sexual feelings by imagining good times ahead. Relaxing, mentally and physically, is important. A shower works for some, a quiet time alone for others.

Some people complain that all this groundwork is too mechanical and time-consuming. Working at sex, they say, defeats the whole purpose. Ironically, these same people don't grouse over warming up for tennis or deny themselves an appetizer before dinner. One of the real reasons people are shy about making preparations for sex is that it seems sinful. Planning for sex runs counter to much of our early learning. Willfully conjuring up a lusty fantasy is wicked. Even sex within marriage can be tainted for some by too voluptuous an attitude.

People may also avoid planning because whenever you plan you risk disappointment. What if you dab on a little perfume and he isn't interested? What if you shave just before bed and she laughs at your obviousness? The risks feel greatest when you are insecure about yourself or your partner. This can make any negative thing feel like a catastrophe. In fact, I believe the risks in warming yourself up for sex (not every time—let's not get compulsive about this) are trivial compared to the possible benefits. Being embarrassed isn't shattering.

In our rush to celebrate spontaneous sex, we may have forgotten a childhood phenomenon—that waiting for Christmas was a big part of the fun. Can we abandon the trickery of seduction without losing the delicious excitement of the tease? Can we remember that a few solitary moments in the bullpen can make all the difference when we finally get into the game?

Bring Back the Kid Stuff

Poor little petting. Lost in the great big world of grownup sex. Somewhere along the line, kissing and tickling, rubbing and hugging became mere preliminaries to the main event.

A lot more is being lost than you might at first realize. Deprived of touch, many of us get a kind of itchy skin hunger. Sexual petting has been one of the primary ways adults can obtain the comforts of touch. While petting, many lovers murmur of their admiration and affection, talk baby-talk, or whisper and giggle—in a way that's not possible during intercourse. Exchanging endearments creates a special emotional bond. You may smile at the memory of a lover's nickname long after you've forgotten the physical details of sex together. Before we can value such indulgence, however, petting would have to lose the stigma of being kid stuff. As most of us grew up, intercourse was rated X: For Adults Only. It acquired the lure of the forbidden and the status of the big leagues.

At a time when lovers complain about insufficient variety, petting should become more popular. The skin is the largest sex organ, yet many of us have learned to regard as sexual only a tiny percentage of the available acreage. On the Polynesian island of Pnape, partners spend hours petting and nuzzling before they begin to think about intercourse.

Couples who seek out sex therapists because of sexual disinterest or difficulty in sexual function are often thunderstruck to hear that the first homework assignment of the treatment is to pet with each other. They can't imagine how avoiding intercourse and just playing around will help. They want help with "real" sex. Therapists explain that petting will lead their clients to discover (or rediscover) a wide variety of erotic sensations while positive emotions generated by the mutual stroking will strengthen the couple's attachment.

But, as clients soon realize, it may be easier to have intercourse than to hug and kiss! The task is better defined: a clear goal, a standard method, easy-to-locate equipment, and a socially defined endpoint. It can be accomplished with a minimum of communication. With petting, the script is more vague. Over what path do the hands and mouth wander? What words are said? How do you know when you're through?

You can have successful intercourse with a stranger, but you have to like someone to enjoy petting. Because the physical sensations are less intense, much of the reward must come from the closeness. It's joyless and burdensome to cuddle and embrace with someone you neither know well nor want to know better. The petting assignment is very revealing for many couples.

Calling kissing and hugging "foreplay" reveals their status as means to an end. Anything that is sometimes an appetizer and sometimes the main dish is worthy of a name other than foreplay. Let's save that one for something more appropriate—like golf.

Shedding Light on Sex in the Dark

Sex is the only game we play in the dark. Are we ashamed to watch what we're doing, or is darkness necessary to liberate our intimate passions?

In the darkness, lovers are safe from the prying eyes of children, parents, neighbors—and each other. To the extent that you want to deny others knowledge of you as a sexual person, you will welcome the protection of the dark.

Under cover of darkness, we are all beautiful. Flab, sag, spots, and wrinkles are mercifully hidden. With the contortions and grimaces of sexual exertion out of focus, we seem graceful as gazelles. To the extent that you find earthy images of skin and sweat distracting, you seek the camouflage of darkness.

In the permissive darkness, sin is softened. Taboos occur without witness. To the extent that your upbringing stressed the prohibitions surrounding sex, you may require the tolerance afforded by darkness.

Concealed by darkness, cracks in the ceiling—or your life—lose their immediacy. It's just the two of you, close together, with the colored lights flashing in your heads. The details of existence fade away.

Blinded by darkness, we are forced to use our other senses. We rediscover touch, aroma, sound. Covered with clothes, we are chronically deprived of the variety of pleasures and comforts available through touch. To the extent that vision distracts you from concentrating on other sensations, you will prefer darkness.

Screened by darkness, we become bold. Our words and our rhythms reveal a lusty eagerness we might deny by day. Shyness can be slain by the dark. In the privacy of darkness, we can exaggerate and improve our actual experience through imagination. Our wishes fulfilled, we feel deeper love and greater passion. Through illusion, we become more involved in reality. To the extent that imagination enriches the moment, darkness is a friend.

The trouble with darkness is that you can't see what you're doing. You can't see how your partner is reacting. You can't gaze into each other's eyes. Travelers ignorant of the territory tend to stick to familiar and well-marked routes. Sex in the dark often becomes routine. Many people protest that seeing themselves and their partners is immodest. But we're talking here about moonlight and 40-watt bulbs, not airport runway approach beacons.

Yet many of us have the greatest difficulty believing that anyone would enjoy seeing our genitals. We've been told they're cursed, or dirty. Many women are so paralyzed by shame they even avoid medical examination "down there." Modesty is often shame in disguise.

Perhaps because of the taboos on showing and looking, such acts can be the final revelation of trust between lovers. Like all proofs of acceptance, they must be mutual—forced, they become empty gestures of intimacy.

Sex Is an Unnatural Act

I have a T-shirt that reads, "Sex is a natural act." I used to think it was at least amusing, at best profound. If people would only relax and let their natural reactions flow, I thought, sex would be more of a pleasure and less of a Pandora's box.

I'm wiser now. I think the sentiment of the T-shirt distorts the truth. The urge to merge may be natural for birds and bees, but the biological takes a back seat in our own species. We humans are the only ones with a sex drive that isn't solely related to procreation.

Originally, the message that sex is natural was meant to relieve guilt feelings—you can't be blamed for doing what is healthy and normal. Such permission was extremely useful for a time. It enabled many people to break free from choking inhibitions.

But the message was taken too literally. I now meet people who believe hormones control their sex life. They feel no pride when sex is good and have no idea what to do when it is not. Letting Mother Nature do the driving sounds like the lazy person's dream; actually it makes you feel powerless and ignorant.

Belief that sexuality comes naturally relieves our responsibility to acquire knowledge and make choices. You don't have to teach your kids anything special—when the time comes, they'll know what to do. You don't have to talk with your partner about your love life—it'll all just happen automatically.

What happens automatically is often brief, routine, and more in the category of scratching an itch than indulging a beautiful expression. Such a sexual style may satisfy a person for whom sex has a low priority. It is unreasonable to expect mutual pleasure, variety, or emotional intimacy without some information and a lot of practice. If all you need for fulfilling sex comes already built in, then any difficulties must be due to physical breakdown. Many couples seek medical help when what they need is a course on communication. Sexual enrichment workshops mixing film, lecture, discussion, and time for private practice present an approach to sex that emphasizes the relationship.

You can't ignore the way worry and anger affect desire. You need to learn how to give suggestions and feedback without putting each other down. There's no way but trial and error to identify forms of effective stimulation. Most important, the attitude that sex is a natural act implies that great sex occurs early in a relationship and stays constant throughout. A dynamic vision of continuing change and adjustment is more realistic—it's not failing memory that leads some older couples to report that sex keeps getting better.

Unfortunately, most sex education has not caught up with what people need now. High school and college classes dwell at length on statistics, plumbing, and contraception. Students rarely read about connections between sexuality and feelings. Nor do they discuss what influences sexual attraction or how psychological needs are met through sex. Often students enter a course and leave it still thinking that love will guide the way to sexual happiness.

Limiting instruction to issues like birth control and venereal disease prevention may promote public health goals, but it does little to enrich the quality of sexual experience. Techniques of pregnancy prevention don't work to prevent sexual disappointment.

Natural sex, like a natural brassiere, is a contradiction in terms. The human sex act is a product of individual personalities, skills, and the scripts of our times. Like a brassiere, it shapes nature to something designed by human purposes and reflecting current fashion.

Sex as Communication? Save Your Breath!

It seems that every new sex book proclaims, "Sex is the ultimate form of communication." What does this mean? How can I figure out if it's true if I can't figure out what it means?

I go to my local guru. He tells me it means that people are most honest, most open, most truly themselves during sex. I ask why. You never really know a person until you've had sex together, he says. I say, I thought you never really knew a person until you got drunk together, or until one of you got cancer. Same thing, he says. Extreme situations cause people to reveal themselves. I'm dubious. Sex may be an extreme situation, but it makes as many people clam up as open up.

I go to another guru. This one tells me that sex is the ultimate form of communication because sex allows a person to express the broadest range of intimate feelings. People fumble for words, she says. They get tongue-tied and choked by emotion. Ah, but in bed they can let themselves go. Love, fear, tenderness, trust, generosity, sensitivity, respect, even anger. But what about those people whose sexual vocabulary is a one-note song? What about those who can emit volumes over breakfast, but only paragraphs in bed? Is sex the ultimate form of communication for them, too?

Another guru, another explanation. This one tells me sex offers the best hope for communication because words can lie, but bodies tell the truth. But I know bodies can lie. Or, rather, that reading body language can lead as often to misunderstanding as revelation. People mistake fatigue for rejection or disinterest. Physical arousal doesn't necessarily reflect desire for the partner in one's arms. Behavior isn't that easy to interpret; smiles and caresses can be as deceptive as words.

Maybe the best approach is to abandon the jargon. What does one person tell another by means of sex? Is the message unique to sex? Can it be delivered better for some people in words, other gestures of tenderness or intimacy or devotion?

The truth seems to be that people express themselves during love-making just as they do by all their activities. There tends to be a lot of consistency to the messages, as couples in sex therapy frequently discover. If one partner dominates sex so the other can't get a move in edgewise, it's a safe bet the same thing occurs during a discussion of how to discipline little Billy.

The gurus' basic error is overgeneralization. To claim sex is the ultimate form of communication sounds as if something fundamental about sex were being revealed that was true for all people. In fact, some people express their feelings better with caresses than words, but others don't. Some people reveal more of their inner feelings in sex than over coffee; others don't. Some people are closer to their lovers than to other companions, but many are not.

Like all generalizations, this one bulldozes individual differences. And like all hype about sex, it makes most of us wonder what we're missing. The word "ultimate" is the tipoff. No one human activity could possibly be the ultimate everything to anyone. We're just not that much alike.

13.

Friendship, East and West

BHIKHU PAREKH

I have often been asked if lovers can be friends, and my answer is yes. "But," I caution, "it takes more work than most couples are willing to invest." Very few people have written about friendship as simply as Bhikhu Parekh, who identifies six main characteristics of this highly regarded virtue. A brief commentary on Eastern spirituality and friendship concludes this fascinating essay.

HUMAN BEINGS STAND IN different kinds of relationship with each other: parents and children, siblings, husband and wife, neighbors, fellow-ethnics, fellow citizens. As we generally understand it, friendship, although sharing features in common with some of these relationships, constitutes a distinct kind of relationship.

First, it is nonbiological in the sense that unlike parents and children or siblings, it is not based on the ties of blood or heredity. This is not to deny that parents and children or brothers and sisters may become friends, but rather that their natural relationship sets limits to the quality and depth of their friendship and that the latter is irreducible and autonomous in nature.

Second, friendship is a voluntary relationship. Although it is not based on conscious, let alone rational, choices, and often grows unconsciously and involves an elusive "mental chemistry," it contains elements of deliberation, choice, and decision. The parties involved are aware of the development of their relationship, and freely decide whether or not to sustain and intensify it by required acts of reciprocity. Since it is entirely voluntary and neither embedded in a network of other relations nor reinforced by social sanctions, friendship is one of the most mortal of all human relationships.

Third, friendship is a relationship between two individuals. One might have many friends, but one is a friend of each of them individually. Friendship is not and never can be a mass or collective relationship.

Fourth, since friendship has no basis outside of itself and is a free creation of two individuals, it is entirely dependent on what they care to make of it. It takes whatever form they choose to give it, has such content and depth as they succeed in putting into it, is a unique expression of the kinds of persons they are, and reveals their individuality to a much greater degree than most other human relationships.

Fifth, friendship is open-ended and admits of degrees. One person is "just" a friend; another is a "good" friend; yet another is a "close" or an "intimate" friend—a "fast" friend, as Indians call it. Friendship covers a large spectrum ranging from a perceptible degree of warmth to a near total merger of two selves, and often occupies a place somewhere between the two extremes.

Sixth, friendship is reciprocal and involves mutual acknowledgement and a shared understanding. I cannot be your friend unless you are my friend. Friendship cannot come into being and last unless the parties involved acknowledge its existence, are broadly agreed on what it means and entails, and behave towards each other accordingly.

Finally, friendship involves mutual liking and good will. Friends are well disposed to each other, wish each other well, and help each other in times of need. They help each other not because they think they *ought* to help their fellow humans, but because they care for each other's well being and wish to be of mutual help. And they care for each other not because they cannot bear to see *human beings* suffer but because they are attached to each other and cannot bear to see *their friends* suffer or feel unhappy. As friendship deepens, mutual liking generates affection and perhaps even love. Since friendship is based on mutual liking, it is an unmediated relationship between two unique individuals. Friends are friends because, for some reason, they have "hit it off" and enjoy each other's presence. Although their common interests, temperaments, background, and so forth throw some light on why they became or remain friends, these do not determine and explain why their relationship took a specific form, acquired a specific measure of depth, and survived changes in interest and circumstances.

Friendship then is a nonbiological, voluntary, open-ended, informal, uninstitutionalized, and mutually acknowledged relationship between two individuals based on their good will and fondness for each other. Given these and its other constitutive features, it is only possible under certain conditions. Friendship presupposes a society or a culture in which human relationships are not totally structured and formalized, and leave adequate space for informal and self-generated relationships. It also presupposes that individuals are able to rise above their socially defined roles, are willing and able to undertake the adventure of new and unpredictable relationships, and have the courage and the disposition to share their intimate thoughts, feelings, and vulnerabilities with others and mortgage their happiness to others' inherently precarious feelings. It also implies that individuals have the patience, constancy of contact, and emotional energy required for a slowly maturing relationship; that they share enough experiences in common to have something to talk about; that they have the capacity to rise above their narrow self-interest and establish noncalculative relationships with others; that they have the emotional and moral maturity to understand and to adjust to each other's moods and eccentricities; and that they do not take so narrow a view of morality that it leaves no room for partiality and preference. These and related conditions do not obtain in all societies, and hence friendship is not a universal phenomenon. Some societies, such as the tribal, have only a limited space for friendship; some others, such as the modern liberal societies, encourage it up to a point but not beyond; some others such as the communist societies frown on it and prefer the collectivist ethos of comradeship based on dedication to a common cause. Many religious communities discourage friendship because it detracts from the love of God and breeds pockets of deep personal attachments. . . .

The [first distinguishing feature of the] classical Indian conception of friendship extends friendship to the human relationship with gods and even with God. For the Indian, a devotee can relate to God in several ways or *bhāvas*, including those of a child, a beloved, and a friend. Some schools of Indian thought reject this approach, but others such as Vaishnavism regard friendship as one of the four major forms of human relationship to God.

Second, the idea of cosmic friendliness as a desired human orientation towards the other inhabitants of the universe is distinctive to the Indian view, and has few if any parallels in the Western discourse on friendship.

Third, the Indian view of friendship places much greater stress on mutual help and loyalty than is to be found in the Western tradition. Friendship for the Indian is a bonding of hearts, and centers around active goodwill and loyalty. Friends are expected to like and enjoy each other's company, but that is not considered enough or even central. They must also care for each other, promote each other's well-being, help each other out in need, and so on. . . . Friendship therefore has a strong practical orientation. It is a system of mutual support, a basis of mutual favors. Not surprisingly it runs the constant danger of becoming a calculated investment in human relationships, a way of accumulating social capital by building up a network which can then be used to enhance one's social status and political power.

Fourth, since friendship is considered to be primarily a matter of heart, the head is assigned only a limited place in the Indian view. Aristotle said that the good man needs friends in order to share discussions and ideas. Such a view of friendship finds only a limited support in the classical Indian literature. Intellectual discussions do take place, but they are generally between gurus and their disciples and not between friends.

Finally, in the classical Indian view, friendship is a social relation. It is one of several ways in which individuals get bonded and acquire social obligations, and is not qualitatively different from other types of social bonds. Besides, friendship is a relation not merely between two individuals but also with the friend's family. As we saw, friendship is assimilated to kinship, and a friend is deemed to be like a brother. While such a socialization of friendship gives it considerable stability and social depth, it also subjects it to social jurisdiction and control, including specifying who should be one's friend, within what limits, and what one may expect of him or her. Such socialized friendship often has only limited independence and intensity, and is unable to develop at its own pace.

14.

Can Harry and Sally Ever Be Friends?

GILBERT MEILAENDER

Harry and Aristotle sleep in the same philosophical bed: "Men and women can't be friends because the sex part always gets in the way." Professor Meilaender demonstrates that academic writing can be humorous and informative, and kicks these two odd bedfellows out by insinuating that friendship and marriage may be the best combination of all.

IS FRIENDSHIP POSSIBLE between men and women? Or, more modestly put, are there reasons why friendship between men and women may be more difficult to sustain than same-sex friendships?

When we ask this question, the first problem that comes to mind is the one raised by Harry Burns in the 1989 movie *When Harry Met Sally.* In the opening scene, as he and Sally are driving together from Chicago to New York, Harry says: "Men and women can't be friends—because the sex part always gets in the way." . . .

Aristotle suggests that a relation grounded in erotic love will not be the highest form of friendship. He distinguishes a bond like friendship, grounded in a trait of character and involving choice, from a bond grounded in an emotion. And, while there can be friendship between lover and beloved, it will not be the highest form of friendship. It will be a friendship grounded not in character but in pleasure—and it is, therefore, likely to fade. "Still," Aristotle grants, noting how one sort of love may grow from another, "many do remain friends if, through familiarity, they have come to love each other's character, [discovering that] their characters are alike."[1]

It is important to note that *eros* and *philia* are indeed different forms of love, even if they may sometimes go together. In making a somewhat different point, C. S. Lewis suggested the following thought experiment:

> Suppose you are fortunate enough to have "fallen in love with and married your friend. And now suppose it possible that you were offered the choice of two futures: "*Either* you two will cease to be lovers but remain forever joint seekers of the same God, the same beauty, the same truth, *or else,* losing all that, you will retain as long as you live the raptures and ardours, all the wonder and the wild desire of *Eros.* Choose which you please."[2]

In recognizing the reality and difficulty of the choice we discern the difference between the loves. That difference Lewis captures nicely in a sentence. "Lovers are normally face to face, absorbed in each other; friends, side by side, absorbed in some common interest." Friends, therefore, are happy to welcome a new friend who shares their common interest, but *eros* is a jealous love which must exclude third parties.

Lewis believes that friendship and erotic love may go together, but in many respects he agrees with Harry and with Aristotle that the combination is an unstable one. He suggests that friendship between a man and a woman is likely to slip over into *eros* unless either they are physically unattractive to each other, or at least one of them already loves another. If neither of these is the case, friendship is "almost certain" to become *eros* "sooner or later." This is not far from Harry's view of the matter. Having asserted that "men and women can't be friends—because the sex part always gets in the way," Harry adds a caveat when he and Sally meet again five years later: "unless both are involved with other people." But then, in one of his characteristically convoluted pieces of reasoning, he adds: "But that doesn't work. The person you're involved with can't understand why you need to be friends with the other person. She figures you must be secretly interested in the other person—which you probably are. Which brings us back to the first rule." A little more optimistic than Harry, Lewis suggests that lovers who are also friends may learn to share their friendship with others, though not, of course, their *eros*. Still, however, that does not address Harry's chief concern: the instability of friendships with members of the opposite sex when those friendships are not shared with one's beloved. . . .

It is wiser to grant the point. Friendship between men and women will always have to face certain difficulties that will not be present in same-sex friendships. There will almost always be what J. B. Priestley calls "a faint undercurrent of excitement not present when only one sex is involved." This may even give to the friendship a tone not easily gotten any other way. Thus, as Priestley again puts it: "Probably there is no talk between men and women better than that between a pair who are not in love, have no intention of falling in love, but yet who *might* fall in love, who know one another well but are yet aware of the fact that each has further reserves yet to be explored." Priestley offered this opinion in a little book titled *Talking: An Essay,* published in 1926 as one of several volumes in the Pleasures of Life Series. But he might well have been describing what many viewers found appealing in *When Harry Met Sally.* Consider the scene in which Harry and Jess are talking while hitting some balls in a batting cage:

JESS: "You enjoy being with her?"

HARRY: "Yeah."

JESS: "You find her attractive?"

HARRY: "Yeah."

JESS: "And you're not sleeping with her?"

HARRY: "I can just be myself, 'cause I'm not trying to get her into bed."

And yet, not too much later comes the party at which Harry and Sally dance together—and themselves recognize the presence of Priestley's "faint undercurrent," which we call *eros*. This is a problem for friendships between men and women, even if it may also be enriching. *Eros* always threatens; for, unlike friendship, *eros* is a love that is jealous and cannot be shared. . . .

When Harry finally realizes that he loves Sally and wants to marry her, he ticks off the reasons: the way she's cold when it's 71 degrees outside; the way it takes her an hour and a half to order a sandwich; the way she crinkles up her nose when she looks at him. All these might be only the signs of an infatuated lover looking at the beloved, not of a friend who stands beside the friend and looks outward. But last in Harry's litany of reasons is that Sally is "the last person I want to talk to before I go to bed at night." And J. B. Priestley—though worrying that spouses' lives may be "so intertwined, that they are almost beyond talk as we understand it"— has a view not unlike Harry's: "Talk demands that people should begin, as it were, at least at some distance from one another, that there should be some doors still to unlock. Marriage is partly the unlocking of those doors, and it sets out on its happiest and most prosperous voyages when it is launched on floods of talk."

In marriage, if we are patient and faithful, we may find that "balance and sanity" which friendship between men and women offers, and we may find it in a context where *eros* also may be fulfilled without becoming destructive. Against the view of Critobulus we may, therefore, set the wisdom of Ben Sira: "A friend or companion is always welcome, but better still to be husband and wife."[3]

15.

Building Trust in Romantic Relationships

SUSAN D. BOON

I give this article to many of my counseling clients, for it is the most comprehensive and concise overview of the importance of trust in relationships. Dr. Boon, an assistant professor at the University of Calgary, describes four key issues—dependability, responsiveness, conflict resolution, and faith—that partners need to embrace in order to develop a mature capacity to trust.

JUST AS A PAIR of mountain climbers must coordinate their movements in order to maintain their precarious grip and keep from plummeting to the hard ground below, so, too, becoming intimately involved with another is a venture in which two individuals strive to reconcile their needs, goals, and desires and to maintain the delicate balance required to preserve the relationship intact. Extending the analogy further, as time passes and a relationship expands in depth and breadth of involvement—as the climbers ascend higher and higher on the mountain wall—the elements of risk associated with depending on another actually increase. First, the level of interdependence is intensified and, in correspondence, the stakes to be lost rise substantially. Furthermore, it becomes increasingly apparent that the efforts of neither partner alone can achieve the balance required to maintain the relationship. A solo climber is a foolish

---

Editor's note: For a listing of the references to this chapter, see Susan D. Boon's article "Dispelling Doubt and Uncertainty: Trust in Romantic Relationships," which appears in Steve Duck's anthology, *Dynamics of Relationships* (Thousand Oaks, CA: Sage Publications, 1994).

climber, and if either partner loses his or her grip, both may plunge head-
long to the valley floor beneath.

This analogy highlights a number of elements important to understanding the interface between trust and risk. Every day in our relationships we must make decisions: decisions to commit further or to
withdraw, to take this course of action in response to a situation of conflict versus some alternative action, to make use of a particular opportunity or to let it pass us by. Often these decisions are difficult and risk laden,
compelling us to confront our hopes and fears about depending on another for our own needs to be met. In the same very real way that mutual
trust enables a pair of mountain climbers to conquer the mountain, it
provides the critical platform from which relationship partners may con-
fidently approach the task of decision making. It provides the implicit
contract of good intentions that permits the negotiation of situations that
conspire to awaken us to the ways in which we are vulnerable in our relationships. . . .

Dependability

At the most elementary level, establishing a partner's dependability is
fundamental to proving his or her trustworthiness. A trustworthy partner is one on whom a person can depend, who can be relied on time and
time again and in all manner of situations to act honestly, considerately,
and with the best of intentions. A dependable partner is reliable and con-
sistent, the kind of person whose motives and intentions one can be certain of.

Responsiveness

Attributions of responsiveness, in contrast to attributions of dependability, extend beyond assessments of a partner's general character to his or
her disposition toward the person in particular. Feelings of security in a

relationship are strengthened when a partner's actions are geared toward the person's particular needs, that is, when such actions signal a special consideration of the person's needs and preferences—a unique interest in promoting a relationship with that person rather than with any other.

As with many other dispositions, responsiveness is best expressed in situations in which the partner's actions are counter to his or her own wishes. By choosing to put aside his or her own preferences in order to satisfy those of the other, a partner demonstrates that he or she truly cares about the person and is intrinsically motivated in the relationship. Such self-sacrificing moves serve to validate the person's needs and desires, and to reassure him or her that the partner accepts who he or she is. According to Reis and Shaver (1988), patterns of responsiveness and validation of this sort are integral to the process by which the affectional bond between intimates is formed, maintained, and intensified.

A Capacity to Resolve Conflict

In addition to establishing that a partner is dependable and responsive, it is also necessary that a person be confident that conflicts that arise in the course of the relationship can be successfully resolved in a manner that does not either neglect partner's needs and concerns or jeopardize the relationship. If such a feeling of efficacy in the couple's ability to face conflict does not exist, the growth of trust may be seriously stunted. Issues of disagreement that remain unresolved tend to persist undiminished and resurface later in other areas, often larger and more intractable than they were initially. Furthermore, repeated experiences of failure in a couple's efforts at problem solving are apt to generate a "terminal hypothesis" (Hurvitz, 1970), a belief that the relationship is in fact doomed to fail because the couple is unable to coordinate effective solutions to the problems they face.

Effective conflict resolution requires open and constructive engagement of the contentious issue. Such an approach affords a natural opportunity for partners to exercise their trust in each other and, through succeeding in their negotiation efforts, the opportunity to bolster their confidence in the belief that it is safe to depend on the integrity and benevolence of the other's motives (Holmes, 1991). By opening the source of their disagreement to discussion, each must assume the vulnerable stance of expressing his or her feelings to the other, boldly facing the threat of rejection or rebuff. In addition, successful problem solving typically requires some degree of compromise, some concession or self-sacrifice on the part of one or both partners. Those who dare to cross this risky terrain may emerge from the other side with a greatly intensified sense of mutual trust as their reward.

Faith

Rempel et al. (1985) describe faith as an emotionally charged sense of closure regarding the question of a partner's trustworthiness and the relationship's future. Others have described it as a construction erected to "curtail feelings of uncertainty once commitments have been made," (Boon & Holmes, 1991, p. 206), enabling an individual to extinguish any residual doubts about the partner's motives that may remain even after the criteria of dependability, responsiveness, and ability to cope with conflict have been satisfied. As discussed previously, the evidence supporting such faith can never be conclusive. Yet if a person is to feel secure relating to an intimate partner in a sometimes unsettled world, this fact must assume secondary importance to the working assumption that trust is well deserved.

Faith is linked to the extent to which an individual's view of the partner incorporates both his or her good and bad points, that is, the extent to which a person is able to come to terms with a partner's faults. When a person is able to effectively consolidate both his or her positive and negative attitudes toward the partner within a single relatively coherent and unified attitude structure, the transformation of working hypothesis ("I hope I can trust my partner") into so-called fact ("I know I can trust my partner") eliminates the need for a vigilant appraisal process and allows feelings of insecurity and vulnerability regarding trust to be abandoned. (Brickman, 1987; Holmes, 1991). Conversely, when negative aspects of a partner are suppressed or denied rather than contextualized within the broader network of positive beliefs, feelings, and experiences, situations that prime such negative elements of the representation will ultimately fail to prime the wealth of positive elements that might have served to defuse the negative impact. (Brickman, 1987). In this case, pockets of attributional uncertainty may remain, tagged to the isolated and compartmentalized body of negative attitudes, handicapping a person's ability to relax his or her fears and make the leap of faith required to fully legitimize trust. Thus the success of this process of integrating the good with the bad—experiences of hurt and disappointment with experiences of validation and caring—may determine the breadth and depth of a person's capacity to trust.

16.

Do Happy Marriages Exist?

JUDITH S. WALLERSTEIN AND SANDRA BLAKESLEE

The authors, well known for their research on divorce, have identified many of the elements that make relationships work. Based upon their groundbreaking study of fifty couples, this essay concludes with a list of nine essential tasks that couples need to address.

FOR EVERYONE [in our research study] happiness in marriage meant feeling respected and cherished. Without exception, these couples mentioned the importance of liking and respecting each other and the pleasure and comfort they took in each other's company. Some spoke of the passionate love that began their relationship, but for a surprising number love grew in the rich soil of the marriage, nourished by emotional and physical intimacy, appreciation, and fond memories. Some spoke of feeling well cared for, others of feeling safe, and still others of friendship and trust. Many talked about the family they had created together. But all felt that they were central to their partner's world and believed that creating the marriage and the family was the major commitment of their adult life. For most, marriage and children were the achievements in which they took the greatest pride.

For these couples, respect was based on integrity; a partner was admired and loved for his or her honesty, compassion, generosity of spirit, decency, loyalty to the family, and fairness. An important aspect of respect was admiration of the partner as a sensitive, conscientious parent. The value these couples placed on the partner's moral qualities was an unexpected finding. It helps explain why many divorcing people speak so vehemently of losing respect for their former partner. The love that people feel in a good marriage goes with the conviction that the person is worthy of being loved.

These people were realists. No one denied that there were serious differences—conflict, anger, even some infidelity—along the way. No one envisioned marriage as a rose garden, but all viewed its satisfactions as far outweighing the frustrations over the long haul. Most regarded frustrations, big and small, as an inevitable aspect of life that would follow them no matter whom they married. Everyone had occasional fantasies about the roads not taken, but their commitment to the marriage withstood the impulse to break out.

Above all, they shared the view that their partner was special in some important regard and that the marriage enhanced each of them as individuals. They felt that the fit between their own needs and their partner's responses was unique and probably irreplaceable. In this they considered themselves very lucky, not entitled.

Their marriages had benefited from the new emphasis in our society on equality in relationships between men and women. However they divided up the chores of the household and of raising the children, the couples agreed that men and women had equal rights and responsibilities within the family. Women have taken many casualties in the long fight to achieve equality, and many good men have felt beleaguered, confused, and angry about this contest. But important goals have been achieved: marriages today allow for greater flexibility and greater choice. Relationships are more mature on both sides and more mutually respectful. A couple's sex life can be freer and more pleasurable. Today's men and women meet on a playing field that is more level than ever before.

Unlike many unhappy families, these couples provided no evidence for the popular notion that there is a "his" marriage and a "her" marriage. On the contrary, the men and women were very much in accord. I did not see significant differences between husbands and wives in their goals for the marriage, in their capacity for love and friendship, in their interest in sex, in their desire to have children, or in their love and commitment to the children. They fully shared the credit for the success of the marriage and the family. Both men and women said, "Everything we have we did together."

Although some men were inhibited in their expression of feelings at the beginning of the marriage, as compared with their wives, I did not find much difference between the sexes in their ability to express emotions over the course of their relationship. Both spoke easily of their love for their partner. In response to my questioning, both men and women cried when they contemplated losing the other.

The children were central, both as individuals and as symbols of a shared vision, giving pleasure and sometimes unexpected meaning to the parents' lives and to the marriage. As the couples reported to me in detail, the children reflected their love and pride. And this powerful bond did not diminish when the children left home.

As I compared the happily married couples with the thousands of divorcing couples I have seen in the past twenty-five years, it was clear that these men and women had early on created a firm basis for their relationship and had continued to build it together. Many of the couples that divorced failed to lay such a foundation and did not understand the need to reinforce it over the years. Many marriages broke because the structure was too weak to hold in the face of life's vicissitudes. The happy couples regarded their marriage as a work in progress that needed continued attention lest it fall into disrepair. Even in retirement they did not take each other for granted. Far too many divorcing couples fail to understand that a marriage does not just spring into being after the ceremony. Neither the legal nor the religious ceremony makes the marriage. *People* do, throughout their lives.

What is the work that builds a happy marriage? What should people know about and what should they do? On the basis of the study I proposed nine psychological tasks that challenge men and women throughout their life together. These tasks, the building blocks of the marriage, are not imposed on the couple from the outside; they are inherent in a relationship in today's world. If the issues represented by each psychological task are not addressed, the marriage is likely to fail, whether the couple divorces or remains legally married. The tasks begin at the start of the marital journey and are continually renegotiated. A good marriage is always being reshaped so that the couple can stay in step with each other and satisfy their changing needs and wishes.

The first task is to detach emotionally from the families of childhood, commit to the relationship, and build new connections with the extended families. Husband and wife help each other complete the transition into adulthood or, in a second marriage, detach from a prior relationship and commit emotionally to the new partner.

The second task is to build togetherness through intimacy and to expand the sense of self to include the other, while each individual carves out an area of autonomy. The overarching identification with the other provides the basis for bonding. As one man put it succinctly, "In a good marriage, it can't be Me-Me-Me, it's gotta be Us-Us-Us." Exactly! But within the new unity, there must be room for autonomy; otherwise there is no true equality. These two early tasks launch the marriage.

The third task is to expand the circle to include children, taking on the daunting roles of parenthood from infancy to the time when the child leaves home, while maintaining the emotional richness of the marriage. The challenge of this task is to maintain a balance between raising the children and nurturing the couple's relationship.

The fourth task is to confront the inevitable developmental challenges and the unpredictable adversities of life, including illness, death, and natural disasters, in ways that enhance the relationship despite suffering. Every crisis carries within it the seeds of destruction as well as the possibility of renewed strength. Managing stress is the key to having a marriage that can reinvent itself at each turning rather than one that becomes a shadow of its former self.

The fifth task is to make the relationship safe for expressing difference, anger, and conflict, which are inevitable in any marriage. All close relationships involve love and anger, connectedness and disruption. The task is to find ways to resolve the differences without exploiting each other, being violent, or giving away one's heart's desire. Conflict ran high among several couples in this group, but I saw no evidence that conflict by itself wrecks a marriage.

The sixth task is to establish an imaginative and pleasurable sex life. Creating a sexual relationship that meets the needs and fantasies of both people requires time and love and sensitivity. Because a couple's sex life is vulnerable to interference by the stresses of work and by family life, and because sexual desire changes, often unpredictably, over the life course, this aspect of the marriage requires special protection in order to flourish.

The seventh task is to share laughter and humor and to keep interest alive in the relationship. A good marriage is alternately playful and serious, sometimes flirtatious, sometimes difficult and cranky, but always full of life.

The eighth task is to provide the emotional nurturance and encouragement that all adults need throughout their lives, especially in today's isolating urban communities and high-pressure workplaces.

Finally, the ninth task is the one that sustains the innermost core of the relationship by drawing sustenance and renewal from the images and fantasies of courtship and early marriage and maintaining that joyful glow over a lifetime. But these images, nourished by the partners' imaginations, must be combined with a realistic view of the changes wrought by time. It is this double image that keeps love alive in the real world.

I have learned from these happily married couples that marriages come in different shapes and sizes. Under today's looser rules a marriage can be custom-made by the couple to an extent their grandparents never dreamed possible. I have therefore suggested a typology of marriage to capture what I have observed in this study. This typology includes romantic, rescue, companionate, and traditional marriages. Second marriages can belong to any of these groups. I suspect that more types will emerge in the future as marriage continues to reflect people's changing emotional needs and values.

No marriage provides for all the wishes and needs that people bring to it. Although every good marriage provides many satisfactions, each type maximizes different rewards and exacts a different price. In each type the psychological tasks are resolved differently. The kind and degree of to-getherness and autonomy vary, as does the importance of children, work, and sexual passion. The values on which the marriage is built differ among the types, although they overlap. Children growing up in each kind of marriage have quite different experiences.

Moreover, the various types of marriages require different kinds of support from society. For traditional marriages to succeed, society must offer jobs that pay enough money for one parent to support the family while the other raises the children. Society also must provide economic and educational opportunities for the child-rearing parent when the children have grown up. Similarly, for companionate marriages to flourish, society must ensure that workplace demands are not allowed to over-whelm the marriage and the family. Companionate couples also need good-quality child care and enlightened personnel policies so that they do not have to make anguished choices between the demands of work and of family, especially at times of crisis.

I [Wallerstein] have tried to show the importance of the fit between the couple and the kind of marriage they create. The idea that different people seek different kinds of marriages has important practical implications. If couples understand in advance that each kind of marriage poses different hazards and requires different tending, they can anticipate where problems are likely to develop and take steps to resolve them. The deepest satisfaction of the romantic marriage is that it gratifies the desire for passionate love, which in some cases is reinforced by the powerful wish to restore a beloved figure lost in childhood. By their nature, ro-mantic marriages absorb most of a couple's emotional investment, and one hazard is that the children may feel peripheral to the couple's rela-tionship.

The rescue marriage is often less emotionally intense than the ro-mantic marriage; its great contribution is in allowing people to revise their sorrowful expectations of life. People who have suffered severe trau-mas are freed to pursue their lives, because the marriage gives them strength. But there is danger that the old problems will reemerge, either in the couple's relationship or between parent and child. Romantic and rescue marriages are not subject to voluntary choice, but in each type the tasks can be resolved and the marriage shaped to avoid the most likely hazards.

Companionate marriage does represent a choice, based on the couple's commitment to two careers or economic necessity or both. At its best, companionate marriage provides the gratifications of family life and the rewards of a successful career for both partners. But each individual's separate path may supersede the togetherness that happy marriage requires, leading to the loss of intimacy and emotional connectedness. Or child care may be delegated to others to the point that neither parent is primary in the child's upbringing.

Traditional marriage can meet people's needs for a home and a stable family life and provide comfort and nurturance for both adults and children. But the danger in a traditional marriage is that the partners' lives may become increasingly separate. And at midlife, when the all-absorbing tasks of child rearing are over and the tasks of the marriage need to be negotiated anew, the partners may feel estranged from each other.

A good marriage, I have come to understand, is transformative. The prevailing psychological view has been that the central dimensions of personality are fully established in childhood. But from my observations, men and women come to adulthood unfinished, and over the course of a marriage they change each other profoundly. The very act of living closely together for a long time brings about inner change, not just conscious accommodation. The physical closeness of sex and marriage has its counterpart in psychological closeness and mutual identification.

As the men and women in good marriages respond to their partner's emotional and sexual needs and wishes, they grow and influence each other. The needs of one's partner and children become as important as one's own needs Ways of thinking, self-image, self-esteem, and values all have the potential for change. The second marriages show clearly that the capacity of men and women to love each other passionately revives in their relationship despite early disappointments. The power of marriage to bring about change is especially evident in rescue marriages. As I have described, people who have been severely traumatized during childhood are able, with the help of a loving relationship, to restore their self-esteem.

A willingness to reshape the marriage in response to new circumstances and a partner's changing needs and desires is an important key to success. All of the couples in the study understood that unless they renegotiated the tasks of the relationship at key points, one or both partners would be unhappy. There are shaky times in every marriage. Many life-course changes, such as the birth of a baby or a child's adolescence, can be anticipated, but others, such as major illness or job loss, cannot. At all of these times, emotional changes in the individual coincide with external changes. If the couple does not take steps to protect it, the marriage may be in peril. These couples succeeded in reshaping their relationship at each major crossroads so that it continued to fit their needs. All mentioned that they had experienced many different marriages within their one enduring relationship.

I have learned a great deal about the intimate connectedness of a good marriage. It became clear to me early on that popular notions about marital communication failed to capture the subtlety of the daily interactions between these men and women. They had learned that a little tact goes a long way, that sometimes silence is golden, and that timing is everything. They listened carefully to each other and tried to speak both honestly and tactfully. But they recognized intuitively that true communication in marriage extends far beyond words. It involves paying attention to changing moods, facial expressions, body language, and the many other cues that reveal inner states of mind. It means knowing each other's history and catching the echoes and behaviors that reverberate from the past. It includes knowing enough about the other so that at critical times one can take an imaginative leap inside the other's skin. That is what empathy in a marriage is about.

These were not talents that came naturally to all of these people, nor were these individuals necessarily empathic in other domains of their lives. They learned to listen and to be sensitive to their partner's cues because they wanted the marriage to work; they had learned that by anticipating a partner's distress, they could protect themselves and the marriage.

These couples also understood that symbolically a marriage is always much greater than the sum of its parts. It is enriched by the continued presence of fantasy. When the marriage is successful, it represents a dream come true, the achievement of full adulthood. Tragically, when it fails, the symbolic loss may cause enormous suffering. The home these couples created gave them both real and symbolic pleasure because they felt strongly that it was their own creation. Their pleasure in each other, especially during times of leisure and reflection, represented more than current satisfaction; it represented the fulfillment of wishes extending way back to the dreams of early childhood.

Finally, I learned again, as I have learned many times over from the divorced couples I have worked with, the extraordinary threats that contemporary society poses to marriage. The stresses of the workplace and its fierce impact on the couple are writ large in the lives of these families, no matter what their economic level. Their stories told and retold how few supports newly married couples have to keep them together and how many powerful forces pull them apart. As the younger couples made clear, the whole world seems to invade the couple's private time together.

Americans today work long hours, yet during the early years of marriage, money is often hard to come by, even in professional occupations. Working for a big firm can be exciting for someone ascending the ladder of success, but it does not provide the latitude for creativity that many crave or the individuality that everyone needs. And because the corporate world is so impersonal, the emotional bonds of the couple and family are even more important, but the time and energy to enjoy them are substantially and cruelly curtailed.

Marriage is hard work partly because raising children is hard work; there is insufficient time before bedtime each day and not enough hands for the tasks that were supposed to have been cut by laborsaving devices but somehow weren't. Marriage is also hard because so many people come from unhappy families, whether the family split up or remained together; those who grew up in such families often carry deep hungers from childhood. Marriage is a high-risk venture because the threat of divorce is everywhere, as these couples all knew.

Because of societal pressures and the essential loneliness of modern life, marriage serves many purposes in today's world. It is our only refuge. The couples in the study were realistically aware that they had to fulfill many needs for each other; there are not many opportunities at work or elsewhere in society for gratifying our desires for friendship, comfort, love, reassurance, and self-expression. These couples wanted a marriage that could respond to all these complex needs without breaking. They discovered anew each day the many ways in which they helped each other and how pleased and proud they were of the marriage they had created.

A good marriage is more than the happy possession of an individual couple and their children. It is this unit, which represents us at our civilized best, that shapes adults and children. More than any other human institution, marriage is the vehicle for transmitting our values to future generations. Ultimately it is our loving connections that give life meaning. Through intimate relationships we enlarge our vision of life and diminish our preoccupation with self. We are at our most considerate, our most loving, our most selfless within the orbit of a good family. Only within a satisfying marriage can a man and woman create the emotional intimacy and moral vision that they alone can bequeath to their children.

These findings on marriage are hopeful and reassuring. The guidelines I have developed to help couples as they start out and at later points along the way are realistic. But given the pressures of contemporary American society, it is clear that marriage is a serious game for adult players, whether they begin as adults or become adults in the play.

PART III

What Can We Do When It Isn't Working?

Seldom or never does a
marriage develop into an
individual relationship
smoothly and without crises.
There is no birth of
consciousness without pain.

CARL JUNG

Whether marriage as we know
it is obsolete, I do not know,
but frankly I doubt it. Despite
its shortcomings, marriage is
still the best institution we
have developed to combat
loneliness and to provide a
structure within which two
adults can find intimate
satisfaction and continue
to grow.

BRUNO BETTELHEIM

The Night Has a Thousand Eyes

The night has a thousand eyes,
   And the day but one;
Yet the light of the bright world dies
   With the dying sun.

The mind has a thousand eyes,
   And the heart but one;
Yet the light of a whole life dies
   When love is done.

FRANCIS WILLIAM BOURDILLON

A Fallen Love

It is winter and the leaves have fallen from the trees. One, however, clings tenaciously to an ancient branch—her tender stem weakened by the breeze. She is beautiful, this leaf, golden like the winter sun, delicate and dry. A little summer green remains, that is all, but it is enough to remind me of her youth.

Nestled in her tree, she seems safe and out of reach, but the branch begins to tremble and frees itself from the leaf. Look at how she falls, turning in the morning light! I want to catch her in my palm but she is quick and pulls away. Perhaps the leaf does not want to be held, perhaps she cannot see me. There is a fear that she will crumble in my hand—a death more certain than the ground below. And so she lies on the cool moist earth, between the twigs of the other fallen leaves, waiting for the transformation of time. I want so much to pick her up, to warm her by the fire and give her life.

Inside, behind the painted glass, I wait, learning how to weep.

M. R. WALDMAN

A ll relationships experience periods of conflict and difficulty, which we usually resolve with ease. But sometimes a conflict seems to fester and grow out of control. Why do relationships suddenly break down or falter when we least expect them to? What are the causes, and how do we identify the roots of our relational ills? The answers to these questions are as complex as those surrounding love. They may involve subtle misunderstandings, hidden expectations, secret agendas, fantasies, unrecognized or unacknowledged aspects of our personalities (addictions, depressions, and other shadow aspects of the self), different core values and beliefs, issues about money or parental control, sexual insensitivity, or even a genetic or biochemical insensitivity.

Even maturity can challenge the stability of relationships. For example, some of the most turbulent moments in love can occur when we enter midlife, a time when we often reevaluate our work, our values, and the relationships we are in. Jung noted that midlife can bring yet another challenge, one in which we may experience a reversal in male and female roles. Often, we are not aware of these internal forces, but they can be discovered in the archetypal images of fairy tales, myths, and dreams. In our opening chapter, Allan B. Chinen explores this midlife drama through the metaphor of a Persian fairy tale, about a man and a woman in conflict and a marriage that is on the rocks. We usually think of fairy tales as ending happily ever after, but there are some that describe what happens after the romantic glow wears off. This ancient tale shows us that, deep down inside, we have both a masculine and feminine self; one predominates in the first half of life, and the other emerges later on. At first there is great conflict, as the stubborn husband and stubborn wife portray in Chinen's tale, but with self-reflection and patience we can bring both sides together. When we accomplish this in our relationships, when we marry our masculine and feminine sides, a deeper respect and love can emerge.

In the next chapter, cognitive psychologist Aaron T. Beck explores some of the underlying issues that cause bitter arguments between people. He describes what happens when we become too self-centered and in-sistent on one particular view, and how power struggles erupt when one person refuses to allow his or her identity to merge with the other. When couples fail to understand the dynamics of partnership, unrealistic expectations—governed by private, symbolic meanings—conspire to disrupt their alliance.

Just as there are stages in the development of intimacy, there are also stages or levels of conflict. Low-level conflict, explain Gerald R. Weeks and Larry Hof, is often focused on specific issues, where both individuals maintain a strong sense of "coupleness" as they negotiate legitimate differences and concerns. In medium-level conflict, unconscious patterns of behavior are often at the root of the disturbance, and may require therapeutic intervention to expose the underlying issues. In these situations, one or both individuals may have a weaker sense of self and may be less objective, irresponsible, or more emotionally reactive. With high-level conflict, there is considerably more disturbance in the couple's personal and interpersonal dynamics, and long-term therapy is generally called for.

When there is adequate strength and commitment in the relationship, couples can engage in a process that Weeks and Hof describe as fighting fairly. In their essay, they outline the essential "do's" and "don'ts" of constructive arguing and the rules to govern such interactions. Their strategy provides an effective technique that can easily be incorporated into our relationships.

Although romance is an essential part to love and intimacy, some people confuse it with obsession. In these highly emotional and self-destructive relationships, one or both partners become overly dependent upon the other, imposing fantasies and ideals that can never be realistically engaged. Women, notes Robin Norwood, are particularly susceptible to "loving too much." In her essay, she lists ten characteristics that signify a more autonomous and self-loving approach to relationship. In Stanton Peele's article, he looks at eight key dimensions of love and how they can be viewed in either a healthy or addictive way. Both authors acknowledge how pervasive co-dependency is in our society and how desperate some people can become in their search for genuine love.

When a person fails to acknowledge and talk about the conflicts that normally arise in a marriage, he or she may act out in anger or in hurt. It may be done in subtle ways: through indirect negative comments, by withholding money or sex, or by becoming distant or anxious or depressed. Having an affair is another way that some individuals use to express relational discord, an avenue that may be turned to when communication skills are weak. Infidelity generates other relational problems because it fosters silence and secrecy, and eventually, through indirect and unconscious forms of communication, the secret is exposed. An affair, when uncovered, is certainly painful, but it does not necessarily mean an end to the relationship. As Harriet Lerner portrays in her essay, the disclosure of an infidelity may lead both people into a deeper intimacy and a better understanding of both partners' needs.

But not all conflicts can be resolved, and in such cases the question of divorce or separation can be raised. For most people, it is the most difficult question they will ever have to face, and for those with limited communication skills, therapeutic and legal intervention may be called for in order to avoid destructive patterns of behavior.

Social commentators often speak of the "alarming increase of divorce in America," citing numbers that range between forty-five to sixty percent, but recent studies show that the divorce rate is actually declining. Other studies suggest that a similar rate of divorce has existed in all cultures throughout history. In some tribal societies, the woman is free to leave her husband at any time, for any reason, without fear of retribution or disgrace. In David Buss's remarkable world study of human mating strategies, he discusses the ways that people have historically handled separation:

> Divorce is a human universal that occurs in all known cultures. Our separation strategies involve a variety of psychological mechanisms. We have ways to assess whether the costs inflicted by a mate outweigh the benefits provided. We scrutinize other potential partners and evaluate whether they might offer more than our current mate. We gauge the likelihood of successfully attracting other desirable

partners. We calculate the potential damage that might be caused to ourselves, our children, and our kin by the dissolution of the relationship. And we combine all this information into a decision to stay or leave. . . . These complex social relationships must be negotiated, the breakup justified. The range of tactical options within the human repertoire is enormous, from simply packing one's bags and walking away to provoking a rift by revealing an infidelity.[1]

If we embrace the notion of a conscious relationship during our mating and bonding stages of love, is it possible to discuss the possibility of divorce with a similar degree of awareness, compassion, and understanding? The answer is a qualified yes, and there is now a movement called divorce mediation, a process where both parties sit down together with a counselor to discuss, without hostility, various options and solutions. In such a situation, the partners are attempting to maintain respect and compassion as they establish a new framework in which to talk and interact. To my way of thinking, mediation represents a great transformation in our standards of marriage, love, and divorce. In an essay by Gary J. Friedman, one of this country's leading voices in the field, he reviews some of the basic principles of divorce mediation. If these communication techniques were to be applied when conflicts first arise in relationships, many marriages could be saved from the traumas of divorce. But even when both people can sit down to talk things through, the process is profoundly disturbing, made all the more difficult by a society that frowns upon divorce. As Orli Peter points out in her summary of divorce research, many of the negative notions surrounding divorce are nothing more than media-generated myths that are capable of generating problems where no problem may actually exist. These myths imply that divorce is a negative and unwise choice. However, most women find themselves happier after the process is complete. Additionally, most people do remarry with adequate satisfaction. In many situations, divorce promotes a deeper consciousness of self and other, and the process of separation, painful though it may be, encourages us to develop a more respectful, mature, and realistic approach to love.

17.

Stubborn Husband,
Stubborn Wife

ALLAN B. CHINEN

Through the metaphor of a humorous fairy tale, Jungian therapist Allan Chinen shows us how our struggles and conflicts in marriage have been universal themes throughout history. He points out how, at midlife, hidden dimensions of our personality often emerge. In this case, we see how the feminine sides of men begin to be incorporated, and how the masculine sides of women come to be embraced.

*O*nce *upon a time, a husband had the habit of sitting outside his home every day, while his wife cooked their meals, swept the floor, and washed their clothes. The two quarreled constantly. "Why do you sit there doing nothing?" the wife would ask.*

"I am thinking deep thoughts," the husband would reply.

"As deep as a pig's tail is long!" the wife would retort.

One morning, the calf lowed hungrily in the barn. "Go and tend the calf," the wife told her husband. "It is man's work."

"No," the man declared, "it is for men to speak and women to obey."

"Real men work!" the wife replied sharply.

"I inherited a flock of sheep from my father," the husband countered, "and a shepherd tends them and gives us wool and cheese. I provide for you, so you must feed the calf."

"Provide? Only with misery!" the woman shot back. The two argued all that morning and all that afternoon. Then, in the evening, the husband and wife both had the same idea at the same time.

"Whoever speaks first," they said simultaneously, "will feed the calf from now on!" The two nodded in agreement, and said nothing more. They went to bed in silence.

The next morning, the wife awoke, lit the fire, cooked breakfast, swept the floor, and washed the clothes. Meanwhile, her husband sat on his bench, smoking his pipe. The wife knew that if she stayed home watching her husband do nothing all day, she would say something. So she put on her veil, and went to visit a friend. Her husband saw her leave, and wondered what she was up to.

A short time later, a beggar came by the house and asked the husband for food and money. The husband was about to reply, when he stopped himself. This is my wife's trick! he thought. "She is trying to make me talk." So the husband kept silent. The beggar thought the husband was a deaf-mute, and went into the house. No one was inside, but the cupboards were full of bread and cheese. So the beggar ate everything and left. The husband started to yell at the beggar, but he remembered his wager with his wife and kept silent.

A traveling barber passed by and asked the husband if he wanted his beard trimmed. The husband said nothing. This is another one of my wife's tricks! the stubborn man fumed. The barber thought he was dealing with a deaf-mute, but he wanted to be helpful, so he trimmed the husband's beard. Then the barber motioned for money. The husband did not move. The barber demanded money again, and became angry. "I will shave off your beard and cut your hair so you look like a woman!" the barber threatened. The husband refused to stir, so the barber shaved off the husband's beard, cut his hair, and left in a huff.

An old woman came up next, peddling cosmetics and secrets of beauty. Her eyesight was poor, and she mistook the husband for a young woman. "Dear lady!" the old woman exclaimed, "you must not sit in public without a veil!" Especially, the old woman added to herself, when you are so ugly! The husband said nothing, so the old woman assumed he was a deaf-mute. "You poor thing," she murmured, "ugly as sin, and deaf to boot!"

The old woman had an idea, and took out her cosmetics. She put a wig on the husband's head, rouge on his cheeks, and lipstick on his mouth. "There," she declared, "you look better!" Then she motioned for payment. The husband refused to move or speak, so the old woman reached into his pocket, took all his money, and left. The husband fumed silently: I will avenge myself on my wife!

A thief then approached. He thought it odd for a young woman to be sitting outside alone. But strange situations were often profitable for him, so he went up to the woman. "Dear lady," he said, "you should not be out alone. Have you no husband or brother to look after you?"

The husband almost laughed aloud. My wife will not give up her tricks! he said to himself. The thief assumed the husband was a deaf-mute, went into the house, which was filled full of costly carpets, vases, and clothes, and packed everything in a bag. He left with his loot and waved merrily to the husband.

I will punish my wife for her tricks, the man swore to himself. By then it was midmorning, and the calf in the barn was thirsty. It broke out of its stall, and ran through the village. The wife heard the commotion, and came out from her friend's house. She caught the calf and returned home. Then she saw the strange woman sitting on her husband's bench.

"Who are you?" she demanded, "and where is my husband? I am gone only a few hours and he has taken another wife!"

"Aha!" the husband sprang up. "You spoke first, so you must tend the calf from now on!"

The wife was incredulous. "You shaved off your beard and put on rouge just to trick me!" She stormed into the house and saw that everything was gone. "What happened?" she demanded of her husband. "Who has taken all our things?"

"The man you hired to act like a thief," the husband chortled. "But I did not fall for your deception!"

"I hired nobody!" the wife declared.

"You cannot fool me," the man boasted. "You lost the wager, and so you must tend the calf from now on."

"Foolish man!" the wife exclaimed. "You sat watching a thief steal everything from our house!"

"I knew it was only an act!" the husband gloated.

The wife could barely speak, she was so angry. "You lost your face and your fortune, and all you can think of is our wager!" She glared at her husband, and then said, "You are right, I shall tend the calf from now on. But that is because I am leaving and taking the calf with me. I will not stay with a stubborn fool like you!"

The woman walked to the village square with the calf and asked a group of children if they had seen a man go by carrying a large bag. The children pointed to the desert. In the distance they could see a man hurrying away, carrying a satchel on his back. The woman stared grimly after the thief, fastened her veil securely, picked up the calf's halter, and struck out into the desert. She caught up with the thief at an oasis. She sat across from the man, sighing and batting her eyelashes at him.

The thief was flattered by the wife's attention. "Where are you going all by yourself?" he asked her. "Have you no husband or brother to protect you?"

The wife fluttered her eyelashes at the thief and sighed. "If I did," the wife said sweetly, "would I be walking in the desert with only a calf for company?"

The two started talking and resumed their journey together. The wife kept sighing and glancing at the thief, and he soon asked her to marry him. She agreed, and so they planned to stop at the next village and have the chief marry them. By then evening had fallen, and the wife knew it was too late for a marriage ceremony. When they arrived at the village, the chief said as much, and invited them to stay with him for the night.

After everyone fell asleep, the wife arose and looked in the thief's bag. Sure enough, there were all her valuables—carpets, clothes, vases, and money! She loaded the bag on her calf and started to leave. Then she had an idea. She tiptoed into the kitchen, cooked some flour and water over a candle, and poured the dough into the thief's shoes and the shoes of the village chief. Finally she hurried into the desert with her calf.

When dawn came, the thief awoke and found his bride-to-be missing. He looked out a window and saw the woman hurrying away with his sack of loot. He rushed to put on his shoes, but found his feet would not fit in them. The dough in the shoes had hardened like a brick! The thief grabbed the shoes of the village chief, but they, too, were ruined. Finally, the thief ran out barefoot. The sun had risen by then, heating the desert sand, and his feet were soon blistered and burned. The thief was forced to halt.

For her part, the woman went back home, thinking about her husband. When she arrived at their house, she saw that her husband was not on his bench as usual. She ran inside and found the floor swept, the water drawn, the fire lit, and dinner cooking. But her husband was nowhere inside! She rushed into the courtyard, and there she found him, hanging laundry to dry.

"Stubborn husband," the wife exclaimed, "what are you doing?"

"I lost my face, my fortune, and my wife," the husband replied, "because I was a stubborn fool!"

The wife took the clothes from her husband, and said, "This is woman's work!" At that moment, the calf lowed, demanding water.

"I shall tend to the calf," the husband said.

"No," the wife retorted, "I shall do it." Then the two of them looked at each other and laughed. They came to an agreement, and from that day on, the husband took care of the calf and worked like any other husband, while the wife tended the house and never complained. In the evenings, when they finished their chores, they both sat down on the bench and watched the world go by.

· · ·

THIS AMUSING STORY starts off with a couple who have long since lost the magic and romance of youth. Their domestic life is no happy-ever-after, but a series of endless disputes.

Perhaps the most striking feature of the story is the fact that the husband and wife switch traditional masculine and feminine roles. The husband begins as a stereotypical patriarch, sitting on his bench outside the house while his wife toils inside. He insists that it is his prerogative to tell his wife what to do. Then the husband loses everything—his dignity, his property, and his authority. His beard is shaved off, his face powdered and rouged, and his wife finally leaves him. By the end of the tale, the husband looks like a woman and does housework. He shifts from a traditional masculine role to a stereotypical feminine one.

At the same time, the wife defies her husband, rejects her role as housekeeper, and leaves home, pursuing the thief. She outwits the ruffian and returns triumphantly with her household treasures. Her journey across the desert mirrors the usual quest of the young male hero in fairy tales. The wife throws off feminine stereotypes and adopts a traditional masculine role. This reversal is especially amazing because the story comes from a Moslem culture, a highly patriarchal tradition. Yet similar dramas appear in middle tales from around the world, suggesting that switching gender roles is a major task for men and woman at midlife. . . .

Why would middle tales reverse gender roles? Carl Jung offers an explanation. One of the first psychologists to study adult development, Jung noted that at midlife men begin to struggle with traditionally feminine interests and needs. Middle-aged men put aside the masculine competition for power and status that motivated them in youth. They turn to relationships and feelings, which men usually reject in youth as too feminine.

Conversely, women reclaim their self-assertiveness, autonomy, and sense of adventure—stereotypical masculine traits. Women shed the submissive, self-effacing roles that most societies impose on girls from an early age. As Jung put it, the noon of life involves "the reversal of all the ideals and values that were cherished in the morning."

Systematic research confirms this midlife role reversal. Young men typically make success at work their primary source of personal fulfillment, but at midlife their emphasis shifts to marital happiness and relationships with coworkers. These changes occur in both middle-class and blue-collar individuals, and among the intellectually gifted. Older men even begin to do more chores around the house, and become increasingly concerned about their appearance. Stubborn Husband, Stubborn Wife illustrates this point when the husband is covered with lipstick and makeup. Women, on the other hand, give up traditional homemaker roles to focus on personal achievements, starting new careers or completing educational degrees. They become less concerned with adornment and more with independence. . . .

Stubborn Husband, Stubborn Wife offers detailed insights about the process of role reversals. Although the husband starts off as a patriarch, he is soon humiliated and cast down. His face is painted and rouged like a woman's, and he loses all his property. His midlife encounter with the feminine is a calamity. The same theme appears in other middle tales. Role reversals are traumatic for men. One reason comes from basic masculine psychology. Young men normally repudiate and fear the feminine as part of their development. Boys usually abhor anything "sissy," and would rather die than associate with girls. As teenagers, young men fear being wimpish or effeminate and strive to be macho. Psychoanalysts have explained why this rejection of the feminine is essential to male development. Boys and girls normally develop close attachments to their mothers, but boys must break away from this bond if they are to develop a clear sense of male identity. The relationship with the mother is difficult to give up because it satisfies deep feelings of dependence and the need for intimacy. To make the break boys usually resort to an extreme measure: they reject not only their mothers, but the whole realm of dependency and intimacy, which they equate with the feminine and regard as something shameful. . . .

Stubborn Husband, Stubborn Wife had equally perceptive insights about women's development at midlife. The wife voluntarily leaves home and starts out into the desert. She actively seeks change, in contrast to her husband, who suffers it passively. The story reflects reality here. At midlife, it is frequently the wife who takes the lead, breaking out of familiar habits and developing rapidly. Her changes then force her husband to develop.

The wife's quest to catch the thief is a traditionally masculine, heroic venture. Yet she does not lose her feminine nature. She does not try to defeat the thief by force, which would be a stereotypical masculine strategy. Instead, she tricks him, using a uniquely feminine brand of wisdom. She entices the thief into a marriage proposal in order to steal her belongings back. Since the thief stole her property, she steals his heart! The wife does not rely on strength, but the power of persuasion and relationship.

The wife's feminine wisdom is dramatized by a clever detail in the story—she makes dough and pours it into the thief's shoes. By preventing him from using shoes on the burning desert sands, she stops him from pursuing her. This detail underscores an important point. Although the wife becomes adventurous, independent, and assertive, she does not become a man. She simply becomes herself—a strong, resourceful woman.

The incident with the shoes symbolizes the importance of ordinary, everyday reality.

The wife apparently suffers no qualms or fears when she leaves home and embarks on her heroic journey. In real life, women's reclamation of their masculine qualities is typically anxious and tentative at first. Women fear that they will alienate those close to them if they become assertive. This is a realistic fear. At work there are subtle, unconscious prejudices against outspoken women, and at home husbands often feel threatened when their wives assert themselves. Consciously or not, many husbands initially undermine their wives' development at midlife.

After outwitting the thief, the wife returns to her husband. This might seem odd. Why should she go back to her foolish, chauvinistic mate? Partly, the story reflects cultural realities. Because of patriarchal restrictions on women in Islamic society, it is difficult for them to live independently. Yet there is more here. The story implies that the wife *chooses* to return to her husband after thinking about the matter on the way home. She returns voluntarily, not by necessity, and in triumph, not resignation. From her new position of strength, she affirms her relationship to her husband. If the wife reclaims her aggressive, heroic, masculine side, she does not neglect her feminine strengths—attention to relationship, communion, and intimacy. The story reinforces this point in a small detail. Throughout her heroic journey, the wife keeps her calf with her. Because the calf needs care, it makes a good symbol for the wife's traditional feminine role as someone who nurtures others.

The wife's return is important for another reason. She discovers that her husband has changed his ways. His reformation is astonishing. . . . This willingness to reform is a major difference between those who age well and those who do not.

If flexibility is a virtue at midlife, it is not necessarily so in youth. The young hero or heroine needs perseverance to succeed, rather than flexibility. In many youth tales, heroes and heroines search for a magic object, like a ring or cup. On the way, they are tempted by other magic treasures. If they are distracted, hero and heroine are destroyed. Such a single-minded sense of purpose is essential to young men and women making their way in the real world. But the resoluteness of youth easily becomes pigheadedness at midlife, so middle tales reverse course and emphasize flexibility. . . .

Unlike most fairy tales, Stubborn Husband, Stubborn Wife lacks any magic. There are no elves, enchanted purses, or mermaids. This confirms the importance of the loss of magic. Even more significantly, there is no need for wizardry. The protagonists of youth tales typically require supernatural help to solve their problems. In middle tales, human wisdom suffices. And learning such wisdom is one of the main challenges of midlife. On a deeper level, magic assumes a different form in adulthood. Middle tales do not portray enchanted rings that change people into animals or transform huts into palaces. The stories focus on a more mysterious magic—the transformation of the human heart.

18.

Love Is Never Enough

AARON T. BECK

Often, the more problematic sides of our relationships don't emerge until several years into marriage. Self-centeredness, unrealistic expectations, and miscommunication may lead to serious conflicts and power struggles. In this article, Aaron T. Beck, the father of cognitive therapy, examines some of the underlying issues that can cause a relationship to collapse and the ways in which they can be resolved.

WHY DO BITTER ARGUMENTS break out between people who presumably love and care about each other? During courtship, a natural self-centeredness of the partners dissolves in the fusion of their concerns and even identities. The penetrating rays of love that melt differences in temperament, interests, and goals help to generate altruism and empathy.

The partners *want* to please each other. They are gratified when they can make each other happy, and sad when their partner is sad. In seeking to please, they try to look at everything from their partner's point of view.

For many people, no doubt, part of the pay-off for this self-sacrifice and subordination of self-interest is relief from loneliness. For others, the sheer pleasures of intimate sharing are paramount. It is as if no price can be too great to pay for the sense of belonging and intimacy.

Because the partners' self-interests are closely linked during courtship, they experience little sense of sacrifice of self-interest. And the rewards for fulfilling one's partner's wishes are plentiful. Not only is there direct reinforcement from the satisfaction of pleasing the partner, but indirect as well, through imagining the partner's pleasure. With this continual reinforcement, the motivation to suspend one's egocentricity is strong. A woman in love is altruistic because she wants to be—not because she "should" be. An infatuated man makes sacrifices for his lover because it pleases him to do so.

From Fusion to Fission

What, then, happens to loving altruism? A variety of forces can cause its erosion after marriage. Fortified by the security of marriage, those who felt lonely while single no longer experience the relationship as an antidote to loneliness. Partners may discover that their needs are not well met; they may decide that they are better served by satisfying their own desires, even when these are in opposition to those of their mate. As the gratification from altruism wanes, partners come to be driven more by *shoulds* than by genuine desires to please one another. And once the partners feel obliged to give priority to one another's wishes, the compromises or concessions necessary in any close relationship may appear burdensome to them.

Inevitably, as partners begin to assert their own desires and conflicting interests, disagreements arise. Each mate may regard the other's desires as signs of a resurgent self-centeredness. The mates may then come to regard each other (but not themselves) as selfish, pigheaded, or stingy.

Of course, this sequence does not occur in all marriages. In fact, many couples find that over the course of time their self-centeredness is reduced and evolves into reciprocity, sharing, and caring. But distressed couples I have treated showed, consistently, the progression from altruism to egocentricity.

A crucial aspect of egocentricity in marriage is a genuine difference in the way partners perceive the same circumstances. Whatever the topic, their perspective is filtered through their own special lens, frequently leading to dramatically opposing views. Since people tend to regard their own opinions as reality, a different interpretation can seem unrealistic to them. A wife with a diverging perspective may appear to her husband as "contrary" or "arbitrary." When a husband's views differ, his wife may perceive him as "dumb" or "childish."

When one spouse presses a "wrong" opinion about an important issue, such as child rearing or finances, this action constitutes a challenge that can stir conflicts over who is right and who is wrong, whose view of reality will prevail, who has the dominant voice in the relationship. Some mates respond to such a challenge with an automatic put-down: "You don't know what you're talking about" or "You're full of it." Others may simply dig in their heels and refuse to listen. . . .

The Self-serving Bias

A more insidious problem is the "self-serving bias." Without realizing it, people have a tendency to interpret events in a way that puts them in the most favorable light, or serves their own self-interest. This self-serving bias exerts a strong influence on their perceptions, making them believe they look better in the eyes of others, as well as themselves. Thus, when mates argue over who is the better spouse or parent, who has contributed more to the marriage, or who has made more sacrifices, they will portray their own roles in such a way as to enhance their self-esteem and prove their moral superiority.

The self-serving bias widens the gap in understanding between spouses. Obviously, there can be substantial self-deception in such a process, and it requires an extraordinary amount of effort for us to see ourselves—stripped of pretense—as others see us. As much effort is required to recognize how, without our realization, we select and assemble the "facts" in a given situation to serve our own interests.

As differences in viewpoint become pronounced, a spouse's image starts to change; he or she may assume the specter of a foe, representing a serious threat. Then, even a small disagreement can easily escalate into a fight. The partners may disparage each other with thoughts or statements such as "You're contradicting me just to put me down," "What do you know about it?" or "You're just plain dumb." They fail to realize that their own point of view may be just as biased as that of their partner, and that they appear to be equally thickheaded or self-serving. This combination of egocentricity and intolerance easily leads to arguments that wound and seem incapable of resolution.

Because the marriage bond is such an emotional one, it is much harder for partners to implement the goals of their compact than for them to forge the bonds in other working relationships, such as a business partnership or close friendship. At first, marital partners are usually attracted to one another by qualities like appearance, personality, charm, humor, and empathy—not by their potential to function well as a team. While these personal qualities may cement a solid emotional bond, they have little to do with how well a couple makes decisions and takes care of the essential details of married life. Even the most attractive spouse may prove deficient in the skills necessary for meeting the obligations of marriage. Those skills that turn out to be crucial in maintaining an effective partnership—defining problems, negotiating, assigning responsibilities— often have little relevance to the couple's initial attraction.

A lack of the necessary skills and appropriate attitudes weakens the working relationship, which must be strong if the partners are to carry out the practical goals of marriage (fulfilling the day-to-day requirements of living, maintaining a household, managing finances, raising children) as well as the emotional goals (enjoying leisure time, sex, sharing experiences). All of these goals require a spirit of cooperation, joint planning and decision making, a rational division of labor, and efficient follow-through.

When couples are unskilled and have little background in partnership techniques, disagreements about policies and their execution are likely. When these disagreements occur in a setting of egocentricity, self-serving bias, and competition, they lead to clashes and hostility.

Setting Standards and Judging Your Spouse

Even when mates want to work together, they are apt to judge each other more harshly than anyone else in other working relationships in their lives. The tendency to impose more stringent standards on the mate seems ironic when we consider that marriage grants people the freedom to let down their hair and expose their vulnerable points. These strict expectations are typically concealed in phrases like "You should know" or "It should be obvious." In addition, these hidden standards are particularly high, as shown in the following exchange between Robert, who had just painted some chairs, and Shelly, his wife, who had asked him to complete the chore. He left the brushes soaking in turpentine instead of cleaning them all at once. This bothered Shelly. She had put in a long day looking after toddlers in a day care center, and she tended to be very sensitive to any sign that Robert, who made much more money than she did as a loan officer in a bank, did not really respect what she did or felt too superior to help around the house.

SHELLY: You didn't finish the job.

ROBERT: I did just as good a job for you as I would for anybody else.

SHELLY: [angrily] But I'm not just "anybody else."

While Shelly might not have felt angry at a painter who left brushes soaking, she interpreted Robert's failure to clean up completely as evidence that he was not pulling his own weight. It was not the specific act but its *symbolic meaning* that bothered Shelly. Because of the symbolic meanings attached to ordinary failings such as being late, one spouse may attach a great deal of significance to the other's tardiness: "*Something may have happened to her*" or "*If he really cared about my feelings, he would be on time.*" Fears or self-doubts like these generally lurk behind exaggerated reactions to minor events.

The impact of symbolic meanings may be understood if we examine the unspoken provisions of the unwritten marital compact. In it, as in many other implied compacts at work or in organizations, there is a tacit agreement about the nature of the goals and the procedures for reaching them (for example, setting policy or assignment of tasks). In addition to having vaguely defined rules and provisions for carrying out practical mandates, the marital compact also contains a set of promises and expectations regarding the nature of the relationship (love, caring, devotion, loyalty, and so forth). What complicates the practical component of the compact is that day-to-day performance may be judged for its ability to meet the values and expectations of the emotional provisions of the compact ("Your interests will always come first") rather than for its ability to achieve practical results. Thus, what might be labeled as an "oversight" on the part of a less than meticulous painter becomes an accusation of "unfairness" or possibly "gross negligence" on the part of a spouse.

To repeat, many partners judge one another's actions according to personal, symbolic meaning rather than practical importance. Thus, we hear: "Everybody has a job to do—if my husband doesn't do his job properly, it's because he's trying to get away with something" or "If my wife doesn't do her job, it shows she doesn't care for me."

It is because of the *personal meanings* they attach to each other's actions that spouses are so often less tolerant of each other's lapses than they are of other people's failings. While they accept lapses by service personnel or co-workers, they view what their spouse does as a reflection of the marital relationship.

These lapses in marital standards trigger a sequence of evaluations: Is he acting responsibly? Is she really devoted? Is he entitled to behave that way? If he slips up on his job, he is bad. If she doesn't pull her own weight, she is wrong. If a husband, for example, catches his wife skipping important details, he experiences moral indignation. If a wife suspects her husband of shirking his duties, she experiences righteous rage.

Most spouses are unaware they are rating each other according to moral standards. Interestingly, judgments like those their parents made seep into their own reactions; they see an erring spouse as "bad," just as they were labeled by their parents, and they respond the same way as their parents did—with punishment.

The Intrusion of Symbolic Meanings

Symbolic meanings, perfectionism, and moralistic evaluations greatly compound the difficulties created by poor communication and hidden expectations. The net result is that difficulties the couple could easily re-solve in other relationships are so emotionally encumbered in marriage that the practical problem doesn't get worked out. This breeding ground for conflict leads to anger and mutual recriminations: "She won't listen to my side—she just insists I do it her way. If I don't, she goes nag, nag, nag."

The everyday mechanics of living together take on meanings that go far beneath the surface realities. How well a husband does his chores at home, for example, is evaluated by his wife not just in terms of quality, but also in terms of what she presumes it reveals about his attitudes and feelings toward her. For example, at a counseling session, Shelly said she was furious at Robert.

SHELLY: [sarcastically] Robert never attends to things properly. Some men were working on the roof. I asked him to come home to inspect it before they left. He wouldn't do it. He's always so trusting of people.

ATB: What thoughts did you have about his not coming home when you asked him to?

SHELLY: He doesn't really care. If he cared for me, he would attend to these things because I ask.

ROBERT: She's always bugging me to do things. I have to do them my own way. If she had confidence in me, she wouldn't bug me all the time.

SHELLY: If you really cared for me, you'd do it because I asked.

Actually, Robert had confidence in the roofers but, based on past experi-ence, Shelly had reason to believe they might do a careless job unless their work was inspected.

A "clash of the symbols" is likely when the same event has different—and highly personal—meanings for each partner. Robert's acceding to Shelly's wishes symbolizes to her that he really cares. But being nagged about the roofer symbolizes to Robert that Shelly lacks confidence in him and must interfere in his business. If Robert had agreed to check the roof, as she requested, Shelly would regard such compliance as a positive symbol. But his negative response made her feel helpless and abandoned, and his further accusation "nag, nag, nag" only exacerbated those feelings. For Robert, doing things his own way—without interference—was a positive symbol, whereas being coerced against his better judgment was a negative one. When Shelly "interfered," he sensed not only her no-confidence vote but also her desire to control him.

People like Shelly and Robert enter into marriage with fixed beliefs about the meaning of certain actions, or nonactions, by their spouses. These beliefs lead them to attach exaggerated significance to those actions. When one spouse's actions take on an importance that leads the other to overreact, that act is symbolic of some deeply held values of the reacting mate. When, as in the case of Robert and Shelly, an action has opposite symbolic meanings for each partner, then a clash is likely. When such clashes occur frequently, the working partnership, as well as the general relationship, is weakened.

In this type of conflict, some resolution is possible if the partners can objectively explain, at a time when neither is angry, how they each felt and how they interpreted the other's actions. As they see each other's perspective—sometimes with considerable surprise—the symbolic insult and rejection are defused, leaving them better prepared to agree on guidelines for handling further disagreements.

After they were able to perceive their controversy through each other's eyes, Shelly and Robert were able to arrive at a set of operating principles: Robert agreed to explain, before starting a project, what was involved and to answer any questions Shelly might have along the way; Shelly agreed to ask questions and inform Robert how the project was proceeding, but not to tell him what to do. . . .

Differing Expectations About Roles in the Family

The eye of the storm in many marital disputes centers on the expectations that partners have of their respective family roles: what it means to be a wife or mother, husband or father. Spouses often differ in their beliefs about earning and spending the family income, parenting, social and leisure activities, and the division of labor in the household.

Partners enter marriage with many preconceptions about both practical and emotional matters. These expectations are usually formed early in life, based on childhood experiences. A husband, for example, may model himself after his own father, and expect his wife to assume the role his mother did. Or, if he disliked his parents' behavior, he might try to act differently from his father or expect his wife to be different from his mother.

Often, such expectations about practical arrangements are camouflaged early in the relationship by the aura of love, dreams of permanent happiness, excitement, and romance. As a result, the couple never sit down to deal with practical matters until they have become frustrating problems. Frequently, at this point, the true differences in their expectations surface.

19.

The Art of Fighting

GERALD R. WEEKS AND LARRY HOF

The expression of anger, authorities now agree, is always destructive to relationships. However, conflicts and arguments are unavoidable. When you
and your partner can agree on a specific way to handle emotional conflicts,
the relationship can blossom into intimacy. There is a way to fight fairly,
and the authors (experts in the field of conflict counseling) provide us
with the rules to follow and the steps to take for finding effective solutions
for our problems.

FIGHTING TAKES TIME. Many couples attempt to resolve their differences in a matter of seconds or minutes. The dialogue is often truncated.
A general rule is to discuss an argument as soon as one is aware of it and
has had some time to think it through. Once the person is ready to say
something, s/he should let the other know s/he wants to talk and that the
talk is an argument and will require some time. If it is not an appropriate
time to talk, or if the time is limited, it is advisable to agree on a time to
talk later. The time should be fixed, otherwise the person with the problem may feel that there will not be an opportunity to express the complaint.

When the couple fight at home, it may be useful to designate a fighting place. This place should not be the bedroom or any other place the
couple spend intimate time together. Most couples have some place in
the house that is relatively free of distractions. The partners need to focus
on each other during this time.

They may agree on the amount of time they have to talk before they
begin. We have found that an hour is about the limit, because after that

time partners begin to tire and issues start to recycle. Some arguments can be resolved in an hour; many of the hot issues will take many hours to resolve. The couple needs to know that certain issues may require many hours to solve and, therefore, learn to segment their fighting.

Segmentation simply means breaking the fight up into manageable increments. For the couple beginning therapy, the fight may be confined to the therapist's office and, for others, some combination of work at home and in the office. At the end of each segment at home, the partners agree on when to talk next and then say something positive about the process and about each other. The statement might simply acknowledge that some progress was made in the discussion and indicate appreciation for the understanding received from the other.

Sometimes a fair fight becomes nasty. Rules may be broken, emotions may begin to rule, and personal attacks may be mounted. The partners may not be able to get back on track. We have an escape clause in place for such an occurrence, which stipulates that either partner may unilaterally call a time-out, without a veto from the other person. When a time-out is called, it may be with or without feedback, for the shortest time possible. If a long time-out is called, the person calling it is also responsible for proposing the next time to talk. Long time-outs should be avoided if possible; shorter time-outs may be used to regain perspective and cool off. A partner may call a time-out because of the actions of the partner or for oneself. If a partner is feeling too upset or angry, some time alone may be needed.

Rules to Keep the Fight Clean

The partners need to agree that a fight must have rules in order to keep it clean and constructive. The following list of Do's and Don'ts may be used as a guideline for keeping the fight fair. The couple may be asked to consider which rules they tend to adhere to and which they tend to violate during an argument. Generally, these rules are given at the end of a session as homework.

Essential Do's and Don'ts

1. Be specific when you introduce a gripe.

2. Don't just complain, no matter how specifically; ask for a reasonable change that will relieve one gripe at a time.

3. Confine yourself to one issue at a time. Otherwise, without professional guidance, you may skip back and forth, evading the harder ones.

4. Always consider compromise. Remember, your partner's view of reality is just as real as yours, even though you may differ. There are no totally objective realities.

5. Do not allow counter-demands to enter the picture until the original demands are clearly understood, and there has been a clear-cut response to them.

6. Never assume that you know what your partner is thinking until you have checked out the assumption in plain language; never assume or predict how your partner will react, or what your partner will accept or reject.

7. Never put labels on your partner. Do not make sweeping, labeling judgments about your partner's feelings, especially about whether or not they are real or important.

8. Sarcasm is dirty fighting.

The partners are told to read the rules during the week and come back with a list of which rules they adhere to and which they violate, in rank order. They may also add ideas to the list if they do things not mentioned. The therapist then goes through the list of each partner, affirming what they do that is helpful and asking them what they can do to avoid the behavior that interferes with fair fighting. If the strategy makes sense, the therapist goes on to the next item. If the client cannot state how to avoid the behavior, or if the approach does not seem workable, the therapist helps the person develop a strategy. After each partner has gone through his or her list, the therapist can turn to the other and ask if there are any additional partner behaviors that either further or interfere with the process. These points are then discussed and if the partner needs to change, a strategy is developed.

At the end of this discussion about rules, the therapist once again asks that each partner make a commitment to the rules. The therapist may point out that the commitment is actually to oneself and not to the partner. In other words, one person violating a rule(s) is no excuse for the other to then violate the rules. To do so only escalates the argument. Each person is responsible, and there is no excuse for violating the agreement.

However, the therapist must suggest that no one is perfect and that bad habits are hard to break. It is normal to violate some of the rules from time to time. When this happens the partner should try to catch it, apologize for the violation, and proceed. Otherwise, the partners may fall into the trap of becoming fixated on the violation and then arguing about whether the person really wants to fight fairly. By normalizing slips in the recovery, the therapist is helping the couple stay focused on the process and to keep moving forward.

Sometimes one person does not recognize that s/he has violated a rule, at least not before the partner has noticed it. Therefore, it should be agreed that one partner may calmly and nonjudgmentally confront the other when a violation occurs. When a violation is pointed out, the partner should stop, think about the feedback, and respond accordingly. If the partner cannot see the violation and persists in enacting the behavior, the other may need to call a time-out until the next therapy session.

The situation described can be difficult to tease out from the descriptions offered by the couple. A simple way to avoid this problem is to tape-record all the arguments that occur at home. Consequently, when the couple agree to talk about a problem, they meet at the agreed time, in the prescribed place, turn on the tape recorder, and begin. If they get stuck and cannot get unstuck, they can review the tape and process the interaction, or, if they have different perceptions about the process, they can bring the tape to the next therapy session so the therapist can play that segment and everyone can discuss the process.

Additionally, using a tape recorder puts some couples on their best behavior, which may be helpful in the beginning. Another way to use the tape is to have the partners listen to their arguments in order to do a self-appraisal. The instructions are as follows: "Listen only to how you sounded, what you said, and whether you followed your own rules and the process for constructive fighting. Don't worry about your partner. S/he will do the same thing you are doing."

Steps to Fair Fighting

The next task for the therapist is to teach the couple the mechanics of fair fighting. The steps are described in the following.

Steps to Fair Fighting

Step 1: Listen to yourself. Identify and express that you own your feelings to yourself and to your partner ("I feel angry and hurt right now"). To "own" feelings means to accept them as your feelings in a responsible manner, and not to blame your partner for the way you feel. The overt and underlying angry and hurt feelings must be identified and expressed appropriately before effective and mutual problem solving can be accomplished. This requires a willingness to become vulnerable to your partner, to actively listen to each other in an empathic manner, and to express yourself clearly and concretely.

Step 2: Identify the real issue, which frequently is not the issue originally presented. For example, beneath the statement, "I am angry that you don't spend enough time with the children," may be another issue, "I feel overwhelmed by my responsibilities with the children and abandoned by you, and I want and need some direct support and help from you." Immediate problem solving regarding "more time with the children" by one partner would not necessarily lead to the exposing of the other partner's feeling of being overwhelmed and abandoned. Work together to identify the real issue(s) facing you or your partner.

Step 3: Stay here and now. In other words, don't drag up the past to score points. What is important is what is happening now, what the feelings and issues are now. The past cannot be modified, the present can. (This is not to say that long withheld feelings should not be expressed. At an appropriate place and time, such a disclosure can be extremely helpful to you and your partner.)

Step 4: Use polarization constructively. People sometimes desire or need to get away from each other in the midst of a conflict, either because anger has escalated beyond manageable limits, or just to think more clearly. Such polarization or time apart should be used constructively, to cool off or figure out how to move closer together on the issue at hand and resolve the conflict. Such time should not be used destructively, to figure out how to get even with your partner or perpetuate the conflict. Whoever requests the break or the time-out is responsible for telling the partner when s/he will reinitiate contact and for following through on the commitment.

Step 5: Find out what each of you has in common regarding the issue at hand. The common ground, or items both of you agree on already, is frequently overshadowed by the differences between you. Identification of the common ground helps you to see the differences in perspective, and frequently provides a positive starting place from which you can build a constructive solution.

Step 6: Do mutual problem solving. The two of you identify as many possible solutions to the problem as you can, without prejudging any of them, and then list the positive and negative consequences of each. Make a joint decision to pursue one proposed solution. After you have reached a decision, create an agreed upon action plan that includes specific steps, a time sequence, and an agreement to revisit the problem after some specific period of time to both reassess how the agreement is working and make changes as needed. Consider also what you might do to undermine the agreement and express that to your partner. (Speak only for yourself; let your partner speak for him- or herself.)

Step 7: Come together in celebration. Give some signal to each other, through the use of words or touch, to signify resolution of the conflict, or that you have at least agreed to disagree, that you have gone as far as you can at this time, or that conflict will not remain a permanent barrier between you. Congratulate each other for the hard work and willingness to compromise. Reaffirm your relationship in as many ways as possible. For example, you could use a hug, kiss, or other constructive use of physical touch, including sex. Words might be used, such as, "I love you and I'm glad we worked this out," "Thanks for hanging in there with me," or "Let's put it aside for now and come back to it later." This step should also include processing the experience, identifying what each of you individually and as the couple did that was helpful or unhelpful, and what has been learned.

20.

Drowning in Love

ROBIN NORWOOD

Although the term "co-dependency" is overly vague and often misapplied, it continues to be a serious problem for many individuals who do not have the strength to leave a neglectful or abusive relationship. It is a slow and painful process, explains Robin Norwood, who has helped many women to understand their problems, to recover their self-esteem, and to leave an abusive relationship if an adequate solution cannot be found.

WHEN BEING IN LOVE means being in pain we are loving too much. When most of our conversations with intimate friends are about him, his problems, his thoughts, his feelings—and nearly all our sentences begin with "he . . .", we are loving too much.

When we excuse his moodiness, bad temper, indifference or put-downs as problems due to an unhappy childhood and we try to become his therapist, we are loving too much.

When we read a self-help book and underline all the passages we think would help *him,* we are loving too much.

When we don't like many of his basic characteristics, values, and behaviors, but we put up with them thinking that if we are only attractive and loving enough he'll want to change for us, we are loving too much.

When our relationship jeopardizes our emotional well-being and perhaps even our physical health and safety, we are definitely loving too much.

In spite of all its pain and dissatisfaction, loving too much is such a common experience for many women that we almost believe it is the way intimate relationships are supposed to be. Most of us have loved too much at least once and for many of us it has been a recurrent theme in our lives. Some of us have become so obsessed with our partner and our relationship that we are barely able to function. . . .

Addiction is a frightening word. It conjures up images of heroin users jabbing needles into their arms and leading obviously self-destructive lives. We don't like the word and we don't want to apply the concept to the way we relate to men. But many, many of us have been "man junkies" and, like any other addict, we need to admit the severity of our problem before we can begin to recover from it.

If you have ever found yourself obsessed with a man, you may have suspected that the root of that obsession was not love but fear. We who love obsessively are full of fear—fear of being alone, fear of being unlovable and unworthy, fear of being ignored or abandoned or destroyed. We give our love in the desperate hope that the man with whom we're obsessed will take care of our fears. Instead, the fears—and our obsessions—deepen until giving love in order to get it back becomes a driving force in our lives. And because our strategy doesn't work we try, we love even harder. We love too much.

I first recognized the phenomenon of "loving too much" as a specific syndrome of thoughts, feelings, and behaviors after several years of counseling alcohol and drug abusers. Having conducted hundreds of interviews with addicts and their families, I made a surprising discovery. Sometimes the patients I interviewed grew up in troubled families, sometimes they did not; but their partners nearly always came from severely troubled families in which they had experienced greater than normal stress and pain. By struggling to cope with their addictive mates, these partners (known in the alcoholism treatment field as "co-alcoholics") were unconsciously recreating and reliving significant aspects of their childhood. . . .

I do not intend to imply that women are the only ones who love too much. Some men practice this obsession with relationships with as much fervor as any woman could, and their feelings and behaviors issue from the same kinds of childhood experiences and dynamics. However, most men who have been damaged in childhood do not develop an addiction to relationships. Due to an interplay of cultural and biological factors, they usually try to protect themselves and avoid their pain through pursuits which are more external than internal, more impersonal than personal. Their tendency is to become obsessed with work, sports, or hobbies while, due to the cultural and biological forces working on her, the woman's tendency is to become obsessed with a relationship—perhaps with just such a damaged and distant man. . . .

These are the characteristics of a woman who has recovered from loving too much.

1. She accepts herself fully, even while wanting to change parts of herself. There is a basic self-love and self-regard, which she carefully nurtures and purposely expands.

2. She accepts others as they are without trying to change them to meet her needs.

3. She is in touch with her feelings and attitudes about every aspect of her life, including her sexuality.

4. She cherishes every aspect of herself: her personality, her appearance, her beliefs and values, her body, her interests and accomplishments. She validates herself, rather than searching for a relationship to give her a sense of self-worth.

5. Her self-esteem is great enough that she can enjoy being with others, especially men, who are fine just as they are. She does not need to be needed in order to feel worthy.

6. She allows herself to be open and trusting with *appropriate* people. She is not afraid to be known at a deeply personal level, but she also does not expose herself to the exploitation of those who are not interested in her well-being.

7. She questions, "Is this relationship good for me? Does it enable me to grow into all I am capable of being?"

8. When a relationship is destructive, she is able to let go of it without experiencing disabling depression. She has a circle of supportive friends and healthy interests to see her through crises.

9. She values her own serenity above all else. All the struggles, drama, and chaos of the past have lost their appeal. She is protective of herself, her health, and well-being.

10. She knows that a relationship, in order to work, must be between partners who share similar values, interests, and goals, and who each have a capacity for intimacy. She also knows that she is worthy of the best that life has to offer.

There are several phases in recovering from loving too much. The first phase begins when we realize what we are doing and wish we could stop. Next comes our willingness to get help for ourselves, followed by our actual initial attempt to secure help. After that, we enter the phase of recovery that requires our commitment to our own healing and our willingness to continue with our recovery program. During this period we begin to change how we act, think, and feel. What once felt normal and familiar begins to feel uncomfortable and unhealthy. We enter the next phase of recovery when we start making choices that no longer follow our old patterns but enhance our lives and promote our well-being instead. Throughout the stages of recovery, self-love grows slowly and steadily. First we stop hating ourselves, then we become more tolerant of ourselves. Next, there is a burgeoning appreciation of our good qualities, and then self-acceptance develops. Finally, genuine self-love evolves.

Unless we have self-acceptance and self-love, we cannot tolerate being "known," . . . because without these feelings we cannot believe we are worth loving just as we are. Instead, we try to earn love through giving it to another, through being nurturing and patient, through suffering and sacrifice, through providing exciting sex or wonderful cooking or whatever.

Once the self-acceptance and self-love begin to develop and take hold, we are then ready to consciously practice simply being ourselves without trying to please, without performing in certain ways calculated to gain another's approval and love. But stopping the performances and letting go of the act, while a relief, can also be frightening. Awkwardness and a feeling of great vulnerability come over us when we are just being rather than doing. As we struggle to believe that we are worthy, *just as we are,* of the love of someone important to us, the temptation will always be there to put on at least a bit of an act for him, and yet if the recovery process has progressed there will also be an unwillingness to go back into the old behaviors and old manipulations. . . . When we are no longer willing to make the moves calculated to produce an effect, there is a period of time during which we suffer from not knowing what to do until our *genuine* loving impulses have a chance to be heard and felt and to assert themselves.

Letting go of the old stratagems does not mean we never approach, never love, never nurture, never help, never soothe nor stimulate nor seduce our partner. But with recovery, we relate to another person as an expression of our own essence, rather than because we are trying to elicit a response or create an effect or produce a change in him. What we have to offer instead is who we genuinely are when we are not hiding or calculating, when we are undisguised and unvarnished.

First we must overcome our fear of being rejected if we allow someone to truly see us, truly know us. Then we must learn not to panic when all our emotional boundary lines are no longer in place, surrounding and protecting us. In the sexual realm, this new quality of relating requires not only that we be naked and vulnerable physically, but that we be emotionally and spiritually naked and vulnerable as well.

No wonder this degree of connecting between two individuals is so very rare. Our terror is that without those boundaries we will dissolve.

What makes the risk worthwhile? Only when we truly reveal ourselves can we ever be truly loved. When we relate as we genuinely are, from our essence, then if we are loved it is our essence that is loved. Nothing is more validating on a personal level and more freeing in a relationship. It must be noted, however, that this kind of behavior on our part is only possible in a climate that is free of fear, so we must not only conquer our own fears of being genuine but also avoid people whose attitudes and behaviors toward us produce fear. No matter how willing to be genuine you become with recovery, there will still be people whose anger, hostility, and aggression will inhibit you from being honest. To be vulnerable with them is to be masochistic. Therefore, lowering our boundaries and eventually eliminating them should happen only with those people—friends, relatives, or lovers—with whom we have a relationship bathed in trust, love, respect, and reverence for our shared, tender humanity.

What frequently happens with recovery is that as our patterns of relating change, so do our circles of friends as well as our intimate relationships. We change in how we relate to our parents and to our children. With our parents we become less needy and less angry, and often less ingratiating as well. We become much more honest, often more tolerant, and sometimes more genuinely loving. With our children we become less controlling, less worried, and less guilty. We relax and enjoy them more because we are able to relax and enjoy ourselves more. We feel more freedom to pursue our own needs and interests, and this frees them to do the same.

Friends with whom we could once commiserate endlessly may now strike us as obsessed and unhealthy, and while we may offer to share what has been helpful for us, we will not allow ourselves to carry the burden of their troubles. Mutual misery as a criterion for friendship is replaced by more rewarding mutual interests.

In short, recovery will change your life in more ways than I can predict for you on these pages, and sometimes that will be uncomfortable. Don't let the discomfort stop you. The fear of change, of relinquishing what we've always known and done and been, is what holds us back from our metamorphosis into a healthier, higher, more truly loving self.

It is not the pain that holds us back. We're already enduring alarming levels of pain with no prospect of relief unless we change. What holds us back is the fear, fear of the unknown. The best way I know to confront and combat fear is to join forces with fellow travelers who are on the same journey. Find a support group of those others who have been where you are and who are headed for or have already arrived at the destination you want to reach. Join them on the path toward a new way of living.

21.

Romantic Addictions, Romantic Ideals

STANTON PEELE

Stanton Peele provides an authoritative overview to the nature of addictive behaviors and how they are sometimes confused with love. In this essay, he describes eight key dimensions of love and how they can become relationally distorted and destructive.

I AIM TO DEFINE love in opposition to addiction. The resulting model of love strikes strong chords in some key visions of love, clarifies some pivotal issues in other descriptions of love, and outlines important ways in which love is best approached both individually and culturally. Key dimensions of this definition of love follow.

1. Love as absorption in another person versus love as an expansive experience: The idea that lovers cannot look beyond each other strongly suggests the total focus on a drug in substance addiction. In its place, love should open the individual to other opportunities in the world and facets of the self that were not previously available to the person. Love is an awakening, expansive experience that makes the person more alive, daring, and exposed.

2. Love as idealization and total acceptance of another versus love as a helping relationship: A notion of love predicated on a blindness to a lover's flaws or a willingness to ignore them describes the kind of defensive system addicts employ to convince themselves their drug-induced state is superior to ordinary reality. Love instead is a helping relationship in which people trust each other enough to offer and accept criticism

without feeling that their basic worth is being undermined. Loving a person is to wish another person will be all that person can be.

3. Love as internal adjustment and a private world versus love as an enhanced capacity and outward growth: Addiction is a preoccupation with personal needs; in the case of love addiction, this means a concern solely that another person fulfill one's demands and fantasies. Adjustments required by the addicted lover are designed only to create a more suitable partner; such adjustments actually make the person *less* capable and appealing to others by creating a world whose private standards are incompatible with those of the outer world. These addicted lovers are notable for their dominance or their malleability or, in Fromm's terms, their sadism and masochism.

Love means valuing a relationship and a lover because they are successful in the outer world. It is this feeling that one is a valuable person and that a lover is likewise worthy of admiration, and love, that creates a secure basis for love. Relationships lacking such existential *and* worldly validity flounder in uncertainty, mutual distrust, and jealousy. Certainly everyone is capable of being jealous; but jealousy is not the *hallmark* of a relationship in which each partner is confident of himself or herself and of a lover. Neither partner in such a relationship must direct or be directed by the other, since each is already capable and worthy.

4. Love as painful or as a refuge from a painful world versus love as an intensification of the pleasure in life: Tennov's lovers report their relationships to be terribly painful, and songs about teenage love describe the experience as an incessant ache. Other lovers claim that they find peace only when they are with their loved one, and that time spent on their own is unbearable. The literature and music of romantic love is, on the balance, more about pain than pleasure. The pain in the addicted love is present from the start. People who are susceptible to addictive love are characterized by a pained sense of the world. To say one cannot endure without a lover is to say one cannot tolerate one's life.

Not only should love be pleasurable, but it should inspire and benefit from the joy lovers feel toward life. The passion of genuine love is not an escape from personal desperation, but instead expresses—and intensifies—the passion that a person brings to all he or she does. Love cannot "save" a miserable person; no external experience has such power. Only a person in love with life can love other people.

5. Love as an incapacitating experience versus love as a productive and beneficial experience: Addiction harms and depreciates those engaged in it. Even addicted lovers who succeed in bonding with another person are unable to function outside their lover's presence. Yet they hardly seem concerned about this diminution; indeed, it signals for them that their feelings are real. Neither are their lovers concerned that the person has been diminished. Each partner, out of his or her insecurity, welcomes the incapacity of the other as a better guarantee of fidelity, as a way of making sure a lover cannot escape.

Love is rather an enhancing experience, one that improves its participants. It rewards those in the relationship and the lovers appreciate its rewarding nature. These rewards are concrete—they endure beyond the time spent in each other's presence. No, it is not like a chain letter where those who send the letter along magically find $50,000. The benefits of love are as varied as the things people have to offer and gain from one another. But the benefits are real.

6. Love as accidental and volatile versus love as a natural outgrowth of one's life and a secure part of oneself: Addicted lovers are forever doubting that their love has a substantial existence both because they feel unworthy of love and because they believe the emotion is not an expression of them or of the conduct of the rest of their lives. This accidental thing that has happened to them can disappear in a moment; it cannot be counted on and cannot be planned for. This is why addicted lovers are so desperate and grasping of the experience.

To be a good lover requires one to strive to be a good person. To be valuable to another is to lead a worthwhile life. To love another requires knowing another person (as Romeo and Juliet were not able to do) and having a belief in that person's value and goodness. Linking one's life to another person's is certainly a risky and perilous enterprise. But people get better at relationships as they understand who they are and know what they value in others.

7. Love as an incommensurable experience versus love as an experience continuous with friendship and affection: When the addicted love relationship is over, no relationship between the lovers is possible. In some cases, one partner may have killed the other. Generally, if one lover finds a better version of addicted love ("I found someone I love more"), he or she simply abandons the first lover. After these breakups, there is no basis for further contact between the two, since the "love they had is gone." That is, the relationship was defined as a total, all-or-nothing experience that leaves no trace once a person emerges from it. Like the religious convert or the recovered alcoholic, this lover rejects all that went before.

An opposite view is that love is not different from—although it may be more intense than—ordinary affection. This love is practiced and seasoned by friendship. It may vary gradually: lovers can improve or suffer setbacks in the relationship without being pushed to a brink (while successfully understanding that they need to work to enable the relationship to continue and improve). If their love ceases to be the primary relationship for two people, they are still capable of respecting, appreciating, and dealing with each other.

8. Love as an uncontrollable urge and unconscious motivation versus love as a state of heightened awareness and responsibility: For addicted lovers, love is something that possesses them and determines their actions. They don't know why they love, and they believe they can as easily (it often seems *more* easily) love an undeserving person. Love is a justification for misbehavior including often hurting their lover. In this view, loving a person too much is a logical defense for killing the lover. The epitome of this approach is love as a biological or unconscious state inadvertently activated by the irrational appeal of some casual object.

Love should stand for a fully aware state of being, one that kindles the most elements of feeling and moral awakening. It is this responsibility for selecting and nurturing a love relationship that actually *defines* our humanity and the special human ability to love. . . .

Our society creates attitudes and values that encourage addiction rather than love. The ability to love can be enhanced—especially for children—by teaching them (1) to value friendship, other people, community, (2) to develop broader purposes and goals in life (for example, health, intellect, accomplishment), (3) to examine their relationships and the impact of their behavior on other people (that is, social mindfulness), (4) to accept responsibility for their actions and to insist on responsible treatment from others, and (5) to recognize and reject addictive entanglements. To identify and to disapprove of some ways of relating to others is a legitimate and age-old form of education. That we don't know how to do so or what to encourage or discourage is a symbol of our uncertainty and confusion about basic social values. . . .

People resist addictions, including love addictions, when they have the most emotional and other life ballast operating. So my therapy for long-suffering love addicts emphasizes that they remove their focus from their emotional neediness, which I see to be the root of their malady. In place of this self-concentration, I advise them to become involved in something they are proud of, to be loyal to their friends, and to read a daily newspaper. For the advanced therapy client, I recommend the works of Jane Austen. As a society we face the difficult goal of accepting the advances and benefits that have occurred since Jane Austen's time (for instance, Austen's women characters devoted their genius entirely to the goal of a suitable marriage, from which they derived their chief status and satisfaction), while recognizing what it is we have lost in our cultural consciousness from that time and others, when to love meant to be at one with ourselves and our worlds.

22.

The Secret Affair

HARRIET LERNER

The discovery of an affair is one of the most painful violations of trust. But the affair is not the problem; it is a symptom of deeper conflicts in the relationship. Dr. Lerner, an international authority on women's issues, shows how a careful exploration can lead to a better understanding of both partner's needs, or even a deeper, more respectful intimacy.

JANE HAD BEEN living with her lover, Andrew, for five years when she found herself attracted to Bill, a man she worked with closely in a small veterinary clinic. Their flirtation, playful at first, intensified over time. For several months, they did not act on, or mention, the obvious sexual energy between them. But Bill was on Jane's mind and under her skin. At home, she talked to him in her head and thought about him while making love with Andrew. The nature of their work and the setup of the office kept Jane and Bill in close physical proximity, even had she wished otherwise.

Jane never questioned her primary commitment to Andrew. Not for a moment did she consider leaving him for Bill. She was, however, surprised by the strength of this attraction, and particularly by its emotional hold on her. She was confused about its meaning, not knowing, as she later put it, whether her feelings were "real" or whether she was getting into "some crazy, addictive, crushlike thing." As Jane felt increasingly anxious and driven by the attraction, she concluded that getting to know Bill better, rather than forcing distance, was the only route to gaining greater clarity about her feelings.

In keeping with a mutual agreement to tell each other about sexual temptations, Jane had, until now, been open with Andrew whenever she had felt attracted to someone else. This time was different. Jane feared that he would be inconsolable if he knew how compelling the attraction to Bill was, and she predicted that the emotional atmosphere at home would become so highly charged that she would be pressured to cut off from him entirely. She imagined Andrew anxiously grilling her every day after work, even insisting that she leave the job she loved. Jane wanted the time and space to move toward Bill and to sort out her feelings, time and space that would not be available if she brought the situation out into the open.

Jane also suspected that ending her relationship with Bill at this point would ensure that she'd stay stuck on him, if only in fantasy. She believed their ongoing contact would "normalize things" and "add more reality to the relationship," ultimately helping her to find her way out of the emotional woods. Also, Andrew wasn't asking questions about Jane's relationships at work, suggesting that perhaps he didn't really want to know about any possible rivals.

When Jane slept with Bill for the first time, vowing it would never happen again, she began to feel overwhelmingly anxious at home. In a panicky moment, she revealed everything to Helene, a long-time best friend who was also like a sister to Andrew. Sharing her secret helped alleviate Jane's anxiety only temporarily, because Helene became increasingly uncomfortable in her role as confidante. "I can't keep hearing about this," she finally told Jane during a late-night phone call. "I feel like it's putting a big wedge between me and Andrew, and I'm worried about the whole thing." Jane became terrified that Helene would violate her confidence.

Then Jane became anxiously preoccupied with the idea that she might have contracted the AIDS virus from Bill and passed it on to Andrew. She began having difficulty sleeping through the night and often awoke in the early morning with fear radiating through her bones. Jane had slept with Bill a total of three times and had practiced safe sex each time. Nonetheless, her anxiety and guilt increased, focusing on the chilling thought that she had brought the deadly virus home.

In response to her escalating anxiety, Jane stopped sleeping with Bill and made a concerted effort to renew her closeness to Andrew. When Bill became romantically involved with another woman, Jane felt wounded but ultimately relieved. In the months that followed, Bill became increasingly committed to his new lover and Jane's attachment to him lessened. She still revealed nothing of the affair to Andrew, though, because she was afraid to do so so soon after its occurrence. "Later . . ." she promised herself. And at other times, "What's the point of bringing it up? It's over."

Several months later, about a year after her relationship with Bill first heated up, Jane finally told Andrew about the affair. Helene had been pushing her to get the truth out into the open, because the secret was at Andrew's expense in their close threesome. Jane did not reveal the details easily, or in one sitting, but she did begin the process of laying the facts out on the table. Andrew felt enraged and devastated, but their relationship survived and deepened over time as they ultimately learned to request more from each other in the way of intimacy and self-disclosure. . . .

Why a secret comes out into the open is less important than what happens after it is discovered or revealed. The discovery of an affair can wreak havoc on a marriage, or it can strengthen it, depending on the commitment of both partners to honesty and to each other.

Andrew initially felt devastated by Jane's involvement with Bill. He and Jane alternated between explosive interchanges, marathon late-night talks, and passionate lovemaking. These heightened levels of both positive and negative intensity surprised them both by enlivening their relationship at a time of crisis. Yet emotional intensity, either positive or negative, is often an anxiety-driven response, more likely to impede than foster clear thinking about the relationship. Despite being a necessary first step in processing the pain of sexual betrayal, it is no more than that.

How does a couple process infidelity and rebuild trust? For starters, Jane and Andrew recognized how very distant their relationship had become prior to the affair. They both had become lazy about paying attention to each other. Andrew, for example, was not registering important information about his partner, including obvious signals during the time of the affair that something was different or "not right." When we aren't receiving and processing information from the other person, we become dishonest with ourselves.

We are all responsible, in part, for how our relationships go; we may collude with or even invite dishonesty. But Andrew neither caused Jane's affair nor could he have prevented it. Most importantly, Andrew and Jane used the revelation of the affair as a springboard to deeper levels of truth-telling and self-disclosure. The affair served as a vivid reminder that sexual temptations are a reality of life, especially, but not exclusively, when a primary relationship is distant. Denying that one's partner, or oneself, is vulnerable to powerful outside attractions is a form of sleepwalking. Jane and Andrew both decided they would keep the subject of sexual and romantic attractions in their consciousness and conversation, while trying not to overfocus anxiously on each other. They recognized that trusting each other—when "trusting" meant taking each other for granted and not paying attention—was not useful.

The dishonesty and secrecy of Jane's affair made it intolerable to Andrew, and he wanted to know the facts, no matter how painful. How could they establish an emotional climate in which honesty about sexuality was increasingly possible? Toward this end, they renewed their promise to each other to openly share any outside attraction before acting on it. This would include revealing strong emotional and romantic attractions, not just genital ones. The one listening would try to respond with honest feelings, without punishing the other for honesty by becoming overly reactive or controlling. Both would feel free to ask each other about outside attractions, and to remind each other that honesty, not monogamy, was their most important shared value.

In her book *The Monogamy Myth,* Peggy Vaughan underlines the fact that we cannot assume monogamy without discussing it, nor can we assure it by extracting promises or issuing threats. Only honesty can create the groundwork for monogamy. Attractions kept secret from a partner are far more likely to intensify and be acted on. . . .

. . .

Not all "honest sharing" is motivated by the wish for greater intimacy and deeper levels of self-disclosure with a partner. A friend of mine was married to a man who, early in their marriage, described his lusty fantasies for other women in vivid detail. His wife initially felt jealous, then alienated and put off. When she told him so, he did some soul-searching and recognized that these provocative communications reflected his insecurities and created distance.

Several years later, he approached his wife about his intensifying feelings of sexual attraction to his business partner. He was, as he put it, becoming intoxicated. He was scared to open up this conversation with his wife, but felt it was a matter of conscience to do so. His self-disclosure was fueled by his commitment to keep his marriage primary and to detoxify and defuse the power that attractions have when kept secret. He also wanted to create the conditions in which he would be least likely to act on his desire. Telling his wife ensured that she would continue to ask questions and express her pain. It ensured that he would consider her, even during those moments when he might prefer not to.

His wife, to her credit, recognized that her husband's honesty reflected his wish to protect their marriage and keep himself in line. Thus, she did her best not to distance herself from him, or try to control him, or otherwise punish him for his truth-telling. While her gut reaction to his disclosure was a fight-or-flight one, she managed to move toward him with love, while sharing her own feelings of threat and hurt.

The cost of confessing a sexual betrayal is obvious and immediately felt. In telling, we deal with our partner's pain and rage, with our own conscience or lack of it, with a lengthy process of reviewing and rebuilding intimacy. If the affair is ongoing, we can no longer have our cake and eat it too; either we end the affair, or deal with the consequences of refusing to do so, or else resume lying again.

In telling—in extending the possibilities of truth between two people—we also open the door for greater integrity, complexity, depth, and closeness in a relationship. Concealing an affair, even when it is long past, brief, and unsuspected, creates a subtle distance, disorientation, and emotional flatness in a relationship. Apart from issues of morality and conscience, concealing or confessing an affair has a great deal to do with the amount of distance we want or will tolerate in a primary relationship. And when we say, "I can't tell, because it will cause him too much pain," what we really mean is, "I don't want to deal with his pain and anger"—which is a different matter.

Whether we tell, or are told, also depends on the spoken or unspoken "contract" that evolves between spouses or intimate partners. We may communicate . . . that we had better not find out about an affair because we couldn't take it. We may say this explicitly or we may convey it through our failure to ask questions that will allow us to know our spouse better as a sexual human being.

There is nothing wrong with communicating to our partner that we do not want the entire truth at a particular time about sexual fidelity, or any other issue. Being honest about our vulnerability, and our wish to be spared the whole story, may be a self-loving and self-protective act. Whatever the subject, we can be direct with others about what information we want and are ready to handle. Obviously we do not share information that may evoke violence or precipitate abuse.

But we should be clear with ourselves that extended silence ultimately invites secrecy (which requires lying and deception to maintain it), not only about affairs but about other emotionally painful issues that affect a relationship. It is simplest, of course, to ask our partner to conceal from us what brings pain, to spare us from the truth. But if we go along with such a contract, we narrow the possibilities of truth-telling and connection between two people.

23.

Four Steps to
Conflict Resolution

GARY J. FRIEDMAN

Sometimes our conflicts take us right to the edge of divorce, but divorce is not really a "solution" to any problem; it is simply an interruption or an end. Marital dissolution demands agreement, compromise, and respect for the entire process, and if these skills are not properly applied, a marriage can destructively continue for years. Divorce mediation, which provides a compassionate alternative to litigation, offers us an intriguing paradox: the skills that we are required to use are the very same skills that can save a marriage from crisis. In fact, there is a greater potential in saving the marriage when a couple opts for mediation. As you read through this essay by Gary Friedman—one of this country's leading mediating attorneys—you will see how these techniques can be effectively adapted to address many relational ills.

THERE ARE FOUR interrelated criteria that are indispensable to mediating successfully. If you both meet them, you should be able to go forward with prospects for success. But *each* of you needs to meet all four:

- The motivation to mediate

- Self-responsibility

- The willingness to disagree

- The willingness to agree

1. The Motivation to Mediate. Most, if not all, people who enter mediation have a mixture of motivations, both altruistic and self-serving. But whatever their particular reasons, *both* parties must be motivated for mediation to work. If you are considering mediation to help you end your marriage, it will not be enough for only one of you to be interested in mediating. If in answer to the question "Why are you here?" one of you feels, "Because my spouse wanted me to be," we're going to have to look deeper to see if you have your own reasons to participate.

Nor is it enough if your friend, therapist, or lawyer thinks you ought to mediate. You need to think about why mediation makes sense for *you.* If one of you is not willing and motivated to be together in the same room to face the realities of your situation, then mediation, as it is generally practiced—and as I practice it—is doomed.

A variety of motivations lead people to mediate. Some clients want to *avoid the adversary system*—save money, speed up the separation, or stay away from adversarial lawyers and the legal system. Others are intent on retaining control of the decision making. Still other couples want to minimize hostility between them and set up a way to deal with each other in the future. And some, despite their decision to end the marriage, want to help each other ease the pain of the separation.

Often, as the process develops, some motivations surface that have been hidden, while some that seemed important at the beginning fade. For example, when Norman and Alice first sat down to mediate, Alice was aware only that she wanted to get a divorce as quickly as possible. But after she and Norman resolved in my office the question of which of them would move out of the house, she became aware that the two of them might actually reach a meaningful agreement together. To feel that neither of them had "lost," she realized, was very important to her. Once Alice became aware of this motivation, we all had a fuller picture of why she was there. This, in turn, evoked a similar feeling in Norman. While identifying this motivation didn't point to a specific resolution of their disagreement, it did help us find the way to the resolution. . . .

2. Self-Responsibility. If motivation is the fuel to the process, self-responsibility is the recognition that *both* members of a couple are at the wheel of the decision-making process. Each of you must be willing to take responsibility to participate fully in the process and for the outcome.

Self-responsibility has three parts:

- You each need to do what is necessary to understand your situation thoroughly.

- You each need to understand your own priorities—your needs, your plans for the future, what is important to you.

- You each must be willing to stand up for yourself, and face whatever conflicts arise. This doesn't mean you can't enter mediation unless you've had success in expressing or resolving your disagreements on your own. But it does mean you must be willing to form your own opinion and express it. . . .

Assuming responsibility for yourself can be a difficult task. If you enter the process wholeheartedly, you may discover that you are facing very basic questions, such as what you want to do with your life. This process of self-assessment can be daunting, particularly if you have had no experience in living on your own. But while experience with being responsible for yourself is useful, willingness to figure out your personal responsibilities is indispensable.

In separation decisions, the stakes are high: You are deciding on no less than what each of you needs to make your own life function. It is this that makes honesty so important. Both of you must know or have the capacity to decide what you really want and need to go forward with your lives. . . .

3. The Willingness to Disagree. The willingness to stand up for yourself requires a determination not only to express your point of view, but also to hold out against any decision that would impede you from moving ahead with your life. Although others may register their opinions about what you should do, ultimately you must decide on your own priorities and how your mediated agreement can best reflect them.

My clients and colleagues often find it ironic that I emphasize so strongly the willingness to disagree. "This is mediation," they remind me. "Isn't the goal to agree?" For me, it is crucial that in embarking on mediation, you realize that you may be entering some very bumpy territory. . . .

4. *The Willingness to Agree.* The final requirement is the willingness on both your parts to work toward mutually acceptable decisions. On its face, this may seem obvious, but in my experience it is the failure to meet this criterion that has derailed many a mediation. Consider Barney and Linda. In mediation with me, an agreement was in sight when Linda blurted out, "I know this agreement is going to work for me. I just can't stand the idea that it's going to work for Barney, too."

Some people going through a divorce cannot bear the fact that their spouses are not going to be punished or that, quite simply, their spouses will be able to make their lives work. Linda's ability to voice that concern gave us a chance to talk about it further so she could resolve her need to punish Barney, but for others the sense of personal outrage has brought mediation to a halt.

24.

Seven Myths of Divorce

ORLI PETER

We may, even after many months of serious dialogue and self-reflection, conclude that divorce is the only solution left. Unfortunately, our society places such a stigma on divorce that many people choose to remain married, even when it is detrimental to the psychological health of everyone concerned. But if we confront the many myths of divorce, we may be able to grow through the pain and emerge better prepared to explore more intimate relationships down the road.

THERE ARE MANY stereotypes about divorce that receive a lot of attention in the media but can be quite harmful to both women and men. Here are some of them, contrasted with what recent sociological and psychological studies tell us:

Myth 1: Most men cheat on their wives.

Actually, the best designed study to date indicates that nearly 80% of men report that they have never cheated on their wives.[1]

Myth 2: Most divorcing women are jilted by their husbands.

Many studies have corroborated that the great majority of divorces (two thirds to three quarters, depending on the study) are initiated by women.[2] This makes sense because numerous studies indicate that men are generally happier being married than are women, they report less marital frustration and dissatisfaction, and they are less likely to consider the option of divorce.[3]

Myth 3: Women bitterly regret divorce.

Most divorced women do not regret divorcing. Moreover, *divorced* women are generally happier than *divorced* men. And one large study[4] suggests that many middle-aged women become happier after their divorce. These women showed an increase in positive self-image and self-esteem and were inspired by their divorce to gain more control of their lives. Many enjoyed sex more after their divorce.

Myth 4: Women emerge from divorce more emotionally scarred and psychologically damaged than do men.

This is generally not true. Not only are divorced women happier than divorced men, but they are better off emotionally too. In study after study they consistently outscore divorced men on psychological tests to assess emotional health and well-being.[5]

Myth 5: Ex-spouses are highly antagonistic toward one another, even to the point of acting unethically.

Divorced couples, of course, vary widely in the civility of their interactions. But about half of divorced men and women even describe their relationship with their ex-spouse as friendly or cooperative.[6]

Myth 6: Most divorced men can remarry while most divorced women cannot.

It is true that divorced women are less likely than divorced men to *want* to remarry (after all, they are happier than the men with being divorced). But both groups do remarry at very high rates—and soon. About 80% of divorced men and 75% of divorced women remarry whether or not they have children, and most do so within three years.[7]

Myth 7: The economic consequences of divorce devastate women more than men.

Women are generally worse off financially in the years immediately following a divorce. This has less to do with divorce than with the fact that women generally make less money than men. But one important study indicates that, five years later, after most men and women have remarried, women's household incomes increased slightly more above predivorce levels than those of their ex-husbands.[8] Furthermore, one very recent study indicates that women are generally more satisfied with their divorce settlements than men, and that this satisfaction is stable over time.[9]

Myths such as these offer false lessons regarding both what men and women should expect from each other and how one should behave in divorce. The truth is richer and contains many positive possibilities for both women and men.

PART IV

Sacred Bodies, Sacred Selves

There is a love like a small
lamp, which goes out when
the oil is consumed; or like a
stream, which dries up when
it doesn't rain. But there is a
love that is like a mighty
spring gushing up out of the
earth; it keeps flowing
forever, and is inexhaustible.

ISAAC OF NINEVEH

Love is a flame without smoke.

KRISHNAMURTI

Give All to Love

Give all to love;
Obey thy heart;
Friends, kindred, days,
Estate, good-fame,
Plans, credit and the Muse,—
Nothing refuse. . . .

Though thou loved her as thyself,
As a self of purer clay,
Though her parting dims the day,
Sealing grace from all alive;
Heartily know,
When half-gods go,
The gods arrive.

RALPH WALDO EMERSON

Sacred Ground

I have found the unknown woman in the trees, the sand, the rocks
beneath my feet. She is in the air and the unborn breath of life. Why
have I been so blind? Why have I not seen this before? I am humbled
and I am aroused. I am hungry and filled, desirous for more and
more and more. In every way I turn I am met with the brilliance of
the earth, the mud, the rivers and the streams. Before the journey, no
one special. And after the journey, I am once more no one special.
And this, I think, is grace.

M. R. WALDMAN

We may talk about love in psychological terms—of consciousness and commitment, of sexual strategies and compromise, of articulated values and beliefs—but still a mystery remains. And so, in this final section, I have sought to include those authors who speak about the soul of love in ways that capture the emerging spirituality of our times. But it is a spirituality that has freed itself from traditional religious belief.

To open this section, I have chosen a passage from Thomas Moore, whose writings on the soul reflect what many feel is the core of our inner being. When we look at the soul of relationship, Moore says, we see beyond the mechanics of structural thinking and analysis. We are not so much concerned with how to make a relationship work, but in allowing it to work through us in its own particular way. When we follow the reasons of the heart, "we may live through the mystery of endings, crises, and turning points in love, marriage, friendship, and family, and submit to the life that is always germinating in them." And so we see in Moore, as with the other contributors to this section, an integration of contemporary psychology and religion, informed by modern science but spoken with poetic grace.

I have also included a letter of advice on love, written in 1903 by the great German poet Rainer Maria Rilke. In deep contrast to the Puritan ethics that surrounded his life, Rilke approaches sexuality as a "glorious infinite experience granted us, a gift of knowledge from the world." Rilke tells his friend that he must never lose touch with his innermost consciousness and inner knowing when confronting the forces of love, for it is in the depths of our being, in the silence and physicality of nature, in the insignificant things that often go unnoticed by others, that we discover our patience and strength and the spirituality of everyday life. Rilke's letter remains timeless, capturing the mystery and spirit of love.

Poetry allows us to touch upon dimensions of experience that can't be seen with the ordinary eye. Beginning with a poem by Robert Bly, authors Connie Zweig and Neil Schuitevoerder explore the concept of the Third Body, a presence that emerges between two people in love. They show us, in psychological terms, how to appreciate and nurture this unseen person, symbolic of the relationship as a whole. Their vision embraces both Jungian and transpersonal psychology in an intimate dialogue with the soul.

When discussing the spirituality of love, the heart becomes a central theme. In John Welwood's essay, he sees love evolving through many stages, from conditional love (meeting each other's needs) to unconditional love (accepting in totality the other person's being). But if we confuse these levels of intimacy, then we will falter on the path of the heart. Welwood's writings remind us that there is much more to the human psyche than we can ever grasp with the mind.

In the next three chapters, the authors illuminate various principles of love that have been drawn from Asian spiritual practice. In Thich Nhat Hanh's description of "true presence," we see the similarities between Eastern and Western views of consciousness and love, themes that are similarly expressed by Peck, Tannen, Hendrix, and other contributors to this anthology. In Margo Anand's chapter, she describes how religion and sex were once an integral part of pre-Christian society. She encourages us to reconsider how the power of sacred sexuality can enhance our daily lives, an ancient Tantric view that can be easily integrated into modern spiritual practice. Sacred sexuality is further explored by religious historian Georg Feuerstein, who draws his insights from the Hindu practice of Bhakti-yoga. And so, in every religion, we can find new seeds of love and understanding that can enrich the quality of our relational lives.

In the final chapter, transpersonal philosopher Ken Wilber describes a painfully intimate story about the loss of his wife. Here we witness how a shared spiritual vision can transform an ordinary love into a marital bond that transcends all fears of death. "Real love hurts; real love makes you totally vulnerable and open; real love will take you far beyond yourself; and therefore real love will shatter you." These were his thoughts when Treya lost consciousness for the very last time. "If love does not shatter you, you do not know love." For me, this story symbolizes the remarkable journey of love and how the development of a spiritual psychology can carry one through the darkest storms of life. Even at the moment of death, love can flower between two people who care.

In love, we never need to hide.

25.

Honoring the Mysteries of Love

THOMAS MOORE

No one in America speaks more eloquently about the soul than Thomas Moore, and in this passage he asks us to consider the inexpressible dimensions of love, of its mysteries and the ways in which it can bring us in touch with the spiritual dimensions of life. It is a thoughtful and inspiring piece.

WHEN WE SHIFT our attention from the mechanics and structures of a relationship to its soul, a number of changes occur. We no longer have to carry the weight of guilt about not having done relationship properly, we can give ourselves a pardon for having engaged in folly in our younger days, we can feel the sting of endings without bearing a neurotic degree of responsibility, and we can enjoy the pleasures that a lifetime of relationships has given us. We can end the impossible quest for the perfect structure—the happy family, the completely satisfying marriage, the unbroken friendship. We can find some purpose in the failures, the intimacies that never got off the ground, the possibilities that never took flesh. The soul does not share the spirit's love of perfection and wholeness, but finds value in fragmentation, incompleteness, and unfulfilled promise.

I'm not saying that being soulful allows us to excuse ourselves, deny, avoid, dissemble, and exploit; following the lead of soul we become more responsive, not less, to those whom fate places in our lives. But when we forgo taking on exaggerated responsibility for mistakes in relating, we are able to feel those errors and misjudgments more fully, and to become people of wisdom, sensitivity, and perspicacity. Guilt blunts sensitivity, it doesn't sharpen it. Only by fully embracing the shadows of love and closeness can we be capable of any genuine union of souls.

Relationship is not a project, it is a grace. The difference between these two is infinite, and since our culture prefers to make everything in life a project, to be accomplished with effort and understanding, to be judged pure failure when it doesn't arrive at an expected conclusion, it is not easy for us to treat intimacy as a grace.

Though we try to be expert at life projects, we are not used to dealing artfully with grace. Responding to the grace of relationship, it is important to appreciate, to give thanks, to honor, to celebrate, to tend, and to observe. We can't complain absolutely when that grace is taken away. We feel the pain, but that is not the same as berating ourselves for failed opportunities. Berating is a way of avoiding pain and love's corresponding initiation.

The soul of relationship is not goal-minded, nor is it any one narrow, clearly defined entity. A friendship may not have to endure throughout life in order to leave its eternal mark on the soul. A marriage may not have to live up to its promises of lasting a lifetime in order to generate an eternal union. A family may be riddled with betrayal and misunderstanding, and still offer the soul the cradle it craves. A partnership in work or business may dissolve and yet continue to feed each of the members with gifts of remembrance.

The soul of a relationship doesn't ask for the "right" ways of acting; it wants something even more difficult—respect for its autonomy and mystery. The soulful relationship asks to be honored for what it is, not for what we wish it could be. It has little to do with our intentions, expectations, and moral requirements. It has the potential to lead us into the mysteries that expand our hearts and transform our thoughts, but it can't do that when our primary interest is in pursuing our cherished ideologies of love, family, marriage, and community. The point in a relationship is not to make us feel good, but to lead us into a profound alchemy of soul that reveals to us many of the pathways and openings that are the geography of our own destiny and potentiality.

Ultimately, relationship brings us to the brink of the ultimate family and the absolute lover, who is nameless and indescribable. We get a taste of this eternal love when we experience an ending and glimpse the deep darkness of death that lies in it. Personally, I know it in the mixed feelings that rush upon me in a moment with my daughter, when I'm feeling the bliss of her presence, and at the same moment and because of that bliss I fear for her safety and hope never to lose her.

Relationship is not only about the people who interact with each other. It is a vehicle as well to the absolute factors that shape human life fundamentally. Every relationship that touches the soul leads us into a dialogue with eternity, so that, even though we may think our strong emotions focus on the people around us, we are being set face to face with divinity itself, however we understand or speak that mystery. The Sufi woman poet Rabi'ah bent Ka'b says:

> Love
> an ocean
> with invisible
> shores,
>   with
> no shores.
> If you
> are wise
> you will
> not swim
> in it.[1]

Few have such prudence that they avoid love, and of course it is in our folly that we allow ourselves to be drawn into all kinds of loves, there to be transformed through the acids of love's chemistries into lovers. Love is an alchemical process in which we are the material to be transmuted. And all love invokes one or another divinity who gives love its fathomless depth.

A relationship to the divine is part, in fact the culminating piece, of this discussion of love and loss, friendship and loneliness. Relationship to the divine, hardly discussed in these days of personalism and secularism, satisfies the soul in ways that no substitute can touch. We may well be preoccupied with the theme of interpersonal relationship precisely because we are stuck in a shallow pool of love, unable to arrive at the mystic's view in which the divine is the only satisfying love, the only true soul mate.

What is divinity? What is the nature of this ultimate relationship? He who speaks, the *Tao te Ching* says, does not know. It can't be spelled out in so many words. Many religions teach us that this ultimate intimacy is not separable or even distinct from our day-to-day relationships in family, marriage, community, and friendship. Yet it is a dimension that may be missing if we are closed off to its presence. We could turn to the religions of the world, a vast source of poetry, confession, prayer, and ritual, to be instructed in this dimension of relationship, but ultimately we will find this divine undercurrent in all our relationships in our own unique way. For some it may appear in a moment of ecstasy, for others in a time of torment. It may take the form of utterly satisfying community, or it may appear in a quiet moment of solitude when, with Emily Dickinson, we discover that the hills are our most true friends.

Knowing that relationship has this divine strain, we may be free to enjoy its human elements more fully. We won't be distracted by imperfections in our partners or families. We won't demand that relationship play itself out according to our expectations and ideologies. We won't have to control every inch of the way amid anxiety and judgment. We may even discover that by being kind to others we can learn to be kind to ourselves—a virtue lacking in a time of far-reaching psychological moralism.

Caring for the soul in our relationships, and through them, we can enjoy them both practically and mystically, and with genuine tolerance for individuality in others, in the relationship itself, and in ourselves. We can let unplanned developments happen, allow people to change, tolerate our own idiosyncratic needs and cravings, and enjoy and appreciate a community of individuals who may think differently than we do, live oddly, and express themselves none too rationally. For this is what relationship is about: the discovery of the multitude of ways soul is incarnated in this world.

Every relationship, from the intense closeness of parent and child or partners in marriage to the more distant connections with coworkers and business acquaintances or even the driver of the bus we take daily to work, is an entanglement of souls. The gift in this entanglement is not only intimacy between persons, but also a revelation of soul itself, along with the invitation to enter more deeply into its mysteries. What better expresses the point of human life than engagement with this soul—with its manifest and hidden qualities, its mysterious alchemies and transformative pieties? If we can find the whole world in a grain of sand, we can also find the soul itself at the small point in life where destinies cross and hearts intermingle.

26.

Advice for a Young Lover

RAINER MARIA RILKE

The great German poet Rilke cautions us that we must never lose touch with our inner selves when confronting the challenges of love. Love, he tells us, can take us into the depths of our being where we may encounter and embrace the spirit of nature and life.

I WOULD LIKE TO BEG OF YOU, dear friend, as well as I can, to have patience with everything that remains unsolved in your heart. Try to love the *questions themselves,* like locked rooms and like books written in a foreign language. Do not now look for the answers. They cannot now be given to you because you could not live them. It is a question of experiencing everything. At present you need to *live* the question. Perhaps you will gradually, without even noticing it, find yourself experiencing the answer, some distant day. Perhaps you are indeed carrying within yourself the potential to visualize, to design, and to create for yourself an utterly satisfying, joyful, and pure lifestyle. Discipline yourself to attain it, but accept that which comes to you with deep trust, and as long as it comes from your own will, from your own inner need, accept it, and do not hate anything.

To cope with sexuality is difficult. Yes, but everything assigned to us is a challenge; nearly everything that matters is a challenge, and everything matters. If you would only recognize that and come to the place where you would strive on your own to finally gain your very own relationship with sexuality, always keeping aware of *your* native bent and *your* personality, your *own* experience, your childhood, and your strengths, then you need no longer fear losing yourself and becoming unworthy of your sexuality, your most precious possession.

Physical lust is a sensuous experience no different from innocently viewing something, or from the feeling of pure delight when a wonderful ripe fruit fills the tongue. It is a glorious infinite experience granted us, a gift of knowledge from the world, the fullness and radiance of all knowing. It is not bad that we welcome it. What is bad is that almost all misuse and waste it. They set it out as a lure in dreary places of their lives and use it as a distraction rather than as a focus on great heights.

Man has also transformed eating into something else. Lack on the one hand and excess on the other have clouded the clarity of this basic need. Similarly cloudy have become all the deep and simple human needs in which life renews itself. But the individual can clarify them for himself and can live that clarity—as long as he is not too dependent on others, as long as he has a pact with aloneness.

We can recall that all beauty in animals and plants is a silent and enduring form of love and longing. We can see the animal just as we perceive the plant, patiently and willingly uniting, multiplying, and growing, not from physical desire, not from physical grief, rather from adapting to what has to be. That existing order transcends desire and grief and is mightier than will and resistance. The earth is full of this secret down to her smallest things. Oh, that we would only receive this secret more humbly, bear it more earnestly, endure it, and feel how awesomely difficult it is, rather than to take it lightly.

Oh, that we might hold in reverence our fertility, which is but *one* even if it seems to be either spiritual or physical. Spiritual creativity originates from the physical. They are of the same essence—only spiritual creativity is a gentler, more blissful, and more enduring repetition of physical desire and satisfaction. The desire to be a creator, to give birth, to guide the growth process is nothing without its constant materialization in the world, nothing without the thousandfold consent of things and animals. Its enjoyment is so indescribably beautiful and rich only because it is filled with inherited memories of millions of instances of procreation and births. In one thought of procreation a thousand forgotten nights of love are resurrected and that thought is fulfilled in grandeur and sublimity. They who meet in the night to be entwined and sway in passionate lust are performing a serious work. They are gathering "sweets" and depth and power for the song of some future poet, who shall arise and speak of unspeakable bliss. They beg the future to wait to become the present, and they blindly embrace, believing their wish. Even so, they are mistaken. The future does come; a new human being arises, due to the law of nature. A strong resistant seed forces itself to the ovum that draws it willingly to itself.

Do not allow yourself to be misled by the surfaces of things. In the great depths all becomes law. They who live this mystery badly and ineffectually (and there are many), lose it only for themselves. Even so, they pass it on like a sealed letter without knowing it. Do not be misled by the great number of names and the complexity of cases. Perhaps there is over all a great motherhood expressed as mutual longing.

The beauty of a virgin, a being that, as you so aptly say, has not yet accomplished anything, is motherhood having a presentiment of itself, is in preparation, and has fears and longings. The beauty of the mother is that of a serving motherhood. And within the aged one there dwells an awesome memory.

Within the man, motherhood exists also, it seems to me, both physical and spiritual. His part in procreation is also a type of giving birth, and giving birth it is when he draws strength from his innermost abundance.

Perhaps the sexes are more closely related than one would think. Perhaps the great renewal of the world will consist of this, that man and woman, freed of all confused feelings and desires, shall no longer seek each other as opposites, but simply as members of a family and neighbors, and will unite as *human beings,* in order to simply, earnestly, patiently, and jointly bear the heavy responsibility of sexuality that has been entrusted to them.

But he who has a pact with aloneness can even now prepare the way for all of this that in the future may well be possible for many, and can build with hands less apt to err. Therefore, dear friend, embrace your solitude and love it. Endure the pain it causes, and try to sing out with it. For those near to you are distant, you say. That shows it is beginning to dawn around you; there is an expanse opening about you. And when your nearness becomes distant, then you have already expanded far: to being among the stars. Your horizon has widened greatly. Rejoice in your growth. No one can join you in that.

27

Nurturing the Third Body: The Soul of Your Relationship

CONNIE ZWEIG AND NEIL SCHUITEVOERDER

In this original article, two distinguished therapists use Robert Bly's metaphor of the Third Body to talk about the archetypal and transpersonal dimensions of love, demonstrating how we may learn to appreciate the unseen relationship that embraces and nurtures our soul.

A man and a woman sit near each other,
and they do not long
at the moment to be older, or younger,
nor born in any other nation, or time, or place.
They are content to be where they are,
talking or not talking.
Their breaths together feed someone whom
we do not know.
The man sees the way his fingers move;
he sees her hands close around a book she hands to him.
They obey a third body that they share in common.
They have made a promise to love that body.
Age may come, parting may come,
death will come.
A man and a woman sit near each other;
as they breathe they feed someone we do not know,
someone we know of, whom we have never seen.

ROBERT BLY[1]

IF YOU COUNT among your blessings an intimate, soulful partnership, you may have felt, from time to time, the presence of something beyond the two of you as individuals. You may have sensed a third presence, a palpable container that holds you in something larger than yourselves. This Third Body is the soul of the relationship itself.

When the needs of the Third Body are met, it nurtures you by providing a loving air that hums quietly between you. When it is neglected, it leaves you feeling neglected, dry, and alone. And when the Third Body is wounded, you sense a wrenching tear in the fabric of your love.

Once you form a partnership, it acts like an invisible glue that holds you in unison. You may experience it as a big, fluffy cushion on which to relax or a pliable container in which the relationship can grow. But with your recognition of it, your sense of safety and comfort can deepen. You can risk more vulnerability and authenticity with each other because you feel bound together as if in a joint soul.

The nature of the Third Body is paradoxical: transcendent and immanent. As a transpersonal field it exists beyond time and beyond your individual egos and shadows. As an archetypal image the Third Body represents the sacred marriage, the union of souls that points toward the spiritual possibility of wholeness. You may glimpse this level of life in the magical spark that ignites in a first meeting or in the synchronicities that surround meetings to come.

Yet, at the same time that it is transcendent, or beyond us, it is also immanent, or within us: the Third Body is alive and develops as you do. It is evoked when you meet and first recognize each other as potential partners. And it goes through the stages of bonding, parting, reconnecting, committing, producing, and enjoying, which mirror the stages of individual development.[2]

And, as Robert Bly puts it, even unknowingly you obey this Third Body that you share in common. It guides your actions and shapes your thoughts and feelings as individuals *and* as a whole that is greater than the sum of two. It has values or rules of conduct, such as keeping agreements with each other rather than acting singly, on individual whims. And it has needs of its own: time to work, time to play, time to make love, time to learn, and time out. Each of these activities builds the Third Body, as if you are investing in a joint bank account.

We suggest that an essential part of the art of staying together involves nurturing the Third Body. Like a plant, the soul of your relationship is alive and responsive to its environment. In order to thrive, it needs care and feeding. Let me, Neil, tell you the story of a couple that I treated in therapy in this way.

Henry and Carol had been married for twenty-eight years when they first came to see me. Their repetitive fights had taken such a toll that they began to speak of divorce. Henry, a research physicist, was highly intelligent, analytical, and remote. An immigrant from Eastern Europe, he felt a deep fear of uncertainty and found it difficult to find security in his marriage, his financial situation, or life at large. He disclosed that his mother, a Holocaust survivor, suffered from mood swings, which caused her to treat him inconsistently.

Henry desperately wanted peace of mind. He felt that Carol did not understand the struggles of his provider role. Instead, she frequently criticized him and threatened to leave. When Henry spoke about his wife, he scientifically analyzed the cycles of her "madness" and described how she screamed like a tyrant, destroying the order and safety of his world. He insisted that Carol's disorder was biological and that the right medication would fix their terrible situation.

Carol's father was emotionally cut off and never encouraged her to succeed. In her marriage, she also felt unsupported in her role as wife and mother and in her efforts to begin a new career in teaching. At times, she felt despondent and helpless and erupted in anger, threatening to leave the marriage.

In therapy, Henry and Carol argued incessantly, separating and reconnecting as they accused each other of failing to meet their respective needs. By perceiving each other as unsupportive and uncaring, the couple had created a relationship that served to maintain their individuality rather than their connection. From the point of view of the Third Body, this unconscious process held them together—but it did so in a destructive way. To nurture the soul of the relationship and learn to bond in a constructive way, Henry and Carol needed first of all to learn how to listen to one another more deeply.

Listening unconditionally: In therapy, I taught them the simple practice of unconditional listening. After taking a few deep breaths to relax and center themselves, one person spoke without interruption until he or she was finished. The other took notes, then repeated back precisely what he or she heard—without additions, subtractions, or commentary. Carol spoke passionately about her struggles with juggling her new career and child-rearing, as well as Henry's apparent disinterest in her efforts. She had the courage to speak without anger or blame, and she risked a few difficult comments that she knew might anger or provoke him. In the meantime, Henry took notes, opened his heart, and closed his mouth. When he tried to interrupt, I suggested that he wait his turn.

When Carol had fully explored her feelings, Henry read back to her the words that he had heard. In the beginning, he unknowingly interpreted her comments and missed her intention. So, she repeated back what she meant until he fully understood her. Soft tears ran down her cheeks. For the first time in twenty-eight years, Carol felt supported in her separateness and in their togetherness. Then Henry took his turn to speak and be heard.

When you hear each other with the ears of your childhood, you will inevitably feel blamed, attacked, or abandoned. Responding defensively, you will escalate the conflict and your partner will not feel heard. But when you learn to listen at the level of soul, honoring the intention of your partner's communication, you both may come to feel cherished and understood. If you set aside time to listen to your partner's soul talk at regular intervals, you may discover that this is a sacred art.

Most painful repetitive fights, like Carol and Henry's, stem from unconscious childhood patterns. When you find a romantic partner, your unconscious fantasy image of him or her is, in part, a composite of familiar parental qualities that you inherited through your identification with your mother or father. For instance, Henry's mother, whom he loves and fears, was emotionally chaotic and demanding with him. Carol's father acted distant and unempathic with her. Without their knowing it, the shadow is at work attempting to re-create these early childhood relationship patterns in their adult relationship. The result: Henry finds his mother's worst traits in his wife; Carol finds her father's worst traits in her husband. And the two engage in shadow-boxing, wrestling with childhood projections from the past rather than loving an adult in present time.

But the shadow is not as destructive as it appears. In fact, it has a secret mission—to enable Carol and Henry to become conscious of these patterns, heal old wounds, and feel loved.

Doing shadow-work: When you see each other with the eyes of projection, you react intensely to a trait in others that you fail to see in yourself. ("She's so out of control . . . manipulative . . . withholding." "He's so controlling . . . angry . . . aggressive.") And you judge and condemn it in your partner, turning him or her into the Other, the enemy who hurts and betrays you. But when you learn to identify the projection as your own shadow character, personify it, trace its roots in your history, and relate to it more consciously, then you may uncover its deeper needs. You may find gold in the dark side. And, at the same time, you turn your partner into the Beloved, the ally of your soul. For example, when Henry first listened to Carol, he felt hurt and angry and wished to blame her for their problems, as he had in the past. But as he learned to center himself and listen unconditionally, he began to identify his own shadow projections, which stem from his mother's difficult traits, and to take responsibility for his own issues. As a result, he began to feel more compassion for his wife and to honor her struggle for separateness.

Sharing dreams: Your dreams, perhaps the most eloquent voice of the unconscious, can reveal unknown feelings and unseen attitudes that cannot be discovered in any other way. For example, a shadow character in a dream may enact forbidden wishes or break taboos, such as stealing, lying, or acting sexually aggressive. When you disclose this dream to your partner, he or she then meets this character that contradicts your persona or waking self-image. In this way, you cultivate a wider range of intimacy and build the Third Body rather than a persona relationship, which remains limited to rigid roles and narrow identities.

Your daydreams and fantasies, including your longing for love, also open a portal to a larger realm. For instance, when you expose your dreams of the ideal relationship to your partner, you can shift your focus from a failure of childhood expectations to a promise of building a future together. For some couples, this exploration might include the initial fantasy that arose upon first meeting one another. When Carol told Henry that she saw in him, twenty-eight years ago, a handsome, exotic man with whom she might have a family, he recalled a similar dream arising within him.

Making love: Through the sexual dance of masculine and feminine energies, you weave together the strands of the Third Body. If your hearts open and your feelings of trust build, your bodies open as well, enabling you to experience deeper and deeper levels of intimacy and pleasure. You experience this as stages of developing sexuality: from infatuation and idealization, through the exchange of giving and receiving pleasure, to the experience of something greater when your partner is pleasured. And, finally, as the Third Body unfolds in sexuality, you touch the embodied soul of the relationship—as it breathes, pulses, and glimpses moments of transcendence and mystical unity.

Practicing meditation, prayer, ritual, or other spiritual work: You can also find a communion of souls in a joint spiritual or religious practice. This work has benefits at many levels: Psychologically, if you center yourself regularly, you are less likely to be caught by shadow projections. And, spiritually, if you take time to worship or acknowledge that which is larger than the two of you, your individual intentions will align, and you may find that you are honoring the same gods.

Uncovering your myth: As you begin to uncover these gods and goddesses, you can explore their universal stories in mythology. These archetypal images can lift you out of your personal pain into a larger story. The archetypes, or gods and goddesses, are not fixed, archaic images to be acted out like roles. Rather, they represent dynamic, ever-reappearing aspects of experience that can ignite your imagination. As you begin to uncover whose story you are living—Athena, Hera, Aphrodite, Zeus, Ares, Hermes—you will also find clues to your invisible assumptions, the unconscious patterns that shape your relationship. If you and your partner are living out incompatible stories, you may want to reimagine your life.

In conclusion, when the shadow erupts and you begin to step onto the roller coaster of blame, you now have another option: to honor and nurture this larger field that is the relationship. In this way, as Robert Bly eloquently puts it in his poem, you make a promise to love that body, to feed someone whose presence you feel but cannot see.

28.

Unconditional Love

JOHN WELWOOD

Like Moore and Zweig and Rilke, John Welwood's writings touch deeply upon the spiritual dimensions of the soul. In this essay, we see how relationships can vacillate between the "conditional love" of the head and the "unconditional love" of the heart. We bring much suffering upon ourselves and our partners when we confuse these two distinct levels of love.

AT THE VERY HEART of our experience of being human, each of us has an intuitive sense of the value of unconditional love. We discover the greatest joy in loving when we can suspend judgments and open fully to the vivid reality of another's being. And we usually feel most loved when others recognize and respond to us wholeheartedly. Unconditional love has tremendous power, activating a larger energy which connects us with the vastness and profundity of what it is to be human. This is the energy of the heart.

We often experience glimpses of unconditional love most vividly in beginning and endings—at birth, at death, or when first opening to another being, in love. At these times we feel moved and inspired by the very presence of another person's existence. Tough, frozen places inside us begin to melt and soften as the circulation of love warms us like spring sun. Yet soon enough, especially in intimate relationships, we come up against inner fears, restraints, or cautions about letting our love flow so freely. Will we get swept away? Can we let ourselves feel this open? Will we get hurt? Can we trust this person? Will we be able to get our needs met in this relationship? Can we live with those things that irritate us in the other? These cautions lead us to place conditions on our openness: "I can only be this open and vulnerable with you *if* . . . I get my needs met; you love me as much as I love you; you don't hurt me; etc."

This pull between loving unconditionally and loving with conditions heightens the tension between two different sides of our nature—the personal wants and needs of our conditioned self and the unconditional openness of the heart. Yet this very tension between conditional and unconditional love, if clearly seen and worked with, can actually help us learn to love more fully. The friction between these two sides of our nature can ignite a refining fire that awakens the heart to the real challenge, the outrageous risk, and the tremendous gift of human love.

The expression of unconditional love follows the movements of the heart, which is its source. We could define "heart" as that "part" of us where we are most tender and open to the world around us, where we can let others in and feel moved by them, as well as reach outside ourselves to contact them more fully. The unconditional love that springs from the heart has both a receptive side—appreciating others as they are and letting them touch us—and an active side—going out to meet, touch, and make contact, what the existentialists call "being-with."

It is the heart's nature to want to circulate love freely back and forth, without putting limiting conditions on that exchange. The heart looks right past things that may offend our personal tastes, often rejoicing in another's being despite all our reasonable intentions to maintain a safe distance, play it cool, or break off contact if a relationship has become too painful. Love in its deepest essence knows nothing of conditions and is quite unreasonable. Once the heart has opened and we have been deeply touched by another person, we will most likely feel affected by that person for the rest of our lives, no matter what form the relationship may take. Unconditional love has its reasons which reason cannot know.

Yet, insofar as we are not just pure heart, but also have conditioned likes and dislikes, certain conditions always determine the extent of our involvement with another person. This is inevitable. As soon as we consider the *form* of relationship we want with someone, we are in the realm of conditions. Because we are of this earth, we exist within certain forms and structures (body, temperament, personality characteristics, emotional needs, likes and dislikes, sexual preferences, styles of communication, life-styles, beliefs and values) that fit more or less well with someone else's structures.

Conditional love is a feeling of pleasure and attraction based on how fully someone matches our needs, desires, and personal considerations. It is a response to a person's looks, style, personal presence, emotional support—what he or she does for us. It is not something bad, but it is a lesser form of love, in that it can be negated by a reversal of the conditions under which it formed. If someone we love starts acting in ways we don't like, we may not like him as much anymore. Conditional liking inevitably gives way to opposite feelings of fear, rage, resistance, or hatred when our structures rub up against another person's structures. Yet beyond both conditional yes and conditional no lies the larger unconditional yes of the heart.

Attraction to another person is often most intense when the two orders of love are in accord: this person not only touches our heart, but also fulfills certain conditions for what we want from an intimate partner. On the other hand, it is quite confusing when these two orders do not mesh. Perhaps this person meets our conditions, yet somehow does not move us very deeply. Or else he or she touches our heart, so that we want to say yes, while our personal considerations and criteria lead us to say no to a committed relationship. To clear up some of the confusions in relationships, we need to distinguish between these two orders of love. . . .

As a spontaneous expression of the heart, unconditional love is naturally available to everyone, especially in the early stages of a relationship. Yet it often becomes obscured by a couple's struggles to see if they can fit, communicate, meet each other's needs, or create a working partnership. It may also get buried beneath preoccupation with hassles of everyday life, family responsibilities, and work demands. How can we stay in touch with the revitalizing presence of unconditional love in an ongoing relationship?

The most obvious answer is to learn to trust in the heart. Yet how do we do this? We need an actual way to develop this trust, not as an article of belief or hope, but as a living experience.

The best training I have found for developing this trust is mindfulness meditation, which comes from the Buddhist tradition. The Buddhist term for unconditional love is *maitri,* which means all-encompassing warmth and friendliness toward one's own experience. *Maitri* develops gradually but very concretely through the practice of mindfulness and awareness. Mindfulness involves just sitting and being in the moment, without doing anything, without trying to concentrate on anything, think good thoughts, or even get rid of thoughts. While letting thoughts and feelings arise and pass away, the practice is to keep returning attention to the breath, which is a literal expression of well-being and presence even in the midst of the most unsettling states of mind. Through this practice, we can gradually realize that, underneath all our confusions, we are basically good, simply because we are present, awake, responsive to life, and facing the world with a tender heart. In glimpsing this basic goodness, we can begin to let ourselves be because we do not have to try to *prove* that we are good.

The process of discovering basic goodness can be likened to clarifying muddy water—an ancient metaphor from the Taoist and Buddhist traditions. The basic nature of water is essentially pure and clear, though its turbulence often stirs up mud. Our minds are also like this, essentially clear and open, but muddied with the turbulence of conflicting thoughts and feelings. If we want to clarify the water, what should we do? What else but let the water sit? Not trusting our own basic goodness is like not trusting that water is essentially pure and that mud settles out by itself. In trying to prove that we are good, we struggle against the dirt, but that only stirs up more mud. Taking up self-improvement programs out of self-doubt is like adding bleach to the water. By contrast, relaxing into the basic goodness we begin to feel when we just let ourselves be awakens the natural warmth of the heart.

As this warmth of the heart radiates outward, it soon meets its first challenge: the tight, constricted, closed-off parts of ourselves and others. Although we may be tempted to fight against these tight places in a struggle to get rid of them, this only stirs up more mud. Even if we could get rid of the mud, we would lose many of the essential minerals and nutrients it contains. What allows the dirt to settle, so that the basic goodness hidden within neurotic patterns can emerge, is the attitude of *maitri*—unconditionally opening to and "being-with" those parts of ourselves that seem most unlovable (our fear, anger, self-doubt, etc.).

These parts of us that give us the most trouble are like children in need of our attention, whom we have cut off from our unconditional love. We say to ourselves, in effect, "I can only love me *if* I don't have this fear, etc." However, any part of us that is cut off from our love eventually becomes sick, for it is the circulation of the heart's energy that keeps us healthy. Circulation is an essential principle of health throughout the natural world, as we can see in the constant cycling and flow of water, which is the cradle of life and the predominant element in the human body. To remain clean and life-giving, it must circulate, rising to the heavens from the ocean, then falling on the mountains and rushing in clear streams back to the sea. The sea itself circulates around the globe, its ebb and flow renewing the shores of the earth it touches. The circulation of blood in the body removes toxins and brings new life in the form of oxygen to the cells. Eastern medicine emphasizes a subtle stream of life energy—sometimes called *ch'i* or *prana*—whose circulation throughout the body and between body and world maintains physical health.

Psychologically, it is the circulation of unconditional love that keeps us healthy. Every child intuitively knows this. As children internalize the conditions placed on love by their parents and the world around them, withholding love from certain parts of themselves, these parts get cut off from the stream of life-enhancing awareness and caring. In mythological terms, the parts that are cut off turn into dragons and demons. As Rilke writes, "Perhaps all the dragons in our lives are princesses who are only waiting to see us act, just once, with beauty and courage. Perhaps everything terrible is, in its deepest essence, something helpless that needs our love."[1] In certain spiritual traditions, the alchemy of turning dragons into princesses is called *transmutation*. The Tantric Buddhist tradition, for instance, considers every neurotic pattern to have an enlightened energy—some quality of basic goodness—locked up in it, just as muddy water already contains pure water within it.

Experiences in psychotherapy continually provide examples of this. For example, one client who suppressed her anger and took it out on herself found that when she could befriend this energy, it no longer had a nasty edge. It was more like a radiant fire or a sharp sword of discrimination which allowed her to penetrate through deception, hypocrisy, and muddled states of mind. Another client who always played the victim discovered that feeling sorry for himself was an indirect way of trying to care for himself and acknowledge his basic goodness. A third client discovered in her pattern of always trying to please people one of her greatest strengths: a tremendous sensitivity to others and a real devotion and concern for their well-being. Every neurotic pattern seems to have enlightened potential in it. That is why we do not have to throw out the dirt. Insofar as a therapist can bring caring attention to those places in their clients that are hurt or cut off, helping to awaken the basic goodness lying dormant within them, psychotherapy can be a genuine healing relationship.

29.

True Presence

THICH NHAT HANH

Through the eyes of a Buddhist teacher, we discover the similarities between Western psychology and Eastern spiritual love, of the importance of consciousness, self-reflection, listening, and the need to be fully present in our relationships. Nominated for the Nobel Peace Prize for his work with Vietnamese refugees, Thich Nhat Hanh is an exemplar for spiritual practitioners—Jewish, Christian, and Buddhist—throughout the world.

WHEN YOU LOVE SOMEONE, you have to be truly present for him or for her. A ten-year-old boy I know was asked by his father what he wanted for his birthday, and he didn't know how to answer. His father is quite wealthy and could afford to buy almost anything he might want. But the young man only said, "Daddy, I want you!" His father is too busy—he has no time for his wife or his children. To demonstrate true love, we have to make ourselves available. If that father learns to breathe in and out consciously and be present for his son, he can say, "My son, I am really here for you."

The greatest gift we can make to others is our true presence. "I am here for you" is a mantra to be uttered in perfect concentration. When you are concentrated—mind and body together—you produce your true presence, and anything you say is a mantra. It does not have to be in Sanskrit or Tibetan. A mantra can be spoken in your own language: "Darling, I am here for you." And if you are truly present, this mantra will produce a miracle. You become real, the other person becomes real, and life is real in that moment. You bring happiness to yourself and to the other person.

"I know you are there, and I am very happy" is the second mantra.

When I look at the moon, I breathe in and out deeply and say, "Full moon, I know you are there, and I am very happy." I do the same with the morning star. Last spring in Korea, walking mindfully among magnolia trees, I looked at the magnolia flowers and said, "I know you are there, and I am very happy." To be really present and know that the other is also there is a miracle. When you contemplate a beautiful sunset, if you are really there, you will recognize and appreciate it deeply. Looking at the sunset, you feel very happy. Whenever you are really there, you are able to recognize and appreciate the presence of the other—the full moon, the North Star, the magnolia flowers, or the person you love the most.

First you practice breathing in and out deeply to recover yourself, and then you sit close to the one you love and, in that state of deep concentration, pronounce the second mantra. You are happy, and the person you love is happy at the same time. These mantras can be practiced in our daily life. To be a true lover, you have to practice mindfulness of breathing, sitting, and walking in order to produce your true presence.

The third mantra is: "Darling, I know you suffer. That is why I am here for you." When you are mindful, you notice when the person you love suffers. If we suffer and if the person we love is not aware of our suffering, we will suffer even more. Just practice deep breathing, then sit close to the one you love and say, "Darling, I know you suffer. That is why I am here for you." Your presence alone will relieve a lot of his or her suffering. No matter how old or young you are, you can do it.

The fourth mantra is the most difficult. It is practiced when you yourself suffer and you believe that the person you love is the one who has caused you to suffer. The mantra is, "Darling, I suffer. Please help." Only five words, but many people cannot say it because of the pride in their heart. If anyone else had said or done that to you, you would not suffer so much, but because it was the person you love, you feel deeply hurt. You want to go to your room and weep. But if you really love him or her, when you suffer like that you have to ask for help. You must overcome your pride.

There is a story that is well-known in my country about a husband who had to go off to war, and he left his wife behind, pregnant. Three years later, when he was released from the army, he returned home. His wife came to the village gate to welcome him, and she brought along their little boy. When husband and wife saw each other, they could not hold back their tears of joy. They were so thankful to their ancestors for protecting them that the young man asked his wife to go to the marketplace to buy some fruit, flowers, and other offerings to place on the ancestors' altar.

While she was shopping, the young father asked his son to call him "daddy," but the little boy refused. "Sir, you are not my daddy! My daddy used to come every night, and my mother would talk to him and cry. When mother sat down, daddy also sat down. When mother lay down, he also lay down." Hearing these words, the young father's heart turned to stone.

When his wife came home, he couldn't even look at her. The young man offered fruit, flowers, and incense to the ancestors, made prostrations, and then rolled up the bowing mat and did not allow his wife to do the same. He believed that she was not worthy to present herself in front of the ancestors. His wife was deeply hurt. She could not understand why he was acting like that. He did not stay home. He spent his days at the liquor shop in the village and did not come back until very late at night. Finally, after three days, she could no longer bear it, and she jumped into the river and drowned.

That evening after the funeral, when the young father lit the kerosene lamp, his little boy shouted, "There is my daddy." He pointed to his father's shadow projected on the wall and said, "My daddy used to come every night like that and my mother would talk to him and cry a lot. When my mother sat down, he sat down. When my mother lay down, he lay down. 'Darling, you have been away for too long. How can I raise our child alone?' she cried to her shadow." One night the child asked her who and where his father was. She pointed to her shadow on the wall and said, "This is your father." She missed him so much.

Suddenly the young father understood, but it was too late. If he had gone to his wife even yesterday and asked, "Darling, I suffer so much. Our little boy said a man used to come every night and you would talk to him and cry with him, and every time you sat down, he also sat down. Who is that person?" she would have had an opportunity to explain and avert the tragedy. But he did not because of the pride in him.

The lady behaved the same. She was deeply hurt because of her husband's behavior, but she did not ask for his help. She should have practiced the fourth mantra, "Darling, I suffer so much. Please help. I do not understand why you will not look at me or talk with me. Why didn't you allow me to prostrate before the ancestors? Have I done anything wrong?" If she had done that, her husband could have told her what the little boy had said. But she did not, because she was also caught in pride.

In true love, there is no place for pride. Please do not fall into the same trap. When you are hurt by the person you love, when you suffer and believe that your suffering has been caused by the person you love the most, remember this story. Do not act like the father or the mother of the little boy. Do not let pride stand in your way. Practice the fourth mantra, "Darling, I suffer. Please help." If you really consider her to be the one you love the most in this life, you have to do that. When the other person hears your words, she will come back to herself and practice looking deeply. Then the two of you will be able to sort things out, reconcile, and dissolve the wrong perception.

In our daily lives, we are often caught by wrong perceptions. We are human, and we make mistakes. When we listen unmindfully, we misunderstand the other person. We have to be aware of that. The Buddha said that we are caught many times a day by our wrong perceptions. We have to be careful not to be too sure of our perceptions. You might like to calligraph these three words and put them on your wall as a bell of mindfulness: "Are you sure?" . . .

According to the teaching of the Buddha, love is made of understanding. With understanding, you can love. To understand is to see all the difficulties, pain, and problems the other person is having. If you ignore the suffering and aspirations of the other person, how can you say you love him or her? But to love and understand is also to see the aspirations and hopes of the other person. To understand him more, you can go to him and ask, "I want to make you happy, but I do not understand you.

Please help." If you want to love someone you don't understand, you might make him or her suffer more. A father has to go to his son and ask, "My son, do I understand you enough? Or is my love making you suffer?" Husbands have to ask wives the same question. Otherwise our love can suffocate the other person. It may be just a prison for him or her. The practice of mindfulness helps us be there, look deeply, and understand the other person. We need to say to the other person, "I really want to love you and make you happy, but I need your help. Tell me what is in your heart. Tell me your difficulties. Tell me whether my way of loving is making you happy or unhappy." That is the language of true love. We need the other person's help to love properly and deeply.

All of us are subject to wrong perceptions. We have an idea of happiness and we want the people we love to follow that idea, but by forcing them to do so, we make them suffer. True love is always made of true understanding. That is in the teaching of the Buddha. "Looking with the eyes of compassion" is an expression from the *Lotus Sutra*, describing Avalokiteshvara. When you look at others with the eyes of compassion, not only do they feel pleasant but you also feel very pleasant, because understanding and love pervade your heart. The amount of happiness you have depends on the amount of compassion that is in your heart. Compassion always carries with it joy and freedom. If you love someone without understanding, you deprive her of her freedom.

In Buddhist psychology, we say that our consciousness is made of two levels. The lower level is called store consciousness *(alayavijñana)*, like the basement. We keep all our seeds down there, and every time we or someone else waters a seed, that seed will sprout and manifest itself on the upper level of our consciousness, called mind consciousness *(manovijñana)*. . . .

Our ancestors have transmitted to us seeds of suffering, but also seeds of peace, freedom, joy, and happiness. Even if these seeds are buried deep in our consciousness, we can touch them and help them manifest.

To touch the seeds of joy, peace, and love within you is a very important practice. You can ask your friends to do the same for you. If you love someone, you acknowledge their positive seeds, and practice touching them every day. Touching and watering the seeds in one person is a very concrete practice of love. If you love me, please refrain from watering only the seeds of anger, despair, and hatred in me. If you love me, recognize the seeds of joy, gladness, peace, and solidity in me also and touch them, several times a day. That will help me grow in the direction of health, joy, and happiness.

To practice mindfulness is to practice selective touching. Your happiness and suffering depend on you and the people around you. If they refrain from touching your negative seeds, if they know the art of touching the positive seeds in you, you become a happy person and your suffering will gradually be transformed by that kind of selective touching.

We learn how to touch the beauty of the sky and the autumn leaves even if pain and sorrow are still there. If it is difficult, we have to rely on the presence of a Dharma sister or brother to help us do so. If one mindful person, capable of joy and happiness, sits close to us, her energy of mindfulness and joy will support us and help restore our balance. Suddenly, with her sitting close, we are able to touch the blue sky and the colors of autumn again. I think all of us have had that kind of experience. Alone it may be difficult. But with someone beside you, solid and free, it is less difficult. We profit very much from his or her presence. If you find yourself in a desperate situation and that person is far away, you go to her, because her presence can help you restore your balance and get in touch with the positive elements that are within and around you . . .

The practice of Buddhist meditation is the practice of true love. True love has the power to liberate us and bring happiness to ourselves and to living beings around us. True love is the love that retains liberty and creates joy. We cannot be peaceful and happy if we do not have true love in us.

30.

Sexuality, Religion, and the Tantric Spirit

MARGO ANAND

Margo Anand reminds us that religion and sexuality were once an integral part of society, and that if we were to embrace the power of sacred sexuality, we could greatly enhance our daily lives. This Tantric view has become quite popular in our culture and has even become the topic of scholarly debate throughout the world.

THESE DAYS, it is difficult to imagine a religious practice in which a beautiful woman or man welcomes you at the temple and makes love with you, conveying through sexual union the spirit of the deity you had come to worship.

Yet in the goddess-oriented religion that existed before the spread of patriarchal faiths like Judaism, Christianity, and Islam, that is exactly what happened. Sexuality was embraced as a sacred act. For example, in the worship of Astarte and Ashtoreth in countries of the Middle East, the priestesses, or female custodians of the temple, would freely make love with men who came to worship the goddess. The experience of spiritual union with the goddess would be conveyed through sexual union with her earthly vehicle, the temple priestess, and through this act the goddess was honored as the one who had given to human beings the joy of sacred sexuality.

Even married women could serve in the temple. They could come there on special occasions and, as an act of worship, make love with any man who came by. The children born of such temple unions were respected, regarded as completely legitimate, and lived within the temple precinct, born and raised on holy ground. The priestesses had legal rights, could own property, and generally enjoyed equal status with men. They were multidimensional in their lovemaking skills and could later marry and have husbands. In fact, they were considered to make very good wives.

Similar customs existed in the Cretan culture that preceded the rise of Ancient Greece. It was the priestess who gave access to the "Great Mother," later to become known as Gaia, and who could convey, either through sexual union or through oracular vision, the message of the goddess to those who sought her guidance.

In Europe, the sexual dimension of religious communion was gradually curtailed by the Greco-Roman civilizations—priestesses and seers now had to be untouchable virgins rather than welcoming lovers—and when Christianity arrived on the scene, the sexual aspect of worship was snuffed out altogether. Even popular religious totems like the phallic pillars planted along Roman roadsides had their genitals chiseled off, to be replaced by crosses.

By the way, please note that when I talk about "Christianity" in this context, I am referring to the dogma created several hundred years after Jesus, pieced together in a Roman Empire that was undergoing a puritanical reaction to its own former excesses. This dogma, in my view, bears little or no resemblance to the mystical vision of Jesus himself.

The shift in moral and social values that accompanied the spread of Christianity was dramatic. Women were no longer permitted even to officiate at religious ceremonies, let alone offer themselves as sexual mediums for an incumbent deity. As for sex, it was not only desanctified, it was thoroughly condemned.

It is no secret that the early Christian priesthood despised life on Earth. Mortal existence was regarded as a period of pain and suffering through which one had to pass, avoiding various temptations in order to qualify for admission to an eternal and far more enjoyable afterlife. Accordingly, all earthly forms of pleasure were either suspect, impure, transient, worthless, or a combination of all four.

Sex, the most available and potentially ecstatic of all earthly pleasures, was reluctantly accepted by the priesthood as a necessary activity for perpetuating the faithful and thereby the faith. But in order to receive the church's grudging blessing, sex had to be stripped of all ecstasy and reduced to the functional business of producing babies. It was not to be enjoyed as recreational pleasure, even by a husband and wife.

As a result, sexuality was transformed into a medieval battleground between good and evil, especially in the minds of those unfortunate monks and nuns who, while sincerely striving for purity in thought, word, and deed, found themselves constantly distracted by perfectly natural but theologically undesirable sexual impulses. Those who gave in to these impulses could justify their carnal lust only by protesting that they had been tempted and possessed by the Devil.

Thus, sexuality was joined with magic as one of the chief threats to orthodox religion. In the war between God and the Devil, both sex and magic were delivered as weapons into the hands of the Horned Beast. But a neutral observer in this conflict might see that, beneath the rhetoric, magic was really a rival source of spiritual power that threatened the church's monopoly, while sex was a rival source of ecstasy.

Miraculously, sex and magic have survived the crusades waged against them. After centuries of being condemned to live in the darkness of superstition, they are slowly beginning to reemerge into the light of understanding and appreciation.

Their struggle is not yet over. Even today, a large segment of our culture continues to condemn both arts, but I like to think the day is not far off when sex and magic will take their place in a more natural and compassionate conception of the universe:

A universe in which all opposing forces are seen as complementaries.

A universe in which ecstasy and sexual orgasm are valued as transformative powers.

A universe that is, by its very nature, Tantric.

It is said that when the god Shiva, the embodiment of pure consciousness, merged in sexual union with the goddess Shakti, the embodiment of pure energy, their Tantric embrace resulted in the creation of the Earth, the stars, the moon, the animals . . . in short, their lovemaking resulted in the creation of the universe itself.

This beautiful metaphor contains an important truth, for in our evolving understanding of this mysterious universe it has become apparent that all energy and movement, and therefore all life, occurs between the attraction of polar opposites.

It is the movement between the negative and positive poles that creates electricity. It is the attraction between the male and the female that creates new life. The dynamics of the universe are dialectical, apparently in conflict, but occurring within a larger context of unity and wholeness. This is the understanding of the Tantra vision.

Tantra, in essence, is the path of acceptance, of including the higher and the lower, the earthly and the spiritual. It allows God and the Devil to hold hands, as two poles, or two aspects, of a single energy. It encourages spiritual seekers to practice sacred sexuality as a means of self-realization. It embraces both sex and magic as valuable tools on the path of transformation.

In addition, Tantra recognizes the female principle as being equal to the male, an important step in the cultivation of sexual energy for magical and spiritual purposes. As Chogyam Trungpa notes in his introduction to *Women of Wisdom,* a fascinating account of six Tibetan female mystics: "Western culture splits the feminine between the prostitute and the madonna. In Tantra we see the emergence of female images which are sexual and spiritual, ecstatic and intelligent, wrathful and peaceful."

In Tibet, where the practice of Tantra reached its greatest heights, certain paths of spiritual development included, after long periods of preparation and purification, ritual sexual union between the teacher and the student. In this Tantric embrace, this merging of two bodies, two hearts, two spirits, secret knowledge would be magically transmitted from the master to the disciple.

Sexual energy would be channeled up the spine through certain forms of breathing and visualization, accessing higher and higher states of consciousness. At the auspicious moment, the secret teaching or knowledge would be transmitted energetically as the two beings merged in ecstatic union.

One aim of such sexual practices was, as Chogyam Trungpa describes it, to "dissolve the sense of inner and outer and plug into a sense of all-pervading energized space which is primordial wisdom and a kind of burning transcendental lust and bliss." Another, more specific, aim was to create a "rainbow body of light" that would endure after the physical body ceased to function. Still another was to access certain types of *dakini* energy—qualities of the divine feminine principle—in order to transcend the limitations of the human ego. . . .

The emphasis in sexually transmitted Tantric teachings tends to be mystical rather than magical, but the same approach is used for both arts. It is a matter of choice: whether you wish to reside in a state of mystical union with the universe, or whether you wish to harness the universal powers deriving from that union for the purpose of earthly manifestation.

In the Tantric tradition of Tibet, magic and mysticism flourished side by side. It was left to the initiate to decide how to use such powers. It was really a matter of personal integrity and responsibility, an attitude that is as valid today as it was then.

31

Faith and Surrender in Bhakti-Yoga

GEORG FEUERSTEIN

Georg Feuerstein is an internationally respected historian of religion and Eastern philosophy who fully embraces the principles of sacred sexuality. Here we see in Hinduism (the second largest religion in the world) how sexuality has been lifted to the highest spiritual standards, where surrender and faith can be used to bring us closer to each other and our god. How much our Western spiritual traditions would benefit if we could learn to embrace the East.

"ALL THERE IS IS LOVE . . ." The Beatles and the flower children of the 1960s knew it: Love is what this world is all about. Not the world of competitiveness, apartheid, social problems, espionage, sabotage, economic progress, and war, but the world *in essence.* We have to step out of our daily skins to appreciate this fact, as did, to some extent, the dropouts of twenty or thirty years ago.

Of course, they were incurable romantics, reacting to the buttoned-down mentality of the older generation. But it is regrettable that their troubadour days are over, because our era is in need of the message of love, even simple talk or reminders about love. I do not mean sophomoric crushes, gushy emotionalism, syrupy neighborliness, or even the New Age kind of romantic, idealistic love between soul mates. Rather, what we need is love as an expression of the greater Reality in which we all inhere and where we are all truly united, since all distinctions are obsolete in it.

When we relax our habitual image of ourselves as egos wrapped in flesh, when we cut through our primal fear *(bhaya),* we get in touch with the power of love. Vedanta tells us that our essential nature is bliss *(ananda)* or happiness, which is another word for love. But love suggests a more active involvement than does bliss or happiness. Perhaps it would not be wrong to say that love is the *practice* of happiness.

In the Hindu tradition of *bhakti-yoga,* such love is variously called *bhakti* or *preman.* This love comes not from the mouth or the head. It is a matter of the heart, which epitomizes the entire bodily being. Love wells up from the *anahata-cakra,* the heart center, where the *yogin* perceives the "unstruck" *(anahata)* sound, the boom of eternity.

Love, or bliss, is a radiant force that bubbles up in us and, in its characteristic superabundance, flows out from us. When we are in love with a person, our love spills over to everybody and everything; it is not confined to our beloved. We embrace all, and our loving embrace is infectious. Love is ecstatic, and it engenders love.

There is a great lesson in this, but a lesson that we seldom really learn, because as soon as we fall out of love with our beloved, we fall out of love with everyone and everything, including ourselves. Life looks drab again, or at least no longer quite as extraordinary, whereas our love or abundant happiness infused it with a vibrant vitality that made it enormously attractive.

Few people in our society know such love. It requires a great depth of feeling, and feeling is largely outlawed in our heady, patriarchal world. Feeling is different from emotionality. It is almost an extended form of the sense of touch. By comparison, emotions are mere local disturbances of the bodily field—anger, sorrow, fear, grief, excitement, envy, jealousy, or lust, even such apparently positive emotions as pleasure, self-satisfaction, or warm regard. Feeling transcends them all, just as it transcends our self-sense and our bodily image. In feeling, we reach out beyond the apparent walls of our body-mind.

Feeling—free feeling—is the carrier for the power of love. *Bhakti-yoga* is thus the discipline of self-transcending feeling-participation in the world at large. Significantly, the Sanskrit word *bhakti* comes from the verbal root *bhaj,* meaning "to participate in." Through and in love, we participate in the larger Life, in what the teachers of *bhakti-yoga* call the Divine Person. That transcendental Person, or *purusha-uttama,* is the universal soil from which springs all life.

Perhaps the flower children intuited something of this. But their "Yoga" was an unconscious one. It lacked self-knowledge, discipline, and the renunciation of what clear insight has revealed to be unreal or false about oneself. There can be no Yoga, no spiritual life, without self-understanding, disciplined self-application, and renunciation. So, *bhakti-yoga* contains elements of *jnana-yoga* (the Yoga of discriminative wisdom), *karma-yoga* (the Yoga of self-transcending action), and *samnyasa-yoga* (the Yoga of renunciation).

At the beginning of his *Bhakti-Sutra* ("Aphorisms on Love"), the legendary Sage Narada noted that *bhakti* is not a form of lust because it entails the spirit of renunciation *(nirodha).* He explained renunciation as the consecration of all one's activities, whether religious or secular, to the Divine Person. Through this act of offering up one's works, a state of unification with the Divine is achieved.

This single-minded self-dedication is best epitomized in the spiritual passion of the shepherdesses for the God-man Krishna. According to legend, the shepherdesses *(gopi),* some of whom were married, were filled with a great longing whenever Krishna would play his flute. Like the Pied Piper he beguiled and distracted them from their daily chores, irresistibly drawing them to him. When they had completely fallen in love with him, their hearts would be with the God-man even in his absence.

The story of Radha, Krishna's favorite shepherdess, relates how she pined for him like a love-sick girl. He would fuel her passion by prolonged periods of absence. The story is a wonderful allegory of the play between the psyche and the higher Reality, which reveals itself in all its glory now and again, leaving us with a growing desire for divine union. The love mystics of medieval Christendom, notably Saint Bernard of Clairvaux, Saint Teresa of Avila, and Saint John of the Cross, have bequeathed to us dramatic accounts of that miraculous work in the depth of the human psyche.

Love, then, is not merely a temporary high, a feeling of elation. It must be cultivated as a continuous spiritual disposition. We must love even when we feel slighted, hurt, angered, bored, or depressed—especially in those moments. *Bhakti-yoga* is the steady application of our feeling capacity in all life situations. Even in our worst moments, we must extend our love, or fundamental respect, to all others. Even though life consists of peaks and valleys, our overall commitment must be to what is revealed in our brief spells on the peaks. . . .

In Yoga, as in all other forms of spirituality, . . . surrender consists not so much in any external transaction but primarily in an inner attitude or response. This attitude is one of "standing back" from oneself, a deliberate relaxation of the boundaries of the ego. What this involves is best indicated by the act of emotional and physical surrender between lovers—a further important usage of the word. In fact, when I once spoke on this subject to a group of Yoga enthusiasts, this was their first and foremost association.

Nor was the group's association of surrender with the act of yielding between lovers entirely positive. There was a feeling that such sexual-emotional surrender is usually a unilateral affair, that it is expected of the woman but that it does not match the masculine "aggressive" self-image of the male lover. Undoubtedly, women have widely been and still are exploited sexually, and an ideology of surrender would fit the bill of the male chauvinists perfectly. However, the present consideration does not focus on these social patterns.

Here we are interested in the dynamics of a *true* loving relationship between sexual partners. They are by definition "equal," for their surrender must be mutual. Of course, such mutual surrender presupposes great individual maturity. Starry-eyed teenagers who have "fallen" in love are incapable of this act, although they may seem to outsiders, and to themselves, to be completely absorbed in one another; in fact, their "love" is a subconscious projection of themselves onto the partner. Strictly speaking, they love themselves in the other. Hence, when reality hits, they "fall out of" love again. That not only teenagers but also so-called adults are victims to this "falling in and out of" love is a commentary on their level of maturity.

I am making so much of this because in *spiritual* surrender, the element of mature love is present as well. When the lover surrenders "body and soul" to the beloved, really what she (or more rarely, he) yields up is the usual self-identification with the body and with bodily and emotional and even mental processes. There is a melting away of conventional propriety, shame, and guilt. Indeed, lovers delight in pouring their hearts out to one another, in confiding long-kept secrets or long-cherished hopes, and in "daring" each other to demonstrate their love by overcoming inhibitions and taboos.

They are self-forgetful—or so it seems. At least they are on the way to being self-forgetful. That they never quite succeed is as obvious as it is subtle. Their surrender is necessarily incomplete, because their love is imperfect. This lies in the nature of ordinary human love, however extraordinary it may be by conventional standards.

Perfect love is possible only with regard to a perfect "object" or, to be more precise, when love is without a specific object but includes all possible objects, the whole universe. This, again, means that perfect love is possible only when there is no ego to create the usual barrier—however tenuous—between an experiencing subject and an experienced object. A genuine loving relationship, especially at the height of its sexual expression, approximates this condition of subject-object transcendence. But it only *approximates* it. For this condition of near-genuine love to turn into genuine love, the lovers' images of each other (and of themselves) would have to be sacrificed. In other words, it is only when they come to love the whole person that they love perfectly. And by "whole person" I mean the human being in his or her entirety, comprising both the visible aspects and the invisible dimension; as a manifestation of the Whole (or God) and as that unmanifest Whole itself. . . .

Faith . . . is a *radical openness* of oneself to something (or someone) that one considers of superlative personal significance. One of the great theologians of our day, Paul Tillich, described faith as "the state of being grasped by an ultimate concern." In this sense, faith is part of daily life. There is no one who has no faith. True, the object of a person's faith—his or her "ultimate concern"—may be a most unworthy thing, as when a blindly loving wife "worships" a husband who chronically mistreats her.

Faith has to do with the very depths of one's being. It is the mainspring of one's will to live, one's primary inspiration. Therefore when we are in the throes of a "crisis of faith" we experience a profound disorientation and even fear of annihilation. Just like love, as understood above, faith is not simply an emotion. Rather it is a kind of basic orientation within us—a person's "trajectory"—which can become associated with different emotions. Love, again, is a movement of one's whole being toward overcoming the separation between beings.

The spiritual significance of faith and surrender, then, is that both are deeply felt *responses* to something that exceeds our personal life. They well up within us, coming from untold depths, and through them we can consciously reach those very depths.

32.

For a Radiant Star

KEN WILBER

In this final chapter, we conclude our journey into the heart with a love story, a true and painful tale of the final moments of intimacy between a man and his wife who is facing death. Here, we witness a transcendent peak of love—a "shattering" of love—when consciousness and oblivion meet. May we all find the courage that Wilber found when we face the mortalities of life.

TREYA HAD DECIDED TO DIE. There was no medical reason for her to die at this point. With medication and modest supports, her doctors felt she could live another several months at least, albeit in a hospital, and yes, then she would die. But Treya had made up her mind. She was not going to die like that, in a hospital, with tubes coming out of her and continuous IV morphine drip and the inevitable pneumonia and slow suffocation—all the horrible images that had gone through my mind at Drachenfels. And I had the strangest feeling that, whatever else her reasons, Treya was going to spare all of us that ordeal. She would simply bypass all that, thank you very much, and die peacefully now. But whatever her reasons, I knew that once Treya had made up her mind, then it was done.

I put Treya in bed that evening, and sat down next to her. She had become almost ecstatic. "I'm going, I can't believe it, I'm going. I'm so happy, I'm so happy, I'm so happy." Like a mantra of final release, she kept repeating, "I'm so happy, I'm so happy. . . ."

Her entire countenance lit up. She glowed. And right in front of my

203

eyes her body began to change. Within one hour, it looked to me as if she lost ten pounds. It was as if her body, acquiescing to her will, began to shrink and draw in on itself. She began to shut down her vital systems; she began to die. Within that hour, she was a different being, ready and willing to leave. She was very determined about this, and she was very happy. Her ecstatic response was infectious, and I found myself sharing in her joy, much to my confusion.

Then, rather abruptly, she said, "But I don't want to leave you. I love you so much. I can't leave you. I love you so much." She began crying, sobbing, and I began crying, sobbing, as well. I felt like I was crying all the tears of the past five years, deep tears I had held back in order to be strong for Treya. We talked at length of our love for each other, a love that had made both of us—it sounds corny—a love that had made both of us stronger, and better, and wiser. Decades of growth had gone into our care for each other, and now, faced with the conclusion of it all, we were both overwhelmed. It sounds so dry, but it was the tenderest moment I have ever known, with the only person with whom I could ever have known it.

"Honey, if it's time to go, then it's time to go. Don't worry, I'll find you. I found you before, I promise I'll find you again. So if you want to go, don't worry. Just go."

"You promise you'll find me?"

"I promise."

I should explain that, during the last two weeks, Treya had almost obsessively been going over what I had said to her on the way to our wedding ceremony, five years earlier. I had whispered in her ear: "Where have you been? I've been searching for you for lifetimes. I finally found you. I had to slay dragons to find you, you know. And if anything happens, I will find you again." She looked profoundly at peace. "You promise?" "I promise."

I have no conscious idea why I said that; I was simply stating, for reasons I did not understand, exactly how I felt about our relationship. And it was to this exchange that Treya returned time and again during the last weeks. It seemed to give her a tremendous sense of safety. The world was OK if I kept my promise.

And so she said, at that point, "You promise you'll find me?"

"I promise."

"Forever and forever?"

"Forever and forever."

"Then I can go. I can't believe it. I'm so happy. This has been much harder than I ever thought. It's been so hard. Honey, it's been so hard." "I know, sweetheart, I know." "But now I can go. I'm so happy. I love you so much. I'm so happy."

That night I slept on the acupuncture table in her room. It seems to me that I dreamt of a great luminous cloud of white light, hovering over the house, like the light of a thousand suns blazing on a snowcapped mountain. I say "it seems to me," because now I'm not sure whether it was a dream or not.

When I looked at her early the next morning (Sunday), she had just awoken. Her eyes were clear, she was very alert, and she was very determined: "I'm going. I'm so happy. You'll be there?"

"I'll be there, kid. Let's do it. Let's go."

I called the family. I don't remember exactly what I said, but it was something like, please come as soon as you can. I called Warren, the dear friend who had been helping Treya with acupuncture for the last few months. Again, I don't remember what I said. But I think that my tone said, It's dying time.

The family began arriving fairly early that day, and each member had a chance to have a last open talk with Treya. What I remember most was her saying how much she loved her family; how incredibly fortunate she felt to have each of them; how they were the best family anyone could want. It was as if Treya were determined to "come clean" with every single family member; she was going to burn as clean as ashes, with no unspoken lines left in her body, with no guilt and no blame. As far as I can tell, she succeeded.

We put her to bed that night—Sunday night—and again I slept on her acupuncture table so I could be there if anything happened. Something extraordinary seemed to be going on in that house, and we all knew it.

.   .   .

About 3:30 that morning, Treya awoke abruptly. The atmosphere was almost hallucinogenic. I awoke immediately, and asked how she was. "Is it morphine time?" she said with a smile. In her entire ordeal with cancer, except for surgery, Treya had taken a sum total of four morphine tablets. "Sure, sweetie, whatever you want." I gave her a morphine tablet and a mild sleeping pill, and we had our last conversation.

"Sweetie, I think it's time to go," she began.

"I'm here, honey."

"I'm so happy." Long pause. "This world is so weird. It's just so weird. But I'm going." Her mood was one of joy, and humor, and determination.

I began repeating several of the "pith phrases" from the religious traditions that she considered so important, phrases that she had wanted me to remind her of right up to the end, phrases she had carried with her on her flash cards.

"Relax with the presence of what is," I began. "Allow the self to uncoil in the vast expanse of all space. Your own primordial mind is unborn and undying; it was not born with this body and it will not die with this body. Recognize your own mind as eternally one with Spirit."

Her face relaxed, and she looked at me very clearly and directly.

"You'll find me?"

"I promise."

"Then it's time to go."

There was a very long pause, and the room seemed to me to become entirely luminous, which was strange, given how utterly dark it was. It was the most sacred moment, the most direct moment, the simplest moment I have ever known. The most obvious. The most perfectly obvious. I had never seen anything like this in my life. I did not know what to do. I was simply present for Treya.

She moved toward me, trying to gesture, trying to say something, something she wanted me to understand, the last thing she told me. "You're the greatest man I've ever known," she whispered. "You're the greatest man I've ever known. My champion . . ." She kept repeating it: "My champion." I leaned forward to tell her that she was the only really enlightened person I had ever known. That enlightenment made sense to me because of her. That a universe that had produced Treya was a sacred universe. That God existed because of her. All these things went through my mind. All these things I wanted to say. I knew she was aware how I felt, but my throat had closed in on itself; I couldn't speak; I wasn't crying, I just couldn't speak. I croaked out only, "I'll find you, honey, I will. . . ."

Treya closed her eyes, and for all purposes, she never opened them again.

My heart broke. Da Free John's phrase kept running through my mind: "Practice the wound of love . . . practice the wound of love." Real love hurts; real love makes you totally vulnerable and open; real love will take you far beyond yourself; and therefore real love will devastate you. I kept thinking, if love does not shatter you, you do not know love. We had both been practicing the wound of love, and I was shattered. Looking back on it, it seems to me that in that simple and direct moment, we both died. . . .

Aloha, and Godspeed, my dearest Treya. I will always, already, find you.

"You promise?" she whispered yet again to me.

"I promise, my dearest Treya."

I promise.

Epilogue: The Game

Mark Robert Waldman

I WOULD LIKE to invite you to play a game, first in your imagination, and later with a lover or friend. It is an exercise in communication that has its roots in meditation and the psychoanalytic process of free association. "The Game," as I like to call it, has the power to transform ordinary conversation into a profoundly intimate moment, one that is both exhilarating and extremely vulnerable. It begins with a basic relaxation technique, which I would like you to do while you read the next few paragraphs.

First, find a relaxing place to sit, in a room that is quiet and free from distractions. Make yourself as comfortable as possible. As you read these lines, take a moment to notice how you feel. Take a slow, deep breath and just let go.

Gently, bring your attention to your feet and your legs. Feel how they are touching the surface upon which they rest. Take another breath— softly breathing in and out—relaxing the muscles of your feet. Take another few breaths and relax the muscles in your legs. Continue breathing gently, and with each breath out, relax another part of your body. Now bring your attention to your back. Notice how it rests against the chair. Breathe out and relax the muscles of your back. Breathe in deeply and feel the muscles in your shoulders; breathe out and let them fall a little more. Bring your attention to your arms, and breathing out, let them relax and become a little softer. Take another breath in and feel the muscles in your neck. Breathing out, allow them to relax. Gently roll your head from side to side, and with each breath out, let your neck become more and more relaxed. Finally, relax your jaw and breathe deeply through your mouth, relaxing the muscles of your face, your forehead, your eyes, your temples, and the top of your head.

Take a moment and pause, noticing the rhythm of your breath and the rising and falling of your chest. Close your eyes for a few minutes, and when you feel ready and relaxed, open your eyes and gently gaze at the surroundings.

Notice the space around you, the sounds, the temperature of the room, the colors, and the shadows on the wall. Take another deep breath and return your awareness to your body.

In this next part of the exercise, imagine a conversation taking place between you and a friend. Visualize this person sitting in front of you, breathing in and out and gazing gently back at you. It could be someone you know in the present or from the past, or simply an image of a person you feel you could trust and like. It may help to close your eyes in order to visualize this, but if you can't, just relax as you read the following scenario, which describes the specific technique of the game, to be practiced later with someone you like or love.

As you gaze at your friend, take a deep breath in and notice the first thought that comes to your mind, repeating it silently to yourself. Do not censor anything, letting your feelings and thoughts go wherever they may. Take another deep breath and, using your imagination, share this thought with your friend—a brief sentence or two that completes the impression you have. Imagine the quality of your own voice and how your body feels, speaking out loud if you want.

After you finish talking, take another deep breath and let the thought and feeling fade away, returning your awareness to your body and your breath. Let it go, as if it didn't matter—just a momentary expression that will pass. This is a very important step, so take a moment and see if you have fully let go of the thought.

Now imagine that your friend takes a deep breath and says the first thing that comes to mind, in response to what you said. Let this fantasy person say anything at all, taking another breath and returning to the meditative state, open and relaxed. For the next few minutes, close your eyes and imagine an intimate conversation unfolding. See where your imagination takes you. When the moment feels right, open your eyes, stretch, and notice your state of mind.

This is the basic format of dialogical meditation, to be played with a personal friend or lover. When both of you can enter this relaxed, free-flowing state, a very different form of dialogue takes place. Surprisingly, intimacy emerges quickly—so fast that, in some occasions, a feeling of anxiety can be provoked. But by pausing regularly and returning to your breath, you stay connected with your partner. You also remain grounded to the space around you: you do not lose yourself in your thoughts or the interaction with your friend. In such an environment it becomes easier to talk about vulnerable issues or to address areas of contention. If an uncomfortable thought or feeling emerges, you notice it, share it, and deliberately let it go, returning over and over to a state of deep relaxation. In this "nonlinear" conversation, you might also discover a number of unexpected feelings and memories, some of which may have been long forgotten or suppressed. But when these impressions are shared with someone who is also in an open and receptive space, that person can better understand you and respond with empathy and support. In the briefest period of time, a profoundly personal exchange can unfold, invigorating and illuminating, promoting an intimate bond.

In dialogical meditation, a conversation can end at any time. Even if the game began with a specific topic or goal, no conclusion is consciously strived for. Instead, we watch for a natural pause, or a moment when the flow of dialogue subsides. Sometimes, one partner may feel tired, or overwhelmed by a feeling of anger or irritability that just won't go away. When this occurs, it helps to take a break and reschedule another time to talk. Eventually our dialogue becomes an ongoing natural process, flowing back and forth between informal conversation and conscious communication.

In a conscious relationship, we work together to create a meaningful dialogue and establish the rules we wish to abide by. Ultimately each couple cultivates a flexible style of interaction that is unique and specific to each person's developmental needs. With time, an intimacy can be constructed in which we have the ability to tolerate and forgive the inevitable callous remark, and to hear each other beyond the literal contents of our words.

The essence of this game is not in the communication of words but in the development of a mutually shared and conscious intimacy in which a close exchange can unfold. We are simply *being* with each other, in conversation *and* in silence.[1] In this state, we learn to experience ourselves more fully, feeling our connection to nature and the space between us. In such a state of awareness, the relationship can take on a numinous quality, a term that Jung and James have used to describe a type of spiritual presence—a heightened sense of awareness where our surroundings seem to come alive. It is a transcendent quality that is hard to describe with words, but similar to how one might feel when watching a spectacular sunset or dawn. To engage in conversation in this state can be an especially rewarding experience.

The game appears deceptively simple at first, yet most people, myself included, experience great hesitation when asked to play. The primary reason, I believe, comes from the vulnerability of being open in front of another. In this type of exercise we are asked to drop our defensive shields that are almost always engaged when we talk to others. By doing so, we expose ourselves to our weaknesses as well as our strengths.

It takes courage to share feelings of anger or guilt, to expose pockets of depression or fear. When we carefully look within we may also discover, as the Jungians suggest, a shadow personality in which the worst aspects of humanity reside: greediness, selfishness, murderous and uncaring rage. Do we really want to share such feelings with others? Can they be trusted to understand? There are so many risks to endure when we open ourselves to others.

Even in counseling, it may take many hours of encouragement before a client feels open to confide. We all fear exploring the darkness within, even after years of practice. Once, when I entered psychoanalysis to resolve a crisis, I found myself reluctant to follow the analytic rule: to say whatever came to mind without censoring my feelings or thoughts. It is an important rule—granting access to many realms of the unconscious—but a difficult one to observe. Underneath the surface, I could sense an ocean of emotional turmoil and insecurity. After so many years of therapy, did I really want to feel those feelings again? Would the analyst be supportive, or would he disappoint me, judge my behavior or criticize my beliefs?

To overcome my resistance, I incorporated a meditation exercise that was designed to keep me calm as I plunged into the depths of my soul. I followed the advice of Krishnamurti: to simply observe without judgment, to follow my feelings and thoughts wherever they led in order to see how they worked and discover their roots.[2] The result was astonishing. In just a few sessions, I was fully expressing myself with ease, touching upon issues that I had been oblivious to for years.

Why was it suddenly so easy to free associate without the usual fear and guilt? The key, I discovered, was embedded in the process of breathing and relaxation, a technique that is often used in hospitals and medical programs to lower stress, recover from cancer, reduce heart disease, manage chronic pain, alleviate panic attacks, and correct a variety of psychological ills.[3] By focusing on our breath, the mind becomes calm and clear. Our fears and anxieties diminish, allowing us to communicate with greater ease.

As anyone who has practiced meditation knows, the mind does not like being quiet, and the more we try to calm it, the busier it seems to get. The Buddhists call it a "monkey mind," jumping around incessantly from thought to thought:

> There was a monkey, restless by his own nature, as all monkeys are. As if that were not enough, someone made him drink freely of wine, so that he became still more restless. Then a scorpion stung him. . . . To complete his misery, a demon entered into him. What language can describe the uncontrollable restlessness of that monkey? The human mind is like that monkey; incessantly active by its own nature; then it becomes drunk with the wine of desire, thus increasing

its turbulence. After desire takes possession . . . the demon of pride enters the mind, making it think itself of all importance. How hard to control such a mind! The first lesson, then, is to sit for some time and let the mind run on. The mind is bubbling up all the time. It is like that monkey jumping about. . . . Give it the rein; many hideous thoughts may come into it; you may be astonished that it was possible for you to think such thoughts. But you will find that each day the mind's vagaries are becoming less and less violent, that each day it is becoming calmer.[4]

This form of meditation is similar to the analytic process, for it provides an entry into the deeper labyrinths of the mind, but its goal is somewhat different. By focusing on our breathing and relaxation we learn to develop an awareness that is separate from our thoughts.[5] We simply watch the productions of the mind. We don't react to them. We don't evaluate. By suspending the habitual ways in which we usually respond to our feelings and thoughts, we begin to develop what is known as an *observing self.* It's almost like being of two minds: the familiar one that is so often caught up in itself and another one that is simply quiet, relaxed, and aware. By returning over and over to our breathing and relaxation we stay grounded and alert, where a deeper comprehension of ourselves begins to emerge. It is here that insight is born.

With the help of my colleagues, I brought together various elements from psychoanalysis and meditation to create a therapeutic game called dialogical meditation.[6] When we played this game in workshops, it took only a few minutes before most of the group was in tears. People who had never met before were sharing incredibly personal stories, and their partners were listening with a compassion rarely seen in relationships. We were all surprised at how easy it was, but those who knew each other were more reserved. Perhaps they did not want more intimacy, preferring to keep their boundaries intact. Married couples had the greatest difficulty, often slipping back into habitual patterns of conversation.

Dialogical meditation can be an effective tool in working with couples, particularly for those who are striving for a more intimate union in life. But couples who are in the midst of a heated controversy may not have the tolerance to expose themselves to the levels of intimacy that the game evokes. A therapist's presence often helps to moderate the conflict, allowing space for the game to be taught, and if both parties are willing, the meditational process can rapidly facilitate a more open dialogue between them. But couples will often forget the rules, interrupting each other, overreacting to what the other person says, or becoming so caught up in their own words that they cannot hear what the other person is trying to say. The therapist may intervene and play a version of the game with one, while the other listens and observes. Eventually, by switching back and forth between them, a calmer state is reached. As the couple reengages, the therapist can continue to monitor the conversation, reminding each person to pause and take a breath and return to a meditative state.

When I present this exercise in workshops, some people express concerns about playing it at home. Women, in particular, have doubts about their husbands' willingness to participate. It is a valid concern, as the following story illustrates. I was giving a lecture on dialogical meditation at a local bookstore. Most of the audience were women, with two men sitting in the back. I guided the participants through a simple meditation and then asked for volunteers. Two women responded and sat down, facing each other. They took a deep breath, and shared the first thoughts that arose, which, in this case, was the degree of discomfort they both felt. After another breath and another pause, they then acknowledged each other's courage in volunteering. Taking turns, they shared their reasons for coming: for one, it was a question of divorce; for the other, the loneliness of her life. They were from different cultures, a generation apart, and yet it took only a few minutes before they were crying and supporting each other's dilemma. After a few more minutes, a comfortable pause emerged and we concluded the game. The women hugged and thanked each other, then returned to their chairs.

I asked if there was anyone in the audience who did *not* want to play the game, and the hands of the two men shot up. I asked them why not, and one responded that he was only here because his wife had sent him to gather information. He really wasn't interested. The other man nodded in agreement. Knowing their reluctance, I asked them if they would still consent, and to my surprise they both came forward. A very different conversation took place. Each confided to the other that they felt pressured by their wives to be more communicative, and each shared an intimate story about their feelings. I looked at the audience and every woman, without exception, was smiling. By the time we ended the game, the men acknowledged an intimacy they had rarely felt with others. For the moment, they were friends, and they looked forward to sharing the evening with their wives.

The women expressed their delight at seeing two men talk so openly, but several thought that they were too wordy and intellectual. They felt that the men were protecting themselves from exposing more intimate feelings and thoughts. The men took offense and disagreed; for them, it was a very intimate exchange. The women did not mean to be offensive; they too were being intimate by sharing what they felt. In part, the women were expressing their need for a particular style of intimacy, but they may have also been responding to stereotypical notions that portray men as silent and unemotional.

This scenario shows how sensitive we are under the surface, and how easy it is for us to feel defensive or misunderstood, particularly in intimate moments. We often make assumptions and generalizations without being aware of it, and we also may interpret the other person's words in ways that subtly change the meaning of what he or she intended. Each of us has a unique style of conversation, and although we may never fully comprehend what the other says, we can still engage in a dialogue that is surprisingly rich and varied.

At this time, I would like to clarify some of the assumptions that I have been making about relationships. I am presuming, first, that communication is an essential key to intimacy. Second, I am assuming that a conscious relationship is desired, one in which both parties attempt to know the other person's innermost feelings and are willing to expose their own. Many people, however, choose to live in a more traditional relationship that does not require an in-depth exploration of self and other, and as long as both partners accept this style, life can go smoothly. In many ways, it is far less difficult, for a conscious relationship is filled with challenges and disappointments, and at times, it can be exhausting. In a conscious relationship, very little can be taken for granted. Intimacy becomes an ongoing affair, unfolding deeper and more complex issues at every stage of the game. In the process, we may deconstruct many precious notions we have held about love, intimacy, communication, and commitment. We may destroy a few fantasies along the way, but we might also build new directions and goals. In my experience, the rewards are tremendous, extending as far as the imagination allows. When we approach each other in this way, a relationship becomes co-creative, a learning experience that promises a richer and more satisfying life.

In order to succeed with such a plan, both partners must be willing to consciously develop their communication skills. Therapy and meditation can help, but the real work begins at home when we engage in meaningful dialogue each day. The game can be helpful to this process and can be practiced several times a week. All we need to do is to spend from twenty minutes to an hour in intimate conversation. But dialogical meditation should be treated with care, for too much intimacy can be overwhelming. We need time (sometimes days) to take in and reflect upon our experience and the psychic processes that are stimulated from intensive interaction. And we also need time to relax and play, together and alone.

In psychoanalysis, the basic rule is to speak openly, without censorship. But sometimes I meet couples who believe that it is healthy to be completely open with one's feelings of anger and hurt. However, this type of "honesty" often upsets the stability of the relationship. When we engage in free association, disturbing thoughts can come to mind that could deeply hurt our partners if we simply blurt them out. We must pause for a moment and consider what we are about to say and reflect upon the other person's sensitivity. Are they ready to hear us, and are we ready to handle *their* response? If not, then we can note our thoughts and work with them privately until we are better prepared to meet.

Usually, the game allows us to speak more openly about sensitive issues, but we also need to trust our intuition. If a thought feels too uncomfortable to share, then we simply follow it inwardly, in the silence of the breath. Such thoughts, however, are not to be avoided, for they often hold the key to our resistances and fears of intimacy. Give these thoughts your fullest consideration until you can find a way to discuss them with your partner. The thought will often lead to other important issues that can be shared in a safe and supportive way. We might even tell our partners that we are struggling with an uncomfortable feeling or thought, without disclosing its contents. This, in turn, could lead to an exploration of how we want to be approached or protected when we are engaged in a vulnerable conversation. In this way we learn to respect each other.

So far, we have focused primarily on four dimensions of intimate communication: an awareness of our thinking and feeling processes, the verbal exchange that takes place, the sensitivity that is required when we interact with each other, and the maintenance of a relaxed and observant posture. A fifth component—listening—is also essential to the dialogical process, but it is perhaps the most challenging skill to develop. When we practice the art of self-reflection, when we develop an observing self, we are listening to ourselves. But when we turn to listen to our partners, we must suspend, at least for a moment, the self-reflective act and the inner dialogue of the mind. Only then can we truly listen to another with openness, suspending the judgmental nature of the mind.

It is here that dialogical meditation can offer specific help, for the exercise is designed to help us become less attached to what we say *or* hear. We communicate something to our partners, then consciously let go of the thought, returning to our breathing as our partners speak to us. In this brief silence, where our thoughts are put aside, we develop a different kind of listening and attention. In this free-floating state, we don't do anything with what we hear. We don't interpret or analyze. We simply allow the other person's words to flow through us like a stream. We hear the tone of the voice, the subtle moods and meanings that are embedded between the words and in the rhythms of the speech. When we listen to the sounds of a stream, we don't try to understand it. We feel it, we enjoy it, we take it in, and for a very brief moment we become one with the stream. In relationship, we resonate with the other person's experience.

We are attentive and alert, listening with the third ear. And a beautiful process begins to unfold, where we come to appreciate all that lies beneath the surface of our words.

In the art of staying together, communication and listening become our allies and our friends, the keys for intimacy and the resolution of conflict. When we are willing to share our lives with each other—our hopes and our dreams, our weaknesses and our strengths—we can embrace the mysteries of love and sacredness of life.

> *And in the dark clear moments of being,*
> *I come to see myself in you,*
> *in a tree, the leaf, the budding branch of spring.*
> *We are falling in love, the stars are falling,*
> *we grasp what can't be grasped and weep.*
> *Sadness, joy, surrender . . .*
> *Lost in a vision of God, I find you, once again.*
>
> **M.R.W.**

Notes and References

INTRODUCTION

1. Fromm, E. (1956). *The art of loving.* New York: Harper.
2. The information in this section has been consolidated from, and cross-referenced with, numerous academic histories of love and family dynamics. For a general overview of love, see Diane Ackerman's *A Natural History of Love* (New York: Random House, 1994) and Nathaniel Branden's *The Psychology of Romantic Love* (Los Angeles: Tarcher, 1980).
3. Tayler, R. (1973). *Sex in history.* New York: Harper and Row.
4. Shakespeare, W. (circa 1590). "The tragedy of Romeo and Juliet." In *The complete works of William Shakespeare.* New York: Garden City Publishing (1936). Versions of this story can be found in the Italian and English literatures of the fifteenth and sixteenth centuries, and can be traced back as far as the second century, to Ephesius' Greek tragedy *Anthia and Abrocomas.*
5. Shakespeare, W. (1593). "Venus and Adonis." In *The complete works of William Shakespeare.* New York: Garden City Publishing (1936). This, experts feel, was Shakespeare's first creative work, the source of which dates back to Ovid's *Metamorphoses.*
6. Branden, N. (1980). *The psychology of romantic love.* Los Angeles: Tarcher.
7. Henley, H. (1950). What can we ask of marriage? Reprinted in *Spring 60,* 1997.
8. Bettelheim, B. (1979). "Growing up female." In *Surviving and other essays.* New York: Vintage.
9. Gergen, K. (1990). *The saturated self: dilemmas of identity in contemporary life.* New York: Basic Books. For a fascinating read of these postmodern issues, see Walter Anderson's *The Future of the Self* (New York: Tarcher/Putnam, 1997) or his more sophisticated anthology, *The Truth About the Truth* (New York: Tarcher/Putnam, 1995).
10. Buss, D. (1994). *The evolution of desire.* New York: Basic Books. This is a provocative, well-researched, and often disturbing exploration of the strategies men and women use to

find a mate, based upon the study of more than 10,000 people, spanning thirty-seven cultures worldwide.

11. Nin, A. (1976). *In praise of the sensitive man and other essays.* San Diego: Harcourt Brace.

12. These indirect forms of communication have become a topic of debate in the media, which often points to the differences in conversational styles between women and men. Deborah Tannen's books, particularly *That's Not What I Meant!* (New York: Ballantine, 1986) and *You Just Don't Understand* (New York: Ballantine, 1990), beautifully exemplify these issues. Critics, however, believe that books like these, or John Gray's *Men Are from Mars, Women Are from Venus* (New York: HarperCollins, 1992), oversimplify the situation, ignoring political, social, and ethnic influences. Worse, it may drive a greater wedge between us, leaving us with the notion that dialogue may always be a battleground between the sexes. Current gender research finds that the differences in communication are minimal. Two excellent books that review these issues are Elizabeth Aries's *Men and Women in Interaction* (New York: Oxford University Press, 1996) and Mary Roth Walsh's *Women, Men, and Gender* (New Haven: Yale University Press, 1997), a text that examines eighteen current controversies with opposing views on each subject.

13. Dickson, F. (1995). "The best is yet to be: Research on long-lasting marriages." In Wood, J., and Duck, S., *Understudied relationships.* Thousand Oaks, CA: Sage Publications.

14. Boon, S. (1994). "Dispelling doubt and uncertainty: Trust in romantic relationships." In Duck, S., *Relationship dynamics.* Thousand Oaks, CA: Sage Publications.

15. Rilke, R. M. (circa 1899). "You see I want a lot . . ." In Bly, R., *Selected poems of Rainer Maria Rilke.* New York: Harper and Row (1981).

16. The commentaries in this section and the components of the accompanying chart have been summarized from more than a hundred references and resources, drawn from research in the fields of communication theory, developmental psychology, cross-cultural sociology, evolutionary biology, psychoanalysis, transpersonal psychology, and comparative religions. This particular summary and arrangement reflects my own thinking and biases about relational theory and dynamics.

Of the scholarly works on relationship dynamics, I highly recommend to professionals and students the Sage series on "Close Relationships" and "Understanding Relationship Processes" (Sage Publications, Thousand Oaks, California: 805-499-9774), which contains significant research and information on topics that are little explored elsewhere. Three books (edited by Steve Duck) have been particularly valuable in my research and work: *Confronting Relationship Challenges* (covering shame, anger, grief, codependency, violence, family reconfiguring after divorce, HIV/AIDS, etc.), *Under-Studied Relationships* (covering intercultural relationships, long-lasting marriages, long-distance relationships, internet relationships, gay and lesbian relationships, etc.), and *Dynamics of Relationships* (covering dialogue, trust, meaning, and nonverbal behavior). Also recommended is Sperling and Berman's anthology, *Attachment in Adults* (New York: Guilford, 1994), which reviews current theories of attachment in childhood, adolescence, romance, marriage, parenting, midlife, and aging, and provides substantial clinical and developmental models of intervention.

17. Buss, D. (1988). "Love acts: the evolutionary biology of love." In Sternberg, R., and Barnes, M., *The psychology of love.* New Haven: Yale University Press.

18. Buss, D. (1994). *The evolution of desire.* New York: Basic Books.

19. Bhattacharya, D. (1970). *Love songs of Chandidas.* New York: Grove Press.

20. Adapted by the author from the poetry of Vidyapati and Chandidas, translated by Bhattacharya.

21. Hafiz, (Barks, C., trans.). *The hand of poetry.* New Lebanon: Omega Publications (1993).

INTRODUCTION TO PART 1: THE NATURE OF THE BEAST

1. Turnbull, C. (1972). *The mountain people.* New York: Simon and Schuster.

CHAPTER 6: LANGUAGE, CONSCIOUSNESS, AND THE YEARNING FOR CONNECTION

1. Margulis, L. (1987). "Early Life." In Thompson, W. (ed.), *Gaia.* New York: Lindisfarne Press.

2. Maturana, H., and Varela, F. (1980). *Autopoeisis and cognition.* Boston: Reidel.

3. Tanner, N. (1981). *On becoming human.* Cambridge: Cambridge University Press.

INTRODUCTION TO PART 2: MAKING RELATIONSHIPS WORK

1. Hendrix, H. (1988). *Getting the love you want.* New York: Henry Holt.

2. Tannen, D. (1990). *You just don't understand.* New York: William Morrow & Co.

3. Aries, E. (1996). *Men and women in interaction.* New York: Oxford University Press.

CHAPTER 14: CAN HARRY AND SALLY EVER BE FRIENDS?

1. Aristotle (Oswald, M., trans.). *Nicomachean ethics.* Indianapolis: Bobbs-Merrill Library of Liberal Arts (1962).

2. Lewis, C. (1960). *The four loves.* New York: Harcourt Brace Jovanovich.

3. Xenophon (Marchant, E., trans.). *The oeconomicus.* In *Memorabilia and oeconomicus.* London: William Heinemann (1923).

INTRODUCTION TO PART 3: WHAT CAN WE DO WHEN IT ISN'T WORKING?

1. Buss, D. (1994). *The evolution of desire.* New York: Basic Books.

CHAPTER 24: SEVEN MYTHS OF DIVORCE

1. Laumann, E. O. (1994). *The social organization of sexuality in the U.S.* Chicago: University of Chicago Press.

2. Bloom, B. L., and Hodges, W. F. (1981). "The predicament of the newly separated." *Community Mental Health Journal,* 17: 277–293; Norton, A. J., and Glick, P. C. (1979). "Marital instability in America: Past, present, and future." In Levinger, G., and Moles, O. C. (eds.), *Divorce and separation: Context, causes and consequences.* New York: Basic Books; Zeiss, A. M., Zeiss, R. A., and Johnson, S. M. (1980). "Sex differences in initiation of and adjustment to divorce." *Journal of Divorce,* 4: 21–33.

3. For a review see Bernard (1972). *The future of marriage.* New York: Bantam.

4. Hayes, C. L., and Anderson, D. (1995). *Our turn.* New York: Pocket Books.

5. Chirboga, D. A., and Cutler, I. (1977). "Stress responses among divorcing men and women." *Journal of Divorce* 1: 95–106; Friedman, H. S., Tucker, J. S., Schwartz, J. E., Tomlinson-Keasy, C. T., Martin, L. R., Wingard, D. L., and Criqui, M. H. (1955). "Psychosocial and behavioral predictors of longevity: The aging and death of the 'Termites.'" *American Psychologist* 50 (2): 69–78; Riessman, C. K., and Gerstel, N. (1985). "Marital dissolution and health: Do males or females have greater risk?" *Social Science and Medicine* 20: 627–635; Wallerstein, J. (1986). "Women after divorce: Preliminary report from a ten-year follow-up." *American Orthopsychiatric Association* 56 (1): 65–77; Zeiss, Zeiss, and Johnson (1980).

6. Aarons, C. (1995). *The Good Divorce.* New York: Harper-Collins.

7. Cherlin, A. (1981). *Marriage divorce remarriage.* Cambridge: Harvard University Press. Furstenberg, F. (1982). "Conjugal succession: Reentering marriage after divorce." In Baltes, P., and Brin, O. (eds.), *Life-span development and behavior,* vol. 4, pp. 107–146. New York: Academic Press.

8. Duncan, G. J., and Hoffman, S. D. (1985). "Economic consequences of marital instability." In David, M., and Smeedings, T. (eds.), *Horizontal equity, uncertainty, and economic well being.* Chicago: University of Chicago Press.

9. Sheets, V. L., and Braver, S. L. (1996). "Gender differences in satisfaction with divorce settlements." *Family Relations* 15: 336–342.

CHAPTER 25: HONORING THE MYSTERIES OF LOVE

1. Rabi'ah bent Ka'b (Wilson, P., and Pourjavady, N., trans.). "The wild horse." In *The drunken universe.* Grand Rapids: Phanes Press (1987).

CHAPTER 27: NURTURING THE THIRD BODY

1. Bly, R. (1985). "A man and a woman sit near each other . . ." In *Loving a woman in two worlds.* New York: HarperCollins.

2. As described in developmental psychology, these stages are known as attachment, symbiosis, separation, rapprochement, oedipal triangles, social identity, and independence by such theorists as Kohut, Bowlby, Mahler, Freud, Winnicott, and Erickson.

CHAPTER 28: UNCONDITIONAL LOVE

1. Rilke, R. M. (circa 1900). (Mitchell, S., trans.). *Letters to a young poet.* New York: Random House (1984).

EPILOGUE: THE GAME

1. The notion of "being" with each other as a desirable quality in relationships is given great importance in Asian psychology and religion but has little context in Western literature, be it psychological or spiritual. And yet the power of this experience cannot be underestimated. And the power of conscious silence—it too can greatly enhance the intimate bond. In the practice of meditation, these skills can be enhanced.

2. Krishnamurti was a widely known and respected East Indian teacher and philosopher who encouraged people to find their own path of meditation and self-reflection without the aid of a guru. One of my favorite books is *Krishnamurti's Notebook,* a diary filled with the experiences of his own awakening, with many comments on his approach to meditation.

3. For a comprehensive overview of how meditation and relaxation is used to influence physical and mental health, see *Mind/Body Medicine* (Yonkers, N.Y.: Consumer Reports Books, 1993), edited by Daniel Goleman and Joel Gurin.

4. Swami Vivekananda (1915). *The complete works of Vivekananda.* Almora: Mayavatl Memorial Edition.

5. There are many excellent books on insight (vipassana) meditation. Some of my favorites include Jack Kornfield's *Path with a Heart* (New York: Bantam, 1993), Sylvia Boorstein's *It's Easier Than You Think* (San Francisco: HarperSanFrancisco, 1995), and Joseph Goldstein's *Insight Meditation* (Boston: Shambhala, 1993). All three books integrate meditation with contemporary psychological perspectives.

6. I would like to acknowledge the members of the Los Angeles Transpersonal Interest Group and the Association for Transpersonal Psychology for their encouragement, participation, and support in the development of dialogical meditation ("the game"). Special thanks to Neil Schuitevoerder, who contributed many hours refining it for its adaptation as a therapeutic tool for couples.

Permissions

Chapter 20 has been excerpted from *Women Who Love Too Much,* by Robin Norwood. Copyright © 1985 by Robin Norwood. Reprinted by permission of the author and The Putnam Publishing Group/Jeremy P. Tarcher, Inc. All rights reserved. For inquiries please contact Susan Schulman Literary Agency, 454 West 44th St., New York, NY 10036.

Chapter 21 has been excerpted from the essay "Fools for Love," by Stanton Peele, in *The Psychology of Love,* edited by Sternberg and Barnes. Copyright © 1988 by Yale University Press. Reprinted by permission of Yale University Press.

Chapter 22 has been excerpted from *The Dance of Deception,* by Harriet Lerner. Copyright © 1993 by Harriet Lerner. Reprinted by permission of the author and HarperCollins Publishers, Inc.

Chapter 23 has been excerpted from *A Guide to Divorce Mediation,* by Gary J. Friedman. Copyright © 1993 by Gary J. Friedman. Reprinted by permission of Workman Publishing Company, Inc. All rights reserved.

Chapter 24 is an original essay by Orli Peter. Copyright © 1997 by Orli Peter. Used by permission of the author.

Chapter 25 has been excerpted from *Soul Mates,* by Thomas Moore. Copyright © 1994 by Thomas Moore. Reprinted by permission of HarperCollins Publishers, Inc.

Chapter 26 has been excerpted from *Letters to a Young Poet,* by Rainer Maria Rilke. Copyright © 1992 by New World Library. Reprinted by permission of New World Library, Novato, CA 94949.

Chapter 27 is an original essay by Connie Zweig and Neil Schuitevoerder. Copyright © 1997 by Connie Zweig and Neil Schuitevoerder. Used by permission of the authors. The opening poem, "A Man and a Woman Sit Near Each Other," is from *Selected Poems,* by Robert Bly. Copyright © 1986 by Robert Bly. Reprinted by permission of HarperCollins Publishers, Inc.

Chapter 28 has been excerpted from *Challenge of the Heart,* by John Welwood. Copyright © 1985 by John Welwood. Reprinted by arrangement with Shambhala Publications, Inc., 300 Massachusetts Avenue, Boston, MA 02115.

Chapter 29 has been excerpted from an article by Thich Nhat Hanh, reprinted from *The Mindfulness Bell,* issue 15 (1995–1996) with permission of Parallax Press, Berkeley, CA.

Chapter 30 has been excerpted from *The Art of Sexual Magic,* by Margo Anand. Copyright © 1995 by Margo Anand. Reprinted by permission of The Putnam Publishing Group/Jeremy P. Tarcher, Inc.

Chapter 31 has been excerpted from *Sacred Paths,* by Georg Feuerstein. Copyright © 1991 by Larson Publications, Burdett, NY. Reprinted by permission of Larson Publications.

Contributors

Diane Ackerman has written many books on nature, including *The Natural History of the Senses* and *The Natural History of Love.* Her poetry has been published in many leading literary journals and she has received the Academy of American Poets' Lavan Award. She has taught at several universities and is currently a staff writer for *The New Yorker.*

Margo Anand teachers and lectures on Tantric love and spirituality. She is the author of *The Art of Sexual Ecstasy* and *The Art of Sexual Magic.*

Elizabeth Aries is professor of psychology at Amherst College, specializing in gender studies and communication. She is the author of *Men and Women in Interaction.*

Aaron T. Beck is professor of psychiatry at the University of Pennsylvania. He is recognized as the father of cognitive therapy, having won numerous awards for his research in the treatment of depression and anxiety. He is the author of many articles and books, including *Love Is Never Enough.*

Sandra Blakeslee, an award-winning science writer for *The New York Times,* is the co-author (with Judith Wallerstein) of *Second Chances* and *The Good Marriage.*

Susan D. Boon is assistant professor in psychology at the University of Calgary, specializing in the area of romantic involvement and trust.

Nathaniel Branden is a California psychotherapist and author of numerous books on love and self-esteem, including *The Psychology of Romantic Love, The Disowned Self,* and *The Psychology of Self-Esteem.*

Allan B. Chinen is a Jungian and transpersonally oriented psychiatrist whose writings have focused on the transformational qualities of fairy tales as they relate to midlife and men's issues. He is the author of numerous books, including *Once Upon a Midlife* and *Beyond the Hero*. He is a faculty member at the University of California in San Francisco.

Deepak Chopra is the author of many books and is the director of the Institute for Mind/Body Medicine and Human Potential in San Diego. He has taught at Tufts University and Boston University schools of medicine and was a former chief of staff at New England Memorial Hospital. He is currently serving on the panel for alternative medicine with the National Institutes of Health.

Mihaly Csikszentmihalyi is professor and former chairman of the Department of Psychology at the University of Chicago. His many articles and books, including *Flow: The Psychology of Optimal Experience,* have focused on extensive research into the nature and experience of flow, meaning, and creativity.

Riane Eisler is a cultural historian and co-director of the Center for Partnership Studies in Pacific Grove, California. She is the author of *The Chalice and the Blade* and *The Partnership Way*.

Georg Feuerstein is an internationally known historian of religion and Eastern philosophy, a contributing editor to several national magazines and author of more than twenty books, including *Sacred Paths, Sacred Sexuality, Holy Madness,* and *Yoga: The Technology of Ecstasy*.

Gary J. Friedman is the director of the Center for Mediation and Law in Mill Valley, California, and is the author of *A Guide to Divorce Mediation*. He is one of the founding attorneys in the development of divorce mediation and training.

Thich Nhat Hanh is a Buddhist teacher and Zen Master, poet, and peace activist who was nominated by Dr. Martin Luther King, Jr., for the Nobel Peace Prize for his work with Vietnamese refugees. He is the author of seventy-five books, including *Teachings on Love, Being Peace,* and *Cultivating the Mind of Love*.

Harville Hendrix has authored many books on relationships, including *Getting the Love You Want*. He is a therapist and pastoral counselor, and a former professor at Perkins School of Theology at Southern Methodist University in Dallas.

Larry Hof is clinical assistant professor of pastoral counseling at the University of Pennsylvania. He has authored five books and numerous articles. He is the co-author of *Integrative Solutions: Treating Common Problems in Couples Therapy.*

Ruthellen Josselson is a psychotherapist and professor of psychology at Towson State University. She has been a visiting professor at the Harvard Graduate School of Education. She is the author of *The Space Between Us* and *Finding Herself: Pathways to Identity Development in Women,* co-editor of the annual *The Narrative Study of Lives,* and author of many articles on adolescence and women.

Harriet Lerner, a clinical psychologist at the Menninger Clinic, is an internationally renowned expert on the psychology of women. She is the author of *The Dance of Anger, The Dance of Intimacy, The Dance of Deception,* and *Life Preservers,* and co-author of a recently released children's book, *What's So Terrible About Swallowing an Apple Seed?*

Gilbert Meilaender is professor of religion at Oberlin College. He serves on the editorial boards of several journals in religious ethics and is the author of five books on friendship, love, and virtue.

Thomas Moore is a psychotherapist and former Catholic monk, best known for his books *Care of the Soul, Soul Mates,* and an anthology on the writings of Jungian analyst James Hillman.

Robin Norwood was formerly a marriage, family, and child therapist, specializing in the treatment of chemical dependency and co-dependency. She has authored several books, including *Women Who Love Too Much* and *Why Me, Why This, Why Now.*

Bhikhu Parekh is professor of political philosophy at the University of Hull in England and former vice-chancellor of the University of Baroda in India. Author and editor of many books (including *Gandhi's Political Philosophy*), he also chairs commissions and committees addressing political philosophy and racial equality in England.

M. Scott Peck is the author of many books on relationship, community, and society, the best known of which is *The Road Less Traveled.* He is a psychiatrist and medical director of the New Milford Hospital Mental Health Clinic.

Stanton Peele is a psychotherapist practicing in New Jersey. He is the author of numerous research articles on drug addiction and the co-author of *Love and Addiction.*

Orli Peter is an associate professor of psychology and director and clinical supervisor of the marriage, family, and child counseling program at Mount St. Mary's College in Los Angeles, California. She is a licensed psychologist, divorce mediator, and author of many articles on relationship and divorce dynamics.

Rainer Maria Rilke, who died in 1926, is considered by many to be Germany's greatest poet and is a major literary figure of this century. His poetry merges human love with nature and the divine. *Letters to a Young Poet* is one of his better known works.

Neil Schuitevoerder practices clinical psychology and family therapy in Woodland Hills, California, specializing in industrial psychology, transpersonal theory, and relational psychodynamics, and helping couples honor the Third Body.

Deborah Tannen, professor of linguistics at Georgetown University, is an internationally recognized scholar in the field of language and communication. She has authored many academic and popular books, including *You Just Don't Understand* and *Talking from 9 to 5.*

Leonore Tiefer is associate professor of urology and psychiatry at the Albert Einstein College of Medicine. She is the author of *Sex Is Not a Natural Act,* a collection of essays on the social construction of sexuality.

Judith Viorst is a graduate of the Washington Psychoanalytic Institute. She has received many awards for her poetry, journalism, and psychoanalytic writings. She is the author of children's books and many best-sellers, including *Forever Fifty and Other Negotiations* and *Necessary Losses.*

Mark Robert Waldman is a therapist, ministerial counselor, and senior editor of the *Transpersonal Review.* He is an internationally published author in the field of transpersonal psychology, co-chair of the Los Angeles Transpersonal Interest Group, and the Los Angeles regional coordinator for the Spiritual Emergence Network.

Judith S. Wallerstein, co-author (with Sandra Blakelee) of *The Good Marriage* and *Second Chances: Men, Women, and Children a Decade after Divorce,* is a renowned authority on the effects of divorce upon children and families. She has been a senior lecturer at the University of California in Berkeley.

Gerald R. Weeks is clinical associate professor of psychology at the University of Pennsylvania School of Medicine and past president of the American Board of Family Psychology. He is the author of ten books on marital relationships, including *Integrative Solutions: Treating Common Problems in Couples Therapy*, co-authored with Larry Hof.

John Welwood is a clinical psychologist and professor of psychology at the California Institute of Integral Studies. He is the author of numerous books on relationships and spirituality, including the anthology *Challenge of the Heart*.

Ken Wilber is widely respected for his numerous books and theoretical contributions in the field of transpersonal psychology, religion, and the study of human consciousness. His personal memoir, *Grace and Grit*, describes his journey with his wife, Treya, as she struggled with terminal cancer.

Connie Zweig is a psychotherapist and co-author (with Steve Wolf) of *Romancing the Shadow: A Guide to Finding Gold in the Dark Side*, co-editor (with Jeremiah Abrams) of *Meeting the Shadow: The Hidden Power of the Dark Side of Human Nature*, and founding editor of the New Consciousness Reader series by Tarcher/Putnam.

Acknowledgments

To ALL THOSE PEOPLE who have shared their love and support, my deepest gratitude and thanks. To my friends Susan and Emily and Neil, who have consistently given of themselves in times of need and who have demonstrated that the highest forms of intimacy and care are there for those who gently ask. To my family, who have held their love through time. To my clients who have shared their deepest struggles with love. To Miles Vich and Jeremy Tarcher, who opened their hearts and pushed me through the writer's door. To David Groff, Irene Prokop, Jocelyn Wright, and the wonderful editorial staff at Tarcher. And to all the poets, unknown or great, who have touched young lovers with their song.

About the Editor

MARK ROBERT WALDMAN is a therapist and ministerial counselor in Woodland Hills, California. He was the founding editor of the *Transpersonal Review* and is an internationally published author in the field of transpersonal psychology. He has been a developmental editor for many publications and books covering the fields of psychology, alternative medicine, and spiritual development.

Mark is the co-chairperson for the Los Angeles Transpersonal Interest Group and a regional coordinator for the Spiritual Emergence Network, an organization founded by Christina and Stanislav Grof for helping people in psychospiritual crisis. His work has been deeply influenced by psychoanalytic and Buddhist studies.

He can be reached for telephone consultations through his Woodland Hills Office, 818-888-6690. Correspondence can be mailed care of Jeremy P. Tarcher, Inc., 200 Madison Avenue, New York, NY 10016.

Soon to be published by
Jeremy P. Tarcher/Putnam

Love Games
Intimacy, Dialogue, and the
Path of Conscious Love

Mark Robert Waldman

With contributions from:

Thomas Moore   Eugene Gendlin
Jean Houston   Thich Nhat Hanh
Harville Hendrix   John Bradshaw
Joan Borysenko   John Welwood
Daniel Goleman   Margo Anand
Theodor Reik   Nathaniel Branden
M. Scott Peck   and more
Sharon Salzberg

More than 100 creative exercises to deepen communication,
compassion, and awareness in your relationships:

discovery games   imagination games
listening games   dream games
dating games   drama games
tantric games   history games
psychology games   fun games
sensual games   games people
meditation games   shouldn't play
focusing games